MUSIC, LANGUAGE, AND COGNITION

Music, Language, and Cognition

And Other Essays in the Aesthetics of Music

PETER KIVY

CLARENDON PRESS · OXFORD

OXFORD

UNIVERSITY PRESS

Great Clarendon Street, Oxford OX2 6DP

Oxford University Press is a department of the University of Oxford.
It furthers the University's objective of excellence in research, scholarship,
and education by publishing worldwide in

Oxford New York

Auckland Cape Town Dar es Salaam Hong Kong Karachi
Kuala Lumpur Madrid Melbourne Mexico City Nairobi
New Delhi Shanghai Taipei Toronto

With offices in

Argentina Austria Brazil Chile Czech Republic France Greece
Guatemala Hungary Italy Japan Poland Portugal Singapore
South Korea Switzerland Thailand Turkey Ukraine Vietnam

Oxford is a registered trade mark of Oxford University Press
in the UK and in certain other countries

Published in the United States
by Oxford University Press Inc., New York

© Peter Kivy 2007

The moral rights of the author have been asserted
Database right Oxford University Press (maker)

First published 2007

British Library Cataloguing in Publication Data
Data available

Library of Congress Cataloging in Publication Data
Kivy, Peter.
Music, language, and cognition : and other essays in the aesthetics of music / Peter Kivy.
p. cm.
Includes bibliographical references (p.   ) and index.
ISBN 978-0-19-921766-3 (alk. paper) -- ISBN 978-0-19-921765-6 (alk. paper) 1.
Music--Philosophy and aesthetics. I. Title.
ML3800.K48 2007
781.1'7--dc22   2007003066

Typeset by Laserwords Private Limited, Chennai, India
Printed in Great Britain
on acid-free paper by
Biddles Ltd., King's Lynn, Norfolk

ISBN 978-0-19-921766-3
ISBN 978-0-19-921765-6 (Pbk.)

1 3 5 7 9 10 8 6 4 2

For Leonard Meyer,
who taught me how to *think* about music

Preface

This is the third collection of my essays on what is now called in the profession "the philosophy of music". It includes some of my most recent contributions to journals, anthologies, and conference proceedings, as well as one essay never before published, and two from my earliest work in the field.

The collection has quite naturally fallen into four sections: papers on the history of, broadly speaking, "musical aesthetics"; papers on music and drama; papers on the concept of, and philosophical problems surrounding, musical performance; and papers on what so-called analytic philosophy construes as problems in its domain that Western art music may present. But there is no historical paper that is bereft of critical analysis, and no analytic paper that is not informed by the histories of philosophy and music. I have reason to believe, therefore, that all of them will be of interest both to philosophers and to music historians. Furthermore, since I have tried as much as possible to keep these essays free of technical jargon (which wasn't difficult, as I know very little of it), I have some reason to hope that they will also be of interest to anyone who likes not only to listen to music, but to think about it as well.

The essays comprising Part I reflect my early interest in the history of music aesthetics. Chapter 1 is a spin-off, really, of my research in eighteenth-century British aesthetics and philosophy of art, pursued while a graduate student in philosophy at Columbia University. I was, at the time, more fond, perhaps, than I am now of Handel's music, and deeply fascinated, as I still am, by his relation to the cultural and intellectual life of Enlightenment London. I later returned to this theme in my book on genius, *The Possessor and the Possessed*, in which Handel and Mainwaring play prominent roles.[1] But the present essay still stands on its own as the commemoration of an important pair of events in music history and music aesthetics: the publication of the first book-length biography of a composer, and the anointing of the first *recognized* composer-genius.

[1] Peter Kivy, *The Possessor and the Possessed: Handel, Mozart, Beethoven, and the Idea of Musical Genius* (New Haven: Yale University Press, 2001), chs. 2 and 4.

"Herbert Spencer and a Musical Dispute", Chapter 2 of the present collection, dates back to my earliest research, as a graduate student in the history of music program at Yale University. My work there centered on what at the time was (and still I think is) an obscure incident in the history of music and philosophy: the attempt to discover music's "origins", fuelled by the speculations of Spencer, Darwin, other evolutionists, and their critics. It was an attempt to put an old question, pursued by Rousseau among others during the eighteenth century, on a new—which is to say scientific—footing. Of course they failed, perhaps because the question itself is too vague and ill-formed for us to know exactly *what* an answer to it would look like. Nevertheless, one can learn a lot from the dispute about how *they* viewed the art of music, and how *we* view it now, particularly what they referred to as "primitive music", a phrase that would make any self-respecting ethnomusicologist cringe.

The essays in Part II concern opera and film. Whereas Chapter 1 presents my earliest (published) ideas about Handel, the man, and his music, Chapter 3 presents the latest. It was written as the invited keynote address for a meeting in Siena, Italy, devoted to Handel's operas. The reason for inviting me was that in my book on what I suppose might be called "the philosophy of opera", I had presented a spirited defense of Handelian *opera seria* as a "solution" to what I represented there as "the problem of opera". The invitation to speak in Siena provided me with an opportunity to return to my defense of Handel's works for the operatic stage, about which I was beginning to have some nagging doubts, and to revise it accordingly. But the essay is brief, and the case for (or against) Handel's operas by no means closed, either in the seminar room or in the opera house.

Chapter 4 was written as a response to an article in the *Cambridge Opera Journal* on the supposed anti-Semitism of Wagner's *Meistersinger*. I submitted it to that journal, and it was rejected—an adverse judgment which I did not then, and do not now, agree with (obviously). But as, at the time, I could not think of another place to publish it, I put it away and forgot about the thing, only to recall it again when planning this collection. It is an attempt to vindicate a great work of art, and a great, though deeply flawed, artist, against a false indictment. It is not a vindication of the distinctly unpleasant person whom the genius inhabited.

The topic of Chapter 5 concerns the medium of expression in opera. Of course the medium is *music*, and in particular (but not solely) *singing*. This is all too obvious. However, the peculiar nature of sung drama has posed intriguing problems with regard to what might, loosely speaking, be termed operatic "metaphysics". This is my second attempt to deal with these problems.[2] And I have made this second attempt not because I have grown dissatisfied with the first, but, rather, because I thought it required amplification and clarification. No doubt this second attempt will, in its turn, require amplification and clarification as well. And so it goes.

The essay on music in the movies was commissioned by the editors of a volume devoted to what analytic philosophers of art might have to say about the art of the cinema. My name was proposed to them by my good friend, and world-famous expert on the philosophy of film, Noel Carroll. I am grateful to the editors for having faith in Carroll's recommendation, and to him for having faith in my ability to write about an art form I had never written about before. All three were of immense help to me in revising the essay I produced. It contains an idea I had actually been carrying around with me long before the invitation to write the essay. So it is not as if I had to begin *de novo*. Nevertheless, the essay was written with a bare minimum of technical knowledge of film, or its music, although with plenty of experience of "going to the movies", from the age of 5. The results of my one and only (so far) venture into the philosophy of film I am sure are tentative, at best. But I hope that they tempt other philosophers to give some thought to the peculiar place of music in the movies (although, of course, I am by no means the first to do so). It is, it seems to me, an important, and intriguing topic, and relatively unexplored as yet in the philosophy of art.

The two essays on musical performance, which comprise Part III, have very different motivations. Chapter 7 was the result of informal comments made with regard to my book *Authenticities*, which had some critical things to say about so-called historically authentic performance.[3] I was told, in effect, that I was beating a dead horse; that nobody talked anymore about historically *authentic* performance; rather, it was historically *informed* performance that was at issue, and so my critique was quite irrelevant to the present state of the art. I was very suspicious of this maneuver, for the easiest way to improve a tarnished reputation

[2] Peter Kivy, *The Fine Art of Repetition: Essays in the Philosophy of Music* (Cambridge: Cambridge University Press, 1993), ch. 7.

[3] Peter Kivy, *Authenticities: Philosophical Reflections on Musical Performance* (Ithaca, NY: Cornell University Press, 1995).

is to change your name, and nothing more. And it was that suspicion that I set out to either verify or dispel.

Chapter 8, in contrast, is on a topic I had no intention of writing about until I was invited, by Anthony Pryer, to speak at a conference at Goldsmiths College of the University of London that he was getting together on the topic of "The Future of Musical Performance". He specifically requested that I speak about the possibility of the "perfect" or "ideal" performance. Chapter 8 is the result. But one thing I discovered in writing it is that the question is more complicated than I had thought, and my views, therefore, less strongly held after finishing it than when I started.

The essays in Part IV of this collection cover a wide range of questions in the "philosophy of music". The first two are, in two ways, a matched pair. They are both responses to criticisms brought against my views by my good friend Stephen Davies. And the topics, musical meaning and musical profundity, are closely related, as, on my view, meaning is a necessary condition for profundity; or, put another way, profundity is a subspecies of meaning.

Chapter 9 deals with the attempt to raise, yet again, the question of whether absolute music has "meaning", in any full-blooded sense of the word, and to give an affirmative answer to it. It is a perennial question in musicology, music criticism, and in philosophy of art, and no matter how frequently skeptics like me deny meaning to absolute music, true believers launch new arguments to reinstate it. I am under no illusion that my answer to Davies and his coauthor, Constantijn Koopman, will settle the question. It is hydra-headed.

Profundity in absolute music, the subject of Chapter 10, entered the literature of musical aesthetics, so far as I know, by way of my 1990 book *Music Alone*.[4] In that place I expressed serious doubts about whether pure instrumental music could be "profound", in the sense in which philosophy, say, or, more relevantly, literature could be. I had no idea, when I expressed these doubts, that they would touch such a sensitive nerve in the musical community. But they obviously did; and this is my second attempt since the publication of *Music Alone* to put the question to rest—*in the negative*. I wish it would be the last, although I doubt it will be, given how strongly others wish that they could call absolute music "profound" in a literal, not merely a metaphorical, sense. (I never denied the metaphor to absolute music.)

---

[4] Peter Kivy, *Music Alone: Philosophical Reflections on the Purely Musical Experience* (Ithaca, NY: Cornell University Press, 1990), ch. 10.

Chapters 11 and 12 are a matched pair in one obvious respect, and in one "private" respect, so to speak. In the obvious respect they are each about the work of a single author—the only such in the volume. The private significance lies in the fact that both authors, whom I deeply admire and respect, have had profound influences on my professional career as a philosopher of art.

The essay on Leonard Meyer, Chapter 11, is what is known in the trade as a "review article", which is to say, a book review that is supposed to explore some volume that a journal considers so important that it wishes it to be treated in a depth and extent that exceed the format of the usual scholarly review. The journal *Current Musicology* invited me to do that job for Leonard Meyer's *Style and Music*, and there was no need to twist my arm, for Leonard Meyer's writings on music were part of my "inspiration" (as they were for many others). It was from his first book, *Emotion and Meaning in Music*, that I first learned that one could write about absolute music with the tools of conceptual analysis. *I* wanted to do that too. But no one does it the way Leonard Meyer does. *That* remains an unattainable goal.

In Chapter 12 I pay tribute to the late Frank Sibley—the philosopher whose ground-breaking article "Aesthetic Concepts" inspired my first project in "analytic aesthetics", after receiving my doctorate, and, without exaggeration, changed the face of the discipline. My paper was written for a conference devoted to Sibley's work, which, alas, he did not live to attend. The topic should have been "Aesthetic Concepts", about which I had written extensively in the late Sixties and early Seventies, including a short book.[5] But I found that I could not work my way back into those issues about which I felt I had probably said just about all I had to say. And in any case, it seemed appropriate to pay some attention, in commemorating Sibley's work, to the topic that occupied him in his final days. The philosophy of music is much the poorer for his not having lived to make further contributions, and much the richer for the contribution he did make.

The penultimate essay of the collection was commissioned by the editors of a *Festschrift* for Marx Wartofsky, whose untimely death struck a heavy blow to the philosophical community, the aesthetics community included. I chose for my topic one to which Professor Wartofsky had made a substantial contribution: the concept of *representation*. There is nothing about my essay that is particularly relevant to his concerns,

---

[5] Peter Kivy, *Speaking of Art* (The Hague: Martinus Nijhoff, 1973).

except of course the general topic itself. Nor is representation something that lies at the center of philosophical concern for philosophers of music, at least in the English-speaking world. But, central or peripheral, it is always a proper philosophical task to get things straightened out. And that is what I have tried to do in this essay, with regard to whether or not music can be representational. Of course it can be. It's just that, all things considered, not much hangs on it.

The final essay, from which I have derived the title of the volume, was written in response to an invitation from a somewhat unexpected source: the International Colloquium on Cognitive Science—unexpected because my work has never been in that area, and my knowledge of the subject is restricted mainly to what I have picked up in hallways from my colleagues and graduate students. In the event, my ignorance did not matter much. The topic, Music, Language, and Cognition, was *their* idea, and I certainly had plenty to say on *it*. *They* made the connections to cognitive science, and so, I think, we all learned something (and the food was terrific). If you are ever invited to San Sebastián, in the Basque country, where this meeting took place, *go*. If you aren't invited, *go anyway*.

Chapter 14 is not, I should add, to be construed as in any way a summing up of what this volume is about. But I suppose there is hardly an essay in it that does not touch on one or another of the concepts therein. That is why I chose *its* title for the title of this volume, and *it* for the concluding chapter. You are not to make too much of my choice; but, on the other hand, you are not to make too little of it.

                                                          Peter Kivy

Acknowledgements

The publication history of the essays is as follows.

Chapter 1 appeared originally in the *Journal of the American Musicological Society*, 17 (1964), 42–8. It is reprinted with kind permission of the editor and of the publisher. Copyright © 1964 by the Regents of the University of California/American Musicological Society.

Chapter 2 appeared originally in the *Music Review*, 23 (1964), 317–29.

Chapter 3 appeared originally in the proceedings of the conference, Georg Friedrich Handel e il teatro d'opera, conducted by the Accademia Musicale Chigiana, Siena, Italy, 7–9 November 2002. It is reprinted with kind permission of Guido Burchi, Leo S. Olschki, and the Accademia Musicale Chigiana.

Chapter 4 appears in print here for the first time.

Chapter 5 appeared originally in the *Journal of Aesthetics and Art Criticism*, 52 (1994), 63–8. It is reprinted with kind permission of the editor and of Blackwell Publishing.

Chapter 6 appeared originally in *Film Theory and Philosophy*, ed. Richard Allen and Murray Smith (Oxford: Clarendon Press, 1997), 308–28. It is reprinted with kind permission of Oxford University Press.

Chapter 7 appeared originally in the *British Journal of Aesthetics*, 42 (2002), 128–44. It is reprinted with kind permission of the editor and of Oxford University Press.

Chapter 8 appeared originally in the *British Journal of Aesthetics*, 46 (2006), 111–32. It is reprinted with kind permission of the editor and of Oxford University Press.

Chapter 9 appeared originally in *Contemporary Philosophy, ix: Aesthetics and Philosophy of Art*, ed. G. Fløistad (Dordrecht, 2007). © Springer. It is reprinted with kind permission of Springer Science and Business Media.

Chapter 10 appeared originally in the *British Journal of Aesthetics*, 43 (2003), 401–11. It is reprinted with kind permission of the editor and of Oxford University Press.

Chapter 11 appeared originally in *Current Musicology*, 49 (1992), 66–80. It is reprinted with kind permission of the editor.

Chapter 12 appeared originally in *Sibley, Aesthetic Concepts: Essays after Sibley*, ed. Emily Brody and Jerrold Levinson (Oxford: Clarendon Press, 2001), 199–212. It is reprinted with kind permission of Oxford University Press.

Chapter 13 appeared originally in a *Festschrift* for the late Marx Wartofsky, *Artifacts, Representations and Social Practice: Essays for Marx Wartofsky*, ed. Carol C. Gould and Robert S. Cohen (Dordrecht, Boston, and London: Kluwer Academic Publishers, 1994), 53–67. The volume is number 154 of the series, Boston Studies in the Philosophy of Science. © Springer. It is reprinted with kind permission of Springer Science and Business Media.

Chapter 14 appeared originally in the Proceedings of the Seventh International Colloquium on Cognitive Science, 9–12 May 2001, San Sebastián, The Basque Country: *Truth, Rationality, Cognition, and Music*, ed. Kepa Korta and Jesus M. Larrazabal (Dordrecht, Boston, and London: Kluwer Academic Publishers, 2004). © Springer. It is reprinted here with kind permission of the editors and of Springer Science and Business Media.

Contents

PART I

HISTORY

1

Mainwaring's *Handel*: Its Relation to British Aesthetics

John Mainwaring's *Handel*[1] has long been familiar to students of the composer as an early (if not always reliable) biographical source. It is generally accorded a place in music history—or, rather, the history of musical scholarship—as the first biography of a musician. One might expect from a pioneer effort in musical biography little more than the usual collection of anecdotes, authentic and apocryphal, that surround the great artist. Mainwaring has not disappointed in this respect. But his work is far from being a mere biographical memoir, containing, as it does, an extended section of critical *Observations* on Handel's compositions.[2] These *Observations* embody a critical point of view that owes its existence to developments in criticism and aesthetic theory, characteristic of late seventeenth- and early eighteenth-century British thought.

I

Mainwaring states at the outset of his *Observations* that "Music is founded on established rules and principles". Such rules and principles are a posteriori, "derived from experience and observation, which inform us what particular system or disposition of sounds will produce the most pleasing effects". Acquaintance with the rules constitutes *knowledge*, which alone can make "a tolerable Composer", but never a Master.[3]

¹ [John Mainwaring], *Memoirs of the Life of the Late George Frederic Handel. To which is added a Catalogue of his Works and Observations upon them* (London, 1760).

² A portion of the *Observations* (ibid. 164–75) were contributed, Mainwaring states, by "a Gentleman, who is a perfect master of the subject". O. E. Deutsch, in his *Handel: A Documentary Biography* (New York: Norton, 1954), 529, identifies the "Gentleman" as Robert Price.

³ [Mainwaring], *Memoirs*, 160–1.

Mastery in music is, for Mainwaring, an amalgam of Knowledge and either *invention* or *taste*. Invention bespeaks a disregard for musical convention—rather than follow the rule, it *gives* the rule. "Those who have an *inventive* genius will depart from the common rules, and please us the more by such deviations. These must of course be considered as bold strokes, or daring flights of fancy. Such passages are not founded on rules, but are themselves the foundation of new rules."[4] In short, invention constitutes originality.

Invention is, if you will, the masculine side of music—the strength that defies stricture. Taste is the feminine—the delicate and obeisant. Mainwaring writes, "they who have *taste*, or a nice discernment of the minuter circumstances that please, will polish and improve the inventions of others. These will adhere strictly to rules, and even make them more strict."[5] Both invention and taste must be coupled with knowledge (Mainwaring apparently maintains that only those acquainted with rules are privileged to break them); but invention and taste are seldom, if ever, combined in the same artist since, clearly, one who violates rules in one instance is not likely to keep them in another.

At this juncture the question arises, How are invention and taste acquired? Knowledge of rules can be taught. Is such also the case with invention and taste? In writing of Handel's early training under Zackaw (*sic*), Mainwaring seems to incline towards the position that it is. "The first object of his attention was to ground him thoroughly in the principles of harmony." That is to say, Handel was first taught the *rules*. "His next care was to cultivate his imagination, and form his taste."[6] As we have seen, invention is a "flight of fancy"—a reasonable enough synonym for "imagination" to support the conclusion that cultivating Handel's *imagination* meant, for Mainwaring, cultivating his *invention*. Thus we conclude that Handel was *grounded* in rules, *cultivated* in invention, and *formed* in taste. The vagueness of these terms and their ambiguous use make it impossible to divine whether Mainwaring intended any clear distinction between them. Be that as it may, they all seem to bear the connotation of *teaching*, however that process is to be construed.

But, we cannot rest content with this conclusion; for in the *Observations*, Mainwaring seems rather to maintain that taste and invention are natural endowments—a position, as we shall see, consistent with the general drift of British aesthetics in the early eighteenth century.

---

⁴ [Mainwaring], *Memoirs*, 161–2.   ⁵ Ibid. 162.   ⁶ Ibid. 14.

Thus Mainwaring states that "*taste* implies a natural sensibility ... "; and he describes grandeur (or sublimity)—the product of invention—as "coming purely from Nature ... ".[7] The fact is that he did not hold a completely coherent position with regard to the relation between natural endowments and education.

The terms "grandeur" and "sublimity" being now introduced, we must consider their relevance to the notions of invention and taste. Invention, as I have had occasion to remark, is characterized by strength—the strength of genius that overcomes rules and conventions. Its effects, therefore, are powerful rather than delicate: the lofty effects of grandeur and sublimity. Such effects are likely to offend the man of taste: "as this faculty is of a tender and timid nature, it is apt to consider those bolder strokes and rougher dashes which genius delights in, either as course, or as extravagant."[8] Handel is the composer *par excellence* of sublimity—an apostle of strength. His works contain "such a fulness, force, and energy, that the harmony of HANDEL may always be compared to the antique figure of HERCULES, which seems to be nothing but muscles and sinews" (although with regard to *melody*, he displays "grace and delicacy").[9] Mainwaring writes of the oratorio choruses as abounding in "sublime strokes";[10] "the cast of his mind was *more* towards the great and sublime than any *other* style ... ".[11]

But if there is merit in "sublime strokes", nevertheless, the breaking of rules, to which the artist of invention is prone, must be considered a fault (at least by the man of taste). So Mainwaring maintains, "the merit of HANDEL's Music will be least discerned by the lovers of elegance and correctness. They are shocked with every defect of this sort [of composition] .... "[12] In Handel's "sublime" choruses, "there are great inequalities"; and "In his Music for instruments there are the same marks of a great genius, and likewise some instances of great negligence."[13] The inventive artist, then, is a flawed artist; he must succeed against a

---

[7] Ibid. 163 and 192.   [8] Ibid. 163.
[9] Ibid. 204. "Harmony" here refers to both the harmonic and contrapuntal aspects of Handel's style.
[10] Ibid. 190.
[11] Ibid. 167 n. This is contained in a footnote to Price's remarks. It is not clear whether the footnote is Price's or Mainwaring's.
[12] Ibid. 162–3. Mainwaring goes into some detail with regard to Handel's alleged faults, particularly in his instrumental accompaniment for the voice, which his English contemporaries seemed to find over-elaborate. Consideration of these criticims—interesting though they are—lies outside the purview of the present study.
[13] Ibid. 192 and 201.

deficit inherent in his procedure. Yet, if he does succeed, his effect is far greater than that which the artist of taste can ever achieve, regardless of his perfection. Handel is such a flawed artist—but a Handel with flaws is, nevertheless, "a down-right prodigy". Indeed, writes Mainwaring, "there are no words capable of conveying an idea of his character, unless indeed I was to repeat those which LONGINUS has employed in his description of DEMOSTHENES, every part of which is so perfectly applicable to HANDEL, that one would almost be persuaded it was intended for him."[14] The passage to which Mainwaring refers, besides epitomizing his evaluation of Handel, forms a natural transition to the discussion which follows. We might well, therefore, conclude here with these words of Longinus:

> Whereas *Demosthenes* adding to a continued Vein of Grandeur and to Magnificence of Diction (the greatest Qualifications requisite in an Orator) such lively Strokes of Passion, such Copiousness of Words, such Address, and such Rapidity of Speech; and, what is his Masterpiece, such Force and Vehemence, as the greatest Writers besides durst never aspire to; being, I say, abundantly furnished with all these divine (it would be Sin to call them human) Abilities, he excels all before him in the Beauties which are really his own; and to atone for Deficiencies in those he has not, overthrows all Opponents with the irresistible Force, and the glittering Blaze, of his Lightning. For it is much easier to behold, with stedfast and undazzled Eyes, the flashing Lightning, than those ardent Strokes of the Pathetic, which come so thick one upon the other in his Orations.[15]

II

Whence came this critical point of view? Surely not fully armed from a John Mainwaring! In Britain, its general outline was already discernible as far back as the early seventeenth century. Francis Bacon, for example, wrote in his essay "Of Beauty":

> There is no excellent beauty that hath not some strangeness in the proportion. A man cannot tell whether Apelles or Albert Durer were the more trifler; whereof

[14] [Mainwaring], *Memoirs*, 192–3.
[15] Dionysius Longinus, *Dionysius Longinus on the Sublime*, trans. William Smith, 2nd edn. (London, 1743), 83–4. Smith's was the standard eighteenth-century English translation of the work. Mainwaring refers to section 33; however, there is no mention of Demosthenes in that section. It is clear that the passage Mainwaring had in mind is in section 34. The confusion probably results from the fact that Mainwaring used as a motto for the title-page of his work a quotation from section 33.

the one would make a personage of geometrical proportions, the other by taking the best parts out of divers faces, to make one excellent. Such personages, I think, would please nobody but the painter that made them. Not but I think a painter may make a better face than ever was, but he must do it by a kind of felicity (as a musician that maketh an excellent air in music), and not by rule.[16]

Two aspects of Mainwaring's position are prefigured here. First, beauty is said to be created "not by rule" but "by a kind of felicity"—that is to say, by a natural endowment. Second, beauty contains "some strangeness in the proportion"; it does not conform to the rule. The beautiful, then, is for Bacon very much what the sublime is for Mainwaring, in two respects: it is the product of natural ability rather than knowledge, and is often contrary to the accepted standards of "correct" composition.

If Mainwaring's position is adumbrated by Bacon, it appears almost entire in Sir William Temple's "Of Poetry" (1690). *Genius*, for Temple, "can never be produced by any Art or study, by Pains or by Industry, ... cannot be taught by Precepts or Examples, and therefore is agreed by all to be the pure and free Gift of Heaven or of Nature, and to be a Fire kindled out of some hidden spark of the very first conception". Yet genius, though necessary to the great poet, is not sufficient for his success; it must be tempered with art. "But tho' Invention be the Mother of Poetry, yet this Child is like all others born naked, and must be Nourished with Care, Cloathed with Exactness and Elegance, Educated with Industry, Instructed with Art, Improved by Application, Corrected with Severity, and Accomplished with Labour and with Time, before it Arrives at any great Perfection or Growth." A union of invention and knowledge wins the day. Acquaintance with rules alone can "hinder some men from being very ill Poets, but not make any man a very good one".[17]

Incipient in Temple's theory of poetry is the distinction between the beautiful and the sublime, so important to the eighteenth century (and to Mainwaring). In comparing Homer with Virgil, Temple writes, "To speak in Painters Terms, we find in the Works of *Homer* the most Spirit, Force, and Life; in those of *Virgil*, the best Design, the truest Proportions, and the greatest Grace ... ". It is clear that Homer embodies, for Temple, qualities which were soon to be associated almost

---

[16] Francis Bacon, *Essays, Advancement of Learning, New Atlantis, and Other Pieces*, ed. R. F. Jones (New York: Odyssey Press, 1937), 125.

[17] Sir William Temple, "Of Poetry", in J. E. Spingarn (ed.), *Critical Essays of the Seventeenth Century* (Bloomington, Ind.: Indiana University Press, 1957), iii. 80 and 85.

completely with the concept of the sublime: "Spirit" and "Force"; and Virgil represents the correct, the beautiful: "the best Design, the truest Proportions". The English, unlike the French, were never happy with the canons of strict neoclassicism; they recognized that the poets' genius lay elsewhere. Temple, like a true Englishman, shies from the correct, and opts for "Spirit" and "Force", even using the term "sublime". "Upon the whole, I think it must be confessed that *Homer* was of the two, and perhaps of all others, the vastest, the sublimist, and the most wonderful *Genius* ...."[18] The distinction that Temple draws corresponds to that of Mainwaring's between invention (the source of the sublime) and taste (the source of the beautiful); and both concur in placing the *forceful* above the *correct*.

Whatever influence seventeenth-century criticism wielded in the development of such aesthetic concepts as genius, sublimity, natural endowments, and the like, it is overshadowed by one force: *Longinus*.[19] The pseudo-Longinian treatise *Peri Hupsous* (*On the Sublime*), had been translated into English as early as 1652. But its rise to popularity in England did not begin till after 1674—the date of Boileau's influential French translation of the work. "Boileau's translation was the turning point of Longinus's reputation in England and France."[20] By the 1730s, Longinus was in apogee; the number of editions both in Greek and in English was enormous; and the frequency with which they were quoted drew this acid verse from Dean Swift:

> A forward Critick often dupes us
> With sham Quotations *Peri Hupsous*:
> And if we have not read *Longinus*,
> Will magisterially out-shine us.
> Then lest with *Greek* he over-run ye,
> Procure the Book for Love or Money,
> Translated from *Boileau's* Translation,
> And quote Quotation on Quotation.[21]

The general effect of Longinus was a rupture with neoclassicism, brought about through the emphasis upon the sublime as a separate aesthetic category: "*Beauty* came to include, generally speaking, those

---

[18] Sir William Temple, "Of Poetry", 82–3.
[19] For these general remarks on Longinus and the sublime, I am indebted to the classic study of the subject, Samuel H. Monk's *The Sublime* (Ann Arbor: University of Michigan Press, 1960).
[20] Ibid. 21.   [21] Quoted ibid. 23.

qualities and gentle emotions that neoclassic art sought to embody; *sublimity* might contain anything else that seemed susceptible of giving aesthetic pleasure provided it was grand enough and might conceivably 'transport'."[22]

Mainwaring was borne on the tide of Longinian tradition in England. When he came to write his *Handel*, in 1760, this tradition was common property. That Mainwaring followed the Longinian tradition is apparent even from the title-page of his book, which bears as a motto these words of Longinus: "I readily allow, that Writers of a lofty and tow'ring Genius are by no means pure and correct, since whatever is neat and accurate throughout, must be exceedingly liable to Flatness."[23]

We have seen that Longinus's characterization of Demosthenes was, for Mainwaring, commensurate with his own characterization of Handel as an artist of the sublime. And the motto with which he chooses to adorn his biography presents the notion of the sublime artist as a flawed artist—a notion which Mainwaring thought particularly applicable to Handel. For that matter, almost the complete arsenal of Mainwaring's critical weapons can be found in Longinus. The concept of sublime genius as a natural gift, suggested in the description of Demosthenes, is clearly formulated elsewhere. Longinus writes of "Elevation of Thought" as "rather a natural than an acquired Qualification ... ".[24] Yet the sublime "is not altogether lawless, but delights in a proper Regulation". So, for Longinus, as well as for Temple, Mainwaring, and many others, natural gifts must be combined with "learning". "Genius may sometimes want the Spur, but it stands as frequently in need of the Curb."[25] What Longinus lacks is a distinct division between the beautiful and the sublime; and that, as has been shown, had already begun to emerge as early as 1690, reaching a climax in Edmund Burke's *A Philosophical Enquiry into the Origin of our Ideas of the Sublime and Beautiful* (1757). Mainwaring, then, did not lack models for any of his critical views.

III

Mainwaring can scarcely be considered an innovator in criticism; nor, indeed, can he even be thought of as in the avant-garde with respect to

[22] Ibid. 55.
[23] Longinus, *Dionysius Longinus on the Sublime*, 78–9. I am grateful to Dr Lawrence A. Gushee of Yale University for his help in locating this passage.
[24] Ibid. 18.   [25] Ibid. 4–5.

his acceptance of other men's opinions. Was Mainwaring, however, at least original in his application of such critical theories as he found at hand to music in general, or Handel in particular? It would appear that here too Mainwaring has been anticipated in certain major respects, although with regard to the notion of the artist as originator and lawgiver, one recent writer has pointed out that " ... John Mainwaring in his life of Handel (1760) was among the first to apply the idea to a composer."[26]

The concept of musical invention as contrary to or apart from the rule was, as we have seen, propounded by Bacon, who wrote of the "musician that maketh an excellent air in music" doing so "by a kind of felicity ... and not by rule". Francis North, in his *A Philosophical Essay of Musick* (1677), made a distinction between "allowable Musick"—that is, music according to rules,—and "Excellent Musick"—music which, if not contrary to rules is, nevertheless, not susceptible of production through rules alone.[27] Roger North (Francis's brother) further amplifies this idea. He writes (*c.*1715–20): "Ayre is no more to be taught than witt, or a good style in wrighting." It is the product of "Nature, and not discipline," although rules are necessary "partly to direct or rather give aim to a composer, that he may know his mark, and how to steer his fancy, which let run loose, will prove like babble in discourse, impertinent and frivolous; and partly for a standard, which applyed may determine the justice, and demonstrate the errors, of a composition ... ".[28] Alexander Malcolm, in *A Treatise of Musick* (1721), takes a similar position. *Melody*, he writes, "is chiefly the Business of the Imagination; so that the Rules of *Melody* serve only to prescribe certain Limits to it ... ". Malcolm concludes: "There is a natural Genius without which no Rules are sufficient ... ".[29] The theories of Roger North and Alexander Malcolm are already familiar to us; for they merely translate Temple's theory of poetry into musical terms.

The notion of Handel as lawbreaker—the bad boy of music— appeared in English music criticism nearly thirty years before the publication of Mainwaring's *Memoirs*. Thus, in the satirical pamphlet *Harmony in an Uproar* (1734), an anonymous supporter of Handel

---

[26] Herbert M. Schueller, "Immanuel Kant and the Aesthetics of Music", *Journal of Aesthetics and Art Criticism*, 14 (1955), 226 n.

[27] [Francis North], *A Philosophical Essay of Musick* (London, 1677), 32.

[28] Roger North, *Roger North on Music*, ed. John Wilson (London: Novello, 1959), 71. Roger North's writings on music remained unpublished in the eighteenth century.

[29] Alexander Malcolm, *A Treatise of Musick* (Edinburgh, 1721), 420 and 546.

addresses this mock criticism to the composer: " ... I understand you have never read *Euclid*, are a declar'd Foe to all proper Modes, and Forms, and Tones of Musick, and scorn to be subservient to, or ty'd up by Rules, or have your Genius cramp'd: Thou *God* and *Vandal* to just Sounds!"[30] This writer alludes to those critical of Handel's disregard for musical convention and "learning", supporting genius's prerogative not to be "ty'd up by Rules". (One is reminded here of a story concerning Beethoven and the composer Anton Halm, related by Czerny. "Halm once brought a sonata of his own composition to him ... and when Beethoven pointed out a few errors, Halm retorted that he [B.] had also permitted himself many violations of the rules, Beethoven answered: 'I may do it, but not you.' "[31])

The identification of Handel with the sublime was also made prior to Mainwaring's biography. In 1753, William Hayes placed Handel first with regard to "the truly *Great* and *Heroic* ... ", characteristics associated with the sublime.[32] Charles Avison, at the same date, gave a description of Handel's style, enumerating many of the usual sublime characteristics, although the term itself is not used.

Mr. HANDEL is in Music, what his own DRYDEN was in Poetry; nervous, exalted, and harmonious; but voluminous, and, consequently, not always correct. Their Abilities equal to every Thing; their Execution frequently inferior. Born with Genius capable of *soaring the boldest Flights*; they have sometimes, to suit the vitiated Taste of the Age they lived in, *descended to the lowest*. Yet, as both their Excellencies are infinitely more numerous than their Deficiencies, so both their Characters will devolve to latest Posterity, not as Models of Perfection, yet glorious Examples of those amazing Powers that actuate the human Soul.[33]

This is the very picture of Handel that Mainwaring gives us: the sublime though flawed genius, triumphing over his inherent faults.

---

[30] Quoted in Deutsch, *Handel*, 349. The pamphlet was once attributed to Arbuthnot, but his authorship is now considered unlikely.

[31] Quoted in Alexander Wheelock Thayer, *The Life of Ludwig van Beethoven* (Carbondale, Ill: Southern Illinois University Press, 1960), ii. 326. Cf. Gluck's statement in the dedication of *Alceste*: "there is no rule I would not have felt in duty bound to break in order to achieve the desired effect." Hedwig and E. H. Mueller von Asow (eds.), *The Collected Correspondence and Papers of Christoph Willibald Gluck*, trans. Stewart Thomson (New York: St Martin's Press, 1962), 23.

[32] [William Hayes], *Remarks on Mr. Avison's Essay on Musical Expression* (London, 1753), quoted in Deutsch, *Handel*, 734.

[33] Charles Avison, *Reply to the Author of Remarks on the Essay on Musical Expression* (London, 1753), quoted in Deutsch, *Handel*, 736.

What of the composer as lawgiver to the art of music? The notion seems at least implicit in Bacon, Roger North, and Alexander Malcolm, with their emphasis upon musical invention as functioning apart from the established rules of composition. Avison comes still closer to Mainwaring's position that the "bold strokes" of inventive genius "are themselves the foundation of new rules".

He expresses the opinion, also held by Mainwaring, that musical principles, based as they are upon experience, are susceptible to evolution and progress in the light of fresh experience—an opinion that in Britain dates back at least to Joseph Addison, who wrote in *The Spectator* (no. 29, Tuesday, 3 April, 1711), that "music, architecture, and painting, as well as poetry and oratory, are to deduce their laws and rules from the general sense and taste of mankind, and not from the principles of those arts themselves ... ".[34] Avison writes: "*Nature* is still superior to *art*: and, as the first principles of all science were primarily deduced from nature, and have been brought, by slow degrees, to their present perfection; so, we may naturally conclude, these improvements may yet be carried higher."[35] If the composer be the source of "these improvements" in the "first principles" of music, he may be considered the musical lawgiver. In any case, Avison recognizes that the "rules" of musical composition are not to be slavishly followed and must, at times, be transgressed by the composer. "In Music, there are express laws relating to *modulation*, as well as to *harmony*; yet, if all composers indiscriminately were confined to these laws, we should soon see an end of all taste, spirit, and variety in their compositions: and I don't know whether, by this means, we should not be deprived of one of the strongest efforts of genius, *viz. that of nobly over-leaping the too narrow bounds of human art.*"[36]

There can be no doubt, I think, that Mainwaring's critical views are entirely derivative. Thus they are of no particular interest in themselves. What *is* noteworthy is that the first musical biographer should have

---

[34] Joseph Addison, *The Spectator* (New York: D. Appleton, 1879), i. 222.

[35] Avison, *Reply to the Author of Remarks on the Essay on Musical Expression*, in *idem*, *Essay on Musical Expression*, 3rd edn. (London, 1775), 193. Cf. Hume's essay "Of the Standard of Taste": "It is evident that none of the rules of composition are fixed by reasonings *a priori*, or can be esteemed abstract conclusions of the understanding, from comparing those habitudes and relations of ideas, which are eternal and immutable. Their foundation is the same with that of all the practical sciences, experience; nor are they any thing but general observations, concerning what has been universally found to please in all countries and in all ages." In *The Philosophical Works of David Hume* (Boston and Edinburgh: Little Brown, 1854), iii. 253.

[36] Avison, *Essay on Musical Expression*, 193–4.

seen so clearly the need of establishing a coherent critical point of view at all. Here he was prophetic. Nor was this unusual characteristic of Mainwaring's work overlooked by his contemporaries. An anonymous reviewer of the *Memoirs* wrote shortly after its publication, "The lovers of harmony will, no doubt, be highly delighted with memoirs, which, indeed, contain but few interesting particulars of the life, but great variety of pretty observations on the compositions of this sublime artist."[37] To be sure, if we weigh Mainwaring's *Handel* against the great musical biographies of the nineteenth century—Winterfeld's *Gabrieli*, Chrysander's *Handel*, Spitta's *Bach*—it will be found wanting. For it was merely a beginning—but not, after all, an unworthy one.

[37] *Critical Review*, 9 (1760), 306.

2

Herbert Spencer and a Musical Dispute

Herbert Spencer, the English philosopher of evolution, seems to have entertained a hearty contempt for criticism and disputation. He once wrote of a critic, "so far as I have observed, he has throughout followed the course which generally characterizes controversy—that of setting up men of straw and knocking them down."[1] One might expect, on the evidence of such a statement, that Spencer would have eschewed controversy. On the contrary, he relentlessly pursued the critics of his writings, defending every proposition as a mother hen her brood. Wrote Ernest Newman, "he is well known to have had an almost invincible repugnance of changing any of his opinions ... ".[2] Nothing characterizes this aspect of Spencer's intellectual life more fully than does the dispute which followed the publication, in 1857, of his essay "The Origin and Function of Music".[3] This "musical dispute" is the subject of the present essay.

SPENCER'S THEORY OF MUSIC

Spencer maintained a theory of music's origin which has been given the label "speech theory". It is based upon an observed affinity between music and the tones of emotional speech. However, analogies between

This article contains portions of an unpublished dissertation, "Herbert Spencer and a Musical Dispute", Department of Music History, Yale University, 1960. I wish to express here my gratitude to Professor William G. Waite of Yale University, who directed this research and critically read the present paper.

[1] Herbert Spencer, *First Principles*, 6th edn. (London: Williams and Norgate, 1904), 472.

[2] Ernest Newman, "A Note On Herbert Spencer", *Weekly Critical Review*, 2 (1904), 579.

[3] Herbert Spencer, "The Origin and Function of Music", *Fraser's Magazine*, 56 (1857). It appeared later, revised and enlarged, in the many editions of Spencer's collected essays.

music and speech did not, by any means, originate with Spencer. Early in the seventeenth century, such speculation was rife in the writings of the Florentine Camerata. Jacopo Peri, for example, writes in the Foreword to his opera *Euridice* (1601), that "in our speech some words are so intoned that harmony can be based upon them ... ".[4] The recognition of musical elements in speech and the conviction that articulate language arose from a primitive language of emotions led to speculation that music also developed from primitive emotive exclamation. Jean Jacques Rousseau expressed such an opinion in his *Essai sur l'Origine des Langues* (*c*.1749). "Accent produced melody ... . To speak and to sing were once the same thing ... ".[5] In England, at an earlier date, Roger North (d. 1733) maintained a similar position, assigning the origin of music to "the use of voices, and language among men".[6]

Spencer's "speech theory" is based upon what he takes to be an axiom of physiology: the direct relationship between mental and muscular activity. Spencer writes: "mental excitement of all kinds ends in excitement of the muscles; and ... the two preserve a more or less constant ratio to each other." In its first beginnings, music was, Spencer believed, a purely vocal activity. And since vocal activity is a species of muscular activity, the same relationship must hold between mental excitement and vocal phenomena as between mental excitement and muscular activity in general.

We have here, then, a principle underlying all vocal phenomena, including those of vocal music and by consequence, those of music in general. The muscles that move the chest, larynx, and vocal chords, contracting like other muscles in proportion to the intensity of feelings; every different contraction of these muscles involving, as it does, a different adjustment of the vocal organs; every different adjustment of the vocal organs causing a change in the sound emitted; it follows that *variations of voice are the physiological result of variation of feeling.* ... [7]

Spencer distinguished five characteristics of vocal utterances: *loudness, quality* or *timbre, pitch, intervals,* and *rate of variation.* The increased

---

[4] Oliver Strunk (ed.), *Source Readings in Music History* (New York: Norton, 1950), 374. Similar observations were made subsequently by Rousseau, Diderot, J. A. Hiller, and many others.

[5] Jean Jacques Rousseau, *Œuvres Complètes* (Paris, 1788–93), xvi, 238.

[6] Roger North, *Memoirs of Music*, ed. E. F. Rimbault (London, 1846), 7. See also pp. 13–14. Other eighteenth-century English writers to maintain this position were John Brown and Daniel Webb.

[7] Spencer, "Origin and Function of Music", 397; my italics.

emotional energy of excited speech tends to increase loudness, increase sonority, raise pitch, widen intervals, and produce a greater variety of sounds. In short, emotional speech begins to resemble music. "Those vocal peculiarities which indicate excited feeling, *are those which especially distinguish song from speech.*"[8] Music, then, is a physiological phenomenon, arising through an exaggeration of the emotional characteristics of human speech. Spencer concludes: "what we regard as the distinctive traits of song are simply the traits of emotional speech intensified and systematized. In respect of its general characteristics ... vocal music, and by consequence all music, is an idealization of the natural language of passion."[9]

From this account of music's origin, Spencer proceeds to an investigation of its function. He draws a connection between the function of music in human life and the general evolutionary process through which it has developed. Spencer states: "alike in occupations, sciences, arts, the divisions which had a common root, but by gradual divergences have become distinct and are now being separately developed, are not truly independent, but severally act and react on one another in their mutual advancement." He concludes: "there exists a relationship of this kind between music and speech."[10]

Spencer recognizes a duality in speech involving both its character and its function. "All speech is compounded into two elements: the words and the tones in which they are uttered—the signs of ideas and the signs of feelings." Now music arose from the tonal and, therefore, the emotional element of speech. But as music has continued to develop, so also has speech, not only the conceptual element but the emotional element as well. "If intellectual language is a growth, so also, without a doubt, is emotional language a growth." Spencer is now prepared to state specifically the dynamic relationship which exists between music and its parent, emotional speech. "Having its root, as we have endeavoured to show, in those tones, intervals, and cadences of speech which express feeling, arising by the combination and intensifying of these, and coming finally to have an embodiment of its own, music has all along been reacting upon speech, and increasing its power of rendering emotion."[11]

Of what importance is this function which music performs? For Spencer it is important indeed. The emotional expression which music

[8] Spencer, "Origin and Function of Music", 400.
[9] Ibid. 402.   [10] Ibid. 406.   [11] Ibid.

helps develop is bound up with Spencer's whole concept of the moral progress of mankind. "The tendency of civilization is more and more to repress the antagonistic elements of our characters and to develop the social ones. ... And while by this adaptation to the social state the sympathetic side of our nature is being unfolded, there is simultaneously growing up a language of sympathetic intercourse—a language through which we communicate to others the happiness we feel, and are made sharers in their happiness." Music helps develop the language of progress, and at the same time, in some way anticipates it. "Those vague feelings of inexperienced felicity which music arouses—those indefinite impressions of an unknown ideal life which it calls up, may be considered as a prophecy, to the fulfilment of which music itself is partly instrumental."[12]

CHARLES DARWIN AND EDMUND GURNEY

The first critic of Spencer's music theory was Charles Darwin, who, in *The Descent of Man* (1871) and *The Expression of the Emotions in Man and Animals* (1872), put forth a theory based on his own evolutionary concepts: a theory which in its general outline was opposed to the position Spencer had taken.[13] Whereas Spencer had maintained that music's origin lay in speech, Darwin, on the contrary, held that music not only *preceded* speech in time, but was in fact *the source* of speech. For Darwin, the origin of music was accounted for by his principle of "sexual selection". According to this principle, the strongest, most active, or most attractive male or female will be the one most likely to gain a mate and, therefore, to reproduce. With respect to birds, the production of pleasing sounds, i.e. "singing", is a primary means of attraction. In *The Descent of Man*, Darwin took pains to point out that in addition to birds, animals much closer to man on the evolutionary scale demonstrate similar patterns of behavior. The ultimate conclusion to be

---

[12] Ibid. 408. Tolstoy, some forty years later, expressed a similar opinion when he wrote: "the evolution of feeling proceeds by means of art—feelings less kind and less necessary for the well-being of mankind being replaced by others kinder and more needful for that end" (*What Is Art?*, trans. Aylmer Maude (London: Oxford University Press, 1959), 231).

[13] For a more detailed account of Darwin's position and his dispute with Spencer, see my article "Charles Darwin On Music", *Journal of the American Musicological Society*, 12 (1959).

drawn is, of course, that primitive man himself depended partly upon the beauty of his voice to attract a mate. Through the process of sexual selection, such characteristics of voice as were attractive to the opposite sex would have been passed on to succeeding generations, resulting ultimately in vocal music. Darwin states his quarrel with Spencer in this way:

> Mr. Spencer comes to an exactly opposite conclusion to that at which I have arrived. He concludes, as did Diderot formerly, that the cadences used in emotional speech afford the foundation from which music has been developed; whilst I conclude that musical notes and rhythm were first acquired by the male or female progenitors of mankind for the sake of charming the opposite sex.[14]

Soon after Darwin's minor foray against Spencer, Edmund Gurney (1847–88) launched a major offensive. Gurney and his older German contemporary Eduard Hanslick have come to represent a position in the aesthetics of music somewhat analogous to that of Clive Bell in painting. This position, often termed "formalist" or "purist", is one which attempts as much as possible to exclude "life-values" from the work of art, emphasizing its formal self-contained character. In music this view is opposed by the traditional theory of emotive expression, accepted by Spencer. Gurney's opposition to Spencer must be viewed in the light of his purist stand with regard to the emotive question in music aesthetics.

Gurney's criticism of Spencer appeared first in an article, "On Some Disputed Points in Music", in the *Fortnightly Review*, 1876. He later reiterated these critical remarks in his major aesthetic work, *The Power of Sound* (1880). Gurney's primary objective in the article of 1876 was to question Spencer's basic characterization of music and emotional speech. As we have seen, Spencer identified five characteristics which distinguish song from speech: loudness, timbre, pitch, size of intervals, and rate of variation. Gurney argued that none of these is a truly definitive element of music. And if these elements do not truly distinguish song from speech, neither can Spencer's account of music's origin be correct, for these are the elements on which the theory rests.

> He [Spencer] considers that song arose from emphasizing and intensifying these peculiarities. On not one of these heads does he seem to me to succeed in making out his case. The first, loudness, is perhaps the most plausible; but loudness though a frequent is by no means a universal or essential element,

14 Charles Darwin, *The Descent of Man*, 2nd edn. (New York, 1897), 572 n. 39.

either of song or of emotional speech. Still less is musical resonance an essential element of the latter.[15]

For Gurney, the characteristics of song are too distinct from those of speech to establish any sort of direct relationship between them. According to Helmholtz, whose opinion Gurney highly valued, the emotional characteristics of the voice exhibit what Gurney calls a "gliding" character and what might more accurately be termed a *glissando* effect. Music, on the other hand, displays a structure of fixed intervals. This disparity, Gurney claims, presents a real difficulty for any theory which attempts to make out a relationship between the material of·speech and that of music. "Music is distinguished from speech in that it proceeds not only by fixed degrees in time but *by fixed degrees in the scale.*"[16] As we shall see, Spencer took hold of this remark and neatly turned it to his own advantage.

Spencer first replied publicly to the critics of his music theory in 1890, although he had, as early as 1872, expressed dissenting remarks to Darwin by letter.[17] His reply of 1890 appeared in the periodical *Mind*, and was later appended to the final version of his essay "On the Origin and Function of Music". Spencer's case against Darwin emphasizes two weaknesses in the Darwinian position. Darwin had assumed, to begin with, that the vocal utterances of animals are concerned for the most part with courting behavior. Spencer points out that this is by no means the case. He writes, for example: " ... I have made memoranda concerning various songbirds dating back to 1883. On February 7 of that year I heard a lark singing several times; and still more remarkable, during the mild winter of 1884 I saw one soar and heard it sing on January 10. Yet the lark does not pair till March."[18] He concludes that Darwin "ignores those multitudinous sounds not produced 'under the excitement of love, rage, and jelousy,' but which accompany ordinary amounts of feelings various in their kinds."[19] Secondly, Spencer maintained that evolutionary evidence did not support Darwin's theory. "Just as we find other traits (instance arms and hands adapted for grasping) becoming more marked as we approach Man; so should we find, becoming more

[15] Edmund Gurney, "On Some Disputed Points in Music", *Fortnightly Review*, new series, 20 (1876), 107.
[16] Ibid. 113; my italics.
[17] Spencer included this letter, dated 16 Nov. 1872, in his *Autobiography* (London: Williams and Norgate, 1904), ii, 238–9.
[18] Herbert Spencer, "The Origin of Music", *Mind*, 15 (1890), 452.
[19] Ibid. 451.

marked, this sexual use of the voice, which is supposed to end in human song. But we do not find this."[20]

Turning to Gurney's criticism, Spencer focuses his attention upon what he takes to be a general misconception of the evolutionary process. Some of Gurney's arguments Spencer attributes to the mistaken notion that "whatever is more highly evolved in general is more highly evolved in every trait". On the contrary, Spencer points out, "very generally, a higher degree of evolution in some or most respects, is accompanied by an equal or lower degree of evolution in other respects. On the average, increase of locomotive power goes along with advance of evolution; and yet numerous mammals are more fleet than man."[21] Gurney had rejected Spencer's contention that song and emotional speech were characterized, in part, by *loudness*. Loudness, says Gurney, is not an essential element of song or emotional speech. Spencer replies: "this criticism implies the above described misconception. If in a song, or rather in some part or parts of a song, the trait of loudness is absent, while the other traits of developed utterance are present, it simply illustrates the truth that the traits of a highly-evolved product are frequently not all present together."[22] Again, Gurney maintains that recitative, which Spencer considers a half-way point between speech and song, instead of displaying more *variation of pitch*—a trait which characterizes a higher level in the evolution of song—displays, on the contrary, a greater *monotony* with respect to *pitch*. Spencer replies to this objection in a similar manner:

But Mr. Gurney overlooks the fact that while, in recitative, some traits of developed emotional utterance are not present, two of its traits are present. One is that greater resonance of tone, caused by greater contraction of the vocal chords, which distinguish it from ordinary speech. The other is the relative elevation of pitch, or divergence from the medium tones of voice: a trait similarly implying greater strain of certain vocal muscles, resulting from stronger feeling.[23]

With regard to Gurney's contention that the determinate pitch structure of music cannot have evolved from the indeterminate *glissando* of speech, Spencer maintains, again, that Gurney has argued from a misconception of the evolutionary process. In this case, Gurney has violated what Spencer takes to be a universal principle of evolution. "Had

[20] Spencer, "The Origin of Music", 454.
[21] Ibid. 458–9.   [22] Ibid. 459.   [23] Ibid. 459–60.

Mr. Gurney known that evolution in all cases is from the indefinite to the definite, he would have seen that as a matter of course the gradations of emotional speech must be indefinite in comparison with the gradations of developed music."[24] According to Spencer's metaphysics of evolution, the evolution from indeterminate to determinate pitch in fact exemplifies the expected course of evolution from *homogeneity* to *heterogeneity* or from the *diffuse* to the *definite* state.

TWO FOREIGN CRITICS

The reappearance of Spencer's speech theory in the form of his answer to Darwin and Gurney brought a new generation of critics to the fore. In 1891 two "foreign" critics, the German ethnomusicologist Richard Wallaschek (1860–1917) and the American psychologist James McKeen Cattell (1860–1944), published critical comments on Spencer's music theory. Wallaschek advanced a theory of music's origin which took rhythm as its ultimate principle. He writes, "it is a well-known fact, established by the observations of travellers and investigators, that the one essential feature in primitive music is rhythm, melody being a matter of accident. ... Rhythm taken in a general sense to include 'keeping in time,' is the essence of music, in its simplest form as well as in the most skilfully elaborated of fugues of modern composers. To recall a tune the rhythm must be revived first, and the melody will easily be recalled." Rhythm, for Wallaschek, is not only a necessary element of music but a sufficient condition for its existence. He concludes, therefore: "the origin of music must be sought in a rhythmical impulse in man."[25]

In taking such a position, Wallaschek placed himself in opposition to both Darwin and Spencer. With regard to Darwin, Wallaschek reiterated Spencer's argument that vocal utterance did not seem to be primarily concerned with courtship behavior. He states: "even if all Darwin's hypotheses are correct, it would not follow that human music and dances were the developed outcome of bird's songs and dancing among animals, for the reason that in a primitive stage of society the

---

[24] Ibid. 460.
[25] Richard Wallaschek, "On the Origin of Music", *Mind*, 16 (1891), 375. Subsequent to Wallaschek's statement of his rhythm theory, Karl Bücher presented an extensive theory of music's origin, based upon rhythm and its relation to work. Bücher first stated his version of the rhythm theory in 1896. See Karl Bücher, *Arbeit und Rhythmus*, 4th edn. (Leipzig and Berlin, 1909).

former have in many cases nothing to do with love."[26] Against Spencer's speech theory, Wallaschek argues in this wise: "Music is an expression of emotion, speech the expression of thought. If we assume that music originates in, and is developed from speech, we must also assume that emotion is developed from thought." The assumption that emotion is developed from thought, Wallaschek is not willing to entertain. He maintains that emotional expression and intellectual expression have their sources in two distinct parts of the brain. "Many cases of aphasia prove that an expression cannot be emotional and intellectual at the same time, the one kind of expression arising in and spreading through different parts of the brain and nervous system from those occupied by the other." Wallaschek concludes: "I think then that music and speech did not arise the one from the other, but that both arose from (or together with) an identical primitive stage in one of their elements."[27] (It should be noted that even if Wallaschek were correct in his assertion that intellectual and emotional expression arise from "different parts of the brain and nervous system", it would by no means exclude the possibility of the one influencing the other. It has long been established, for example, that skills can be transferred from one side of an organism's body to the other, in spite of the fact that the neural connection between the two sides has been artificially inhibited.[28] Such evidence seems to indicate that there might well be a transfer of responses from the linguistic to the musical "faculty", even though it be conclusively demonstrated that the two are neurologically separate and distinct.)

Cattell, the second of the foreign critics, raises an interesting question not as to the origin of music in general but rather as to the origin of one element: *harmony*. In fact, Cattell is in agreement with Spencer and in opposition to Darwin as regards the origin of music. "It is likely", writes Cattell, "that most readers ... will agree with Mr. Spencer in holding that music had its origin in vocal sounds expressing emotions of all kinds, and not solely in vocal sounds prompted by amatory feelings."[29] Now Spencer's theory, as he usually stated it, presented the origin of

[26] Wallaschek, "On the Origin of Music", 379.

[27] Ibid. 383. Wallaschek's views with regard to the distinctness of of the musical and linguistic faculties were shared by a number of his contemporaries, including Jules Combarieu, *Music: Its Laws and Evolution* (London, 1910); Ernest Newman, *A Study of Wagner* (London, 1899); and Salomon Stricker, *Du Language et de la musique* (Paris, 1885).

[28] R. S. Woodworth and S. Schlossberg, *Experimental Psychology* (New York: Holt, 1954), 739.

[29] James McKeen Cattell, "On the Origin of Music", *Mind*, 16 (1891), 386.

unaccompanied song. However, the question naturally arises, "whence harmony?" This question Spencer had completely ignored in the essay of 1857, and, in the article of 1890, he expressed the opinion that the speech theory could not answer it satisfactorily.

It goes without saying that there must be otherwise accounted for that relatively modern element in musical effect which has now almost outgrown in importance the other elements—I mean harmony. This cannot be affiliated on the natural language of emotion; since, in such language limited to successive tones, there cannot originate the effects wrought by simultaneous tones.[30]

Spencer's conclusion with regard to harmony, Cattell rejects.

Cattell had studied psychology in Leipzig with Wilhelm Wundt and was, naturally enough, under the influence of German scientists. In his criticism of Spencer he reveals particularly the influence of Helmholtz. Cattell maintains that the overtone series presents material for the origin of harmony.

Mr. Spencer seems to hold that nothing in a single tone corresponds to a combination of tones, and that the intervals used in music are not found in nature. The facts are, however, different. Rameau and d'Alembert knew, more than a hundred years ago, that the overtones (harmonics) given by a single tone are in harmony with each other, and Helmholtz has shown that all difference in timbre (quality) of sounds rests on the number and strength of the overtones present.

Since the elements of harmony are contained in individual tones, and since melody is the succession of individual tones, Cattell concludes, "harmony has been developed from melody. ... "[31]

Three months after the appearance of Wallaschek's and Cattell's critical remarks, Spencer published his reply. Wallaschek's contention that music arose, not from tones but, rather, from rhythm, Spencer finds quite untenable. He writes, "in this view I cannot coincide, for the reason that it regards music as acquiring its essential character by a trait which it has in common with other things, instead of by a trait which it has apart from other things."[32] Spencer further amplifies this argument in *Facts and Comments* (1902): "We deny the name 'song' absolutely to the rhythmical sounds made by the sparrow, in which there is no combination of notes unlike one another, and we give it to

---

[30] Spencer, "Origin of Music", 466.
[31] Cattell, "On the Origin of Music", 387.
[32] Herbert Spencer, "On the Origin of Music", *Mind*, 16 (1891), 535.

the variously-combined sounds made by the blackbird, though these are entirely unrhythmical. ... "[33] Spencer concludes that "in the absence of combinations of tones there is no music."[34] What Spencer maintains here is that rhythm is not a sufficient condition for music and, indeed, appears not even to be a necessary one. If that is the case, it cannot be asserted that sound becomes music merely through the acquisition of rhythm.

Having dealt with Wallaschek's general position with regard to the origin of music, Spencer attempted to answer his principal criticism. Wallaschek maintained, as we have seen, that the sole office of speech was the expression of thought. This Spencer denies, stating: "it is not true that speech is 'the expression of thought' exclusively, since the cadences which ordinarily constitute part of it habitually express feeling. ... " However, granting that the expression of thought is the *principal* element of speech, Spencer denies that he considers music to be evolved from that element. He writes: "the whole argument of the essay is to show that it is from the emotional element of speech that music is evolved—not from its intellectual element." Wallaschek's mistake Spencer lays at Gurney's door. "As used by Mr. Gurney, 'speech theory' seemed to me very much a nickname; and it has now proved to be a mischievous nickname. ... "[35]

Turning to Cattell's proposal that harmony evolved from melody, Spencer writes: "to establish the evolution of the one from the other, there must be found some identifiable transitions between the combinations of tones constituting *timbre*, which do not constitute harmony to our perception; and those combinations of tones which do constitute harmony to our perception; and I know of no such transitions." After rejecting Cattell's theory of the origin of harmony, Spencer presents his own speculations in this regard. He states: "so far as I know ... harmony commenced with the fugal repetition of a melody in ecclesiastical chants. Though the melody was the same, and the effect was produced by one choir commencing a bar or two after the other, yet the new kind of effect suddenly achieved cannot be considered as *evolved* without stretching somewhat unduly the meaning of the word."[36] Spencer had presented this hypothesis previously in *First Principles*, where he attributes the first polyphony to possible errors in performance. "It became the habit

[33] Spencer, *Facts and Comments* (New York: D. Appleton, 1902), 53.
[34] Spencer, "On the Origin of Music", 535.
[35] Ibid. 536.   [36] Ibid. 537.

(possibly first suggested by a mistake) for the second choir to commence before the first choir had ceased: thus producing a fugue."[37] If we disregard Spencer's rather naive musical vocabulary and his apparent assumption that the earliest polyphony in the West was imitative, his hypothesis seems plausible enough. In fact, recent speculation with regard to the origin of organum includes suggestions of accidental jumps to the fourth and fifth as well as accidental overlap of melodies.[38]

ERNEST NEWMAN

In his first book on Wagner, *A Study of Wagner* (1899), Ernest Newman joined the ranks of Spencer's critics. In this early work, Newman displayed a marked antipathy to the Wagnerian aesthetic. And since Wagner's conception of the relation between *word* and *tone* came very close to Spencer's, it was inevitable that Newman, in considering Wagner's position, should be led to a criticism of Spencer's speech theory. Newman looked at Spencer's theory through a musician's eyes and saw in it an "unmusical" view of music. He could not see in speech the musical potential that the speech theory required.

Speak in your ordinary manner, for example, and then in a slightly intensified manner, and the mental transition is felt to be very slight. Hardly more noticeable is the transition from excited speech to ordinary recitative. ... But sing a song, or play an adagio upon the piano, and you will realize at once that you have got upon quite a different plane of psychology. There is no longer a mere difference of degree ... *there is an absolute difference in kind.*[39]

Newman attacks the contention, central to Spencer's position, that since music and speech have certain characteristics in common, this indicates that the one evolved from the other. Such arguments from analogy, Newman considers inconclusive. He states:

the resemblances between the external characteristics of speech and those of song are only what might be expected, seeing that both are phenomena of sound, and sound can only vary in the ways indicated by Mr. Spencer. There is no necessity, however, to assume merely on the basis of these resemblances, that song is only an intensification of speech; any more than when a man has

---

[37] Spencer, *First Principles*, 289.
[38] For a review of such theories, see Gustave Reese, *Music in the Middle Ages* (New York: Norton, 1940), ch. 9.
[39] Newman, *Study of Wagner*, 163–4; my italics.

a headache and looks pale, we need assume that the paleness is due to the
headache. ...

Newman further maintains that the characteristics common to speech
and music are overshadowed by their differences. He seizes here upon
the element of harmony, pointing out that a theory which is unable to
account for the origin of harmony cannot be considered a satisfactory
theory of music's origin. Newman writes:

the mere resemblance of song and speech in their most external characteristics
is not a proof that one is the outcome of the other, but simply that they have
certain causal phenomena in common; while the internal differences between
them are greater than their resemblances. Mr. Spencer himself admits that his
theory affords no explanation of the place of harmony in music, while many
aestheticians have found it almost as unsatisfactory in respect to the origin of
melody.[40]

In 1902, one year before his death, Spencer completed his final work,
Facts and Comments, a collection of brief essays.[41] In two of these essays,
"The Origin of Music" and "Developed Music", Spencer concerns
himself with the origin of music, answering Newman's criticism and
further clarifying his own position. They represent Spencer's last word
on the question of music's origin. In answering Newman's criticism,
Spencer reiterated an opinion expressed in the first reply to his critics: to
wit, that his theory of origin had been taken for a general theory of music.
Originally Spencer had directed these remarks to Edmund Gurney. It
is not surprising that Newman too should be the butt of such criticism,
for he held a position in this dispute similar to that of Gurney, arguing
from aesthetic considerations, rather than on theoretical grounds. "I
gave an account of the *origin* of music," writes Spencer,

and now I am blamed because my conception of music does not include a
conception of music as fully developed! If to someone who said that an oak
comes from an acorn it were replied that he had manifestly never seen an oak,
since an acorn contains no trace of all its complexities of form and structure, the
reply would not be thought a rational one ... What is every process of evolution
but the gradual assumption of traits which were not originally possessed?

Again, in defending his position with regard to the origin of harmony,
Spencer accused Newman of taking his theory of music's origin for a
theory of its developed aesthetic character. With direct reference to

---

[40] Newman, *Study of Wagner*, 163.
[41] Spencer's unfinished *Autobiography* was published posthumously in 1904.

Newman's assertion that the speech theory cannot account for "the place of harmony in modern music", Spencer states: "with equal reason the assertion that all mathematics begins with finger-counting might be rejected because, if so, no explanation is forthcoming of the differential calculus!" For Spencer, the origin of music was an event lost in the prehistory of primitive man. The origin of harmony, however, he considered a comparatively late event in history, not at all involved with music's primeval beginnings. "History itself shows us", he concludes, "that harmony, being a late development of music, could not possibly be recognized in an account of its origin."[42]

Spencer also considers Newman's contention that the transition from recitative to song is a transition to "a different plane of psychology". Newman admitted, as we have seen, that the transition from ordinary speech to excited speech and from excited speech to recitative are only gradual steps, as Spencer had maintained. But he balks at the transition from recitative to song, claiming that here there is not only a difference in degree but a difference in kind as well. Spencer finds this partial acceptance implausible. "To most it will seem strange that along with the belief that there is a natural transition from excited speech to recitative there should go a denial that there can be any such transition from recitative to song." We reach here an impasse which reveals the conflicting interests in this dispute. In the opinion of Newman and Gurney, Spencer was deaf to the aesthetic qualities of music. To Spencer, the aesthetic point of view seemed irrelevant. Therefore, he merely repeated what to him seemed evident and in no conflict with the distinctive aesthetic character of music. "Such distinction as exists between recitative and melody is a distinction which may be recognized while asserting that the two have a common source: melody rising a step higher than recitative as recitative rises a step higher than excited speech."[43]

Spencer took leave of his critics in the same confident tone with which he had first stated his theory in 1857. He had answered them to his his own satisfaction and had moved not a jot from his original position. In a final act of defiance, Spencer threw up this challenge: "With the established doctrine that from simple vocal signs of ideas language has been developed, there must obviously go the doctrine that from similarly rude beginnings there has been a development of music; and if so there must be faced the question—What rude beginnings?

---

[42] Spencer, *Facts and Comments*, 55–6.   [43] Ibid. 56–7.

Those who reject the answer here given are bound to give another. What
can it be?"[44]

FINALE

In an essay entitled "Herbert Spencer and the Origin of Music",
published in *Musical Studies* (1905), Newman wrote the finale to the
Spencer dispute. That is not to say that he resolved the issues. Newman
had written the last word only because there could be no rejoinder
from Spencer—he had died two years before. In a memorial article
to Spencer, written shortly after his death, Newman re-expresses the
musician's mistrust of the theoretical mind, an attitude which was
revealed, although less explicitly, in his earlier criticism of Spencer.
Newman writes: "Spencer, indeed, great as was his interest in aesthetic
questions, always handled them as a scientist, not as an artist." And with
direct reference to the music theory, Newman states: "nobody can deny
the interest, the fascination of his various essays on the origin, nature,
and development of music; but there is always, to me at least, a sense that
some tiny but essential element is lacking; it is a wonderful achievement
for a man who had not the complete musical psychology, but it falls short
just where the complete musical psychology is requisite."[45] Many years
after these words were written, Newman still displayed this mistrust of
Spencer's theoretical orientation to musical matters. In the final volume
of *The Life of Richard Wagner* (1947), Newman wrote of Spencer's
opinions on Wagner, "it is amusing to see the philosopher ... trying his
best to pass Wagner's complex art through the milling machinery of his
own severely logical mind".[46]

In *Musical Studies*, Newman again reveals his dissatisfaction with
Spencer's method. Newman had maintained in his original criticism of
Spencer that the similarity in certain respects, of music and speech, does
not imply the origin of the one from the other. In *Musical Studies* he
restates this position. "It is unquestionable that, on the whole, a loud
tone in speaking and a loud tone in singing both indicate heightened
feeling; and that in all the other respects enumerated by him [Spencer],
song and speech exhibit precisely the same characteristics. But that does

44 Spencer, *Facts and Comments*, 60.
45 Newman, "Note On Herbert Spencer", 580.
46 Newman, *The Life of Richard Wagner*, iv (London, 1947), 536 n. 12.

not authorise us, in any way, to assert that song has 'grown out of' speech. Spencer argued too hastily from a mere analogy to a cause."[47] In the memorial article, Newman expressed the opinion that this tendency to argue from analogy was a general defect in Spencer's method, and not merely an isolated instance in his theory of music. "If he had a defect as a reasoner," writes Newman, "it was a tendency to rely too much on arguments from analogy. ... The passion for symmetry and for large, comprehensive inductions, is answerable for his weakest as for his strongest efforts." Interestingly enough, Newman himself, in his own writings, shows a strong theoretical propensity; and he was not without admiration for Spencer's rigor. Therefore, he could also write of Spencer: "to read one of his superb demonstrations, with its orderly marshalling of facts, its dexterous gradation of them according to their importance, its almost imperceptible evocation of the desired conclusion, step by step, the whole argument finally bearing down upon you with the irresistible momentum of a magnificent phalanx, was to get not only a lesson in logic but a real aesthetic thrill."[48] To the last, Newman remained an admirer of Spencer's intellectual powers, and yet doubted the applicability of such a mind to questions of an aesthetic nature.

Since the beginning of the twentieth century, the origin of music as a subject of inquiry has all but disappeared from the pages of scholarly literature. Our era is not prone to flights of speculation and synthesis in the historical disciplines; and, despite the relevance of positive science to certain of its aspects, the speech theory will remain, at least in the foreseeable future, a speculative venture. The systematic spirit and speculative disposition which Spencer represents are not in high repute. In the Herbert Spencer Lecture of 1914 at Oxford, Bertrand Russell expressed the following opinion of speculative philosophy in general, and Spencer in particular. "To build up systems of the world ... is not, I believe, any more feasible than the discovery of the philosopher's stone. What is feasible is the understanding of general forms, and the divisions of traditional problems into a number of separate and less baffling questions. 'Divide and conquer' is the maxim of success here as elsewhere."[49] I think Curt Sachs reflected this attitude when he

---

[47] Newman, *Musical Studies* (London and New York, 1905), 193.
[48] Newman, "Note On Herbert Spencer", 579–80.
[49] Bertrand Russell, "On Scientific Method in Philosophy", in *Mysticism and Logic, and Other Essays* (London: George Allen & Unwin, 1951), 113.

wrote with regard to speculation on the origin of music, "instead of guessing how things could have happened, we go back to their earliest preserved form."[50] Yet speculation on ultimate questions will continue to excite people's imaginations. And in a time more congenial to such speculation, the speech theory and the origin of music will again occupy the attention of music theorists. "The feeble beginnings of whatever afterwards becomes great or eminent, are interesting to mankind."[51]

[50] Curt Sachs, *The Rise of Music in the Ancient World* (New York: Norton, 1943), 20.

[51] Charles Burney, *A General History of Music*, ed. Frank Mercer (New York: Dover, 1957), i. 11.

PART II

OPERA AND FILM

3

Handel's Operas: The Form of Feeling and the Problem of Appreciation

Serious artworks of the past, as well as those of the present, may pose a problem of appreciation for even sympathetic and receptive audiences. In one sense it is the *same* problem: the problem of the unfamiliar. But in another, obvious sense it is a different problem. For in the case of contemporary artworks it is the unfamiliarity of the new and the shocking that is the problem; whereas in the case of those problematic artworks of bygone ages, it is the unfamiliarity of the old, the forgotten, the unfashionable. In other words, the problem of appreciating artworks of the past is the problem of lost traditions, the problem of appreciating contemporary artworks, particularly those of the avant-garde, is the problem of no tradition at all: a tradition yet to be or in the making.

With regard to problematic artworks of the past, the villain, needless to say, is the passage of time, during which tribal memory fades and tradition is broken and lost. But it would be a mistake to think that the relationship between time and difficulty is a simple function: that a work from the Renaissance (say) is necessarily less difficult for us than a work from the Middle Ages, and a work from the Middle Ages necessarily less difficult than one from Classical Antiquity. For I dare say, the plays of Dryden, in rhymed couplets throughout, are far greater obstacles to the appreciation of contemporary audiences than the plays of Shakespeare and Sophocles. Nevertheless, we can certainly accept it as a reasonable generalization that the passage of historical time between us and the artwork *tends* always to make for difficulty of appreciation, and must, therefore, be compensated for in some manner or other by anyone wishing to enjoy artworks of the more or less distant past, be it the Middle Ages, Classical Antiquity, or even the eighteenth century.

Certainly the operas of Handel are no exception to this general rule. They have by no means had an easy passage from then to now, and have suffered almost total eclipse from the time Handel turned exclusively to English oratorio. Indeed, it is only in the very recent past that these masterpieces of the musical theater have begun to appear in the repertory.

Even though so much music of the High Baroque, including Handel's, is widely appreciated by concertgoers, Handel's operas seem to present difficulties out of proportion to the time that has elapsed since their heyday. It is this aspect of Handel's operas, these difficulties, which I want to talk about today.

I

In my book *Osmin's Rage*, I located the problem of appreciation with regard to Handel's operas, I am sure to no one's surprise, in the da capo aria, which is, of course, the major structural building block of Handelian *opera seria*. I say to no one's surprise because, as is well known, the da capo aria was already considered a serious stumbling block to musical drama in Handel's waning years, its supposed basic flaw fully exposed. The major charge against it was lack of dramatic verisimilitude. For the operatic aria was, almost universally, the vehicle for the expression of a character's emotional state. And since, to fulfill its musical form, its first section had to be repeated after its second section's close, it presented the strange spectacle of a character expressing, all over again, what had already been expressed. As Francesco Algoratti succinctly put the point, in 1755:

Words are to be [musically] treated in no other manner but according as the passion dictates; and when the sense of an air is finished, the first part of it ought never to be sung over again, which is one of our modern innovations and quite repugnant to the natural process of our speech and passions, that are not accustomed to thus turn about and recoil upon themselves.[1]

Furthermore, to a modern audience, the emotive expression itself of Handel's operatic arias, as I pointed out in my book, is bound to seem stiff, stilted, overly controlled: in other words, completely lacking in that spontaneity and, if I may so put it, that explosiveness we ordinarily associate with the expression of intense feeling states. The Handel arias are, as I put it, emotive set pieces.

[1] Oliver Strunk (ed.), *Source Readings in Music History* (New York: Norton, 1950), 669.

The way I tried to answer this two-pronged indictment of the da capo aria—the driving engine of Handel's operas—was to show that if one takes, so to speak, a historical perspective, one can come to see that these arias are far from unfaithful to the nature and structure of the emotions, as the emotions were viewed by Handel's contemporaries, instantiated in the characters that people his works for the operatic stage. Let me review this defense briefly.

The core of the argument is the simple but incontestable claim that during most of Handel's creative life, and certainly during his operatic years, the prevailing view of the emotions was the Cartesian view, as presented to the world, in 1649, in René Descartes's highly influential book *The Passions of the Soul*. On this view, there are six basic emotions: wonder, love, hatred, desire, joy, and sadness.[2] The proximate cause of each is a specific, particular motion of what Descartes called the "vital spirits", *esprits animaux* in the original French edition—a subtle fluid (or gaseous) substance that flows through the brain and nervous system in the manner of a kind of miniature hydraulic system. Thus the emotions are conceived of as discrete, hard-edged mental states caused to be aroused by six discrete physical motions of a material medium: six emotions, six particular motions of the *esprits animaux*—a one-to-one relationship. So the emotions, on the Cartesian view, are, so to speak, emotive routines: each with a specific, hard-edged behavior pattern of its own. Ambiguity is not in evidence.

Descartes's emotive psychology was very quickly taken up by theorists of musical expression, and may even have been in place in Descartes's inaugural work, the *Compendium musicae* of 1618. It had its most ardent supporter in Johann Mattheson, whose highly influential *Der vollkommene Capellmeister*, completely systematized, in 1739, a Cartesian theory of how music represents the human emotions: a theory that, informally, was already common coin among practicing composers of the High Baroque, including, of course, Bach and Handel.

In essence, the core idea was that music is to represent the emotions by, in effect, representing in musical "motion" the appropriate motions of the vital spirits. This idea can quickly be apprehended by quoting directly from Mattheson:

Since, for example, joy is an expansion of our soul, thus it follows reasonably and naturally that I could best express this affect by large and expanded intervals.

[2] René Descartes, *The Passions of the Soul*, trans. Lowell Bair (New York: Bantam Matrix Books, 1966), 141.

Whereas if one knows that sadness is a contraction of these subtle parts of our body, then it is easy to see that the small and smallest intervals are the most suitable for this. passion.[3]

And so on for the rest of the Cartesian "passions of the soul".

With this concept of the emotions at least implicitly part of his intellectual background, if not fully before his conscious mind, Handel endeavored to "represent" the passions of his operatic characters in music. And, very often, he did it supremely well.

But is it any wonder, then, that we may have a problem hearing the emotive "realism" in Handel's dramatic works? For to the extent that *our* picture of the human emotions differs from the picture prevalent in Handel's day, we will find Handel's musical reflection of *his* picture distorted because, of course, we have *our* picture before our minds, not his, when we listen to them. And the antidote to that predicament is, so I suggested in *Osmin's Rage*, to try to temporarily make ourselves, so to speak, Cartesian listeners, so that we can hear the perfect match that Handel achieved between the music he composed and the emotions as he and his audiences took them to be. Handel's characters express their emotions in ways that seem to us to lack the spontaneity and, if I may so put it, the messiness of the emotive life, not because of Handel's ineptitude, but because he did not see the emotive life as spontaneous and messy. So until we can take Handel's Cartesian point of view as provisionally our own, we cannot fully, or perhaps at all, appreciate the dramatic success of his operatic arias or, therefore, the dramatic success of the operas themselves. Which is to put no more nor no less a burden on us than we must take up if we are to fully appreciate the actions and expression of Oedipus the King or Hamlet the Dane.

So much, then, for the charge that Handel's dramatic characters express their emotions, musically, in unrealistically neat ways, lacking in spontaneity. They are simply behaving as Cartesian creatures will do, under the influence of their Cartesian *esprits animaux*—somewhat stately and hard-edged, by modern standards, but just as they should do, under the influence of the emotive machinery with which they are endowed. But what of the further charge, the charge that the very structure of the da capo aria, the "da capo" itself, makes for a fatally flawed emotive expression? What of Algarotti's charge that people don't

---

[3] Johann Mattheson, *Der vollkommene Capellmeister*, trans. Ernest C. Harriss (Ann Arbor: UMI Research Press, 1981), 104.

repeat themselves in reality, the way the da capo form forces them to do in musical drama? A charge, by the way, that was brought against it again and again.

The answer is simple: Algarotti and the others were just plain wrong. Certain kinds of people, in certain kinds of situations and circumstances, *do* tend to repeat themselves incessantly. And *one* of those kinds of people is the crowd that inhabits the opera librettos Handel and his contemporaries set. What are these characters like?

As you all know, they are, to put it mildly, "larger than life": kings, queens, emperors, princes, princesses, knights, magicians, enchantresses. Furthermore, they are all in the grip of towering passions. Moderation is definitely not one of their virtues. They are, in a word, *obsessed*. When they love, they love obsessively; when they hate, their hate is unrelenting; when they grieve, their grief is inconsolable. They are, indeed, just the kinds of personages we expect would be driven to the repetitive, compulsive expression of emotion that characterizes the da capo aria form. Handel's dramatis personae were made for the da capo aria, and it for them. (There is a supreme irony, therefore, in the notion that, for the sake of dramatic verisimilitude, the da capo arias should be truncated: performed without the second section or the da capo, a procedure that characterized early twentieth-century attempts to revive Handel's operas in Germany and elsewhere. For it is a violation not only of their musical integrity, but of their *dramatic* integrity as well; it is dramatic as well as musical butchery.)

This, then, was my strategy, in *Osmin's Rage*, for answering the charge that the da capo aria, the blood and bones of Handel's *opera seria*, is emotionally and dramatically absurd. It might well be described as the method of Historicism. For it is the proposal that the emotive and dramatic appropriateness of the da capo aria can be perceived and appreciated only if we take, so to speak, the historical point of view, by internalizing the theories and presuppositions of the audiences for which these works were originally composed. It is the method that David Hume recommended, in Handel's own time, when he described, in his luminous essay "Of the Standard of Taste", the *wrong* way for someone to try to appreciate the artworks of the past. "If the work be addressed to persons of a different age or nation, he makes no allowance for their peculiar views and prejudices; but full of the manners of his own age and country, rashly condemns what seemed admirable in the eyes of those for whom alone the discourse was calculated." Such an individual, as Hume put it, "obstinately maintains his natural position, without placing himself in that point of view which the performance supposes".[4]

II

I want to devote the rest of my talk to discussing the plausibility of the Historicist method, not just as an answer to the charge against the da capo aria in Handelian *opera seria*, but as an enduring problem with regard to our appreciation of all the artworks of the past. It's, indeed, one of the central questions in the philosophy of art, which is my particular line of work. It is my hope that this brief excursion into philosophy, with Handel's operas as the center of attention, will put them in a larger perspective, and remind us, if we need reminding, that the problem of their appreciation is not some special flaw in the *opera seria*, as has frequently been asserted, but a problem endemic to all difficult artworks of the past that are worth appreciating at all.

Since the publication of my discussion of Handel's operas, in 1988, I have come to have some serious doubts about the effectiveness of the Historicist method as a defense of their viability as works of art. I have not, to be sure, ceased to think that the historical perspective I have just sketched out is a necessary ingredient in our enjoyment and appreciation of them. I have, however, come to think that there is something missing. What worries me is that I have presented a method that will certainly yield considerable intellectual satisfaction to the listener who adopts it. But is intellectual satisfaction enough? Where's the *emotion*?, the seasoned opera lover is bound to ask. Where is the emotional involvement? We are angry at Count Almaviva, feel sorry for Rosina, and the Grand Inquisitor sends shivers of terror and apprehension down our spines. And who is so jaded as not to have a good cry at *La Bohème*? Indeed, in all serious fiction, not merely in opera, a great part of our satisfaction and understanding involves getting "emotionally involved" with the characters therein. And the question is whether Handelian *opera seria* can do that for us, given the intellectual contortions the method of Historicism dictates that we must perform in order to comprehend its characters emotionally. Can we "feel for" the Cartesian creatures of Handel's operas, as we can for the less

    4 David Hume, *Essays, Moral, Political and Literary* (Oxford: Oxford University Press, 1963), 245.

emotionally remote ones of Mozart's and Verdi's? And if we can't, does it not seem that these Baroque dramas, for all their considerable musical and "intellectual" rewards, can never have anything but a peripheral interest for the vast majority of devoted operagoers?

I hasten to add that I do not have definitive answers to these questions to offer you. What I do have to offer is, I hope, some food for further thought about them.

Let me put up for discussion, at this point, another method of appreciation for artworks of the past as a possible alternative to the method of Historicism. C. S. Lewis, in his little monograph on Milton, *A Preface to Paradise Lost*, happily denominates it the method of the Unchanging Human Heart. Here is how he describes it:

How are these gulfs between the ages to be dealt with by the student of poetry? A method often recommended may be called the method of the Unchanging Human Heart. According to this method the things which separate one age from another are superficial. Just as, if we stripped the armour off a medieval knight or the lace off a Caroline courtier, we should find beneath them an anatomy identical with our own, so, it is held, if we strip from Virgil his Roman imperialism, from Lucretius his Epicurean philosophy, and from all who have it their religion, we shall find the Unchanging Human Heart, and on this we are to concentrate.[5]

The idea, I take it, for present purposes, is that if we can strip away from the Handelian *opera seria* all of the historical baggage, such as the Cartesian theory of the emotions, that it carries along with it, we will find that beneath, common to us all—and by this we can be moved, with this we can become emotionally involved, whether or not we espouse the Cartesian psychology. But if the Unchanging Human Heart is absent, then these works must be declared emotionally dead to us, whatever other satisfactions of a musical and intellectual kind they may afford.

I will return briefly at the end of my talk to the method of the Unchanging Human Heart. But before I do that I want to point out that C. S. Lewis, after so eloquently presenting the method, summarily rejects it. For if we adopt it, he writes, "Our whole study of the poem will then become a battle between us and the author in which we are trying to twist his work into a shape he never gave it, to make him use the loud pedal where he really used the soft, to force into false

---

[5] Lewis, *A Preface to Paradise Lost*, 63.

prominence what he took in his stride, and to slur over what he actually threw into bold relief."[6]

Lewis recommends, instead, a version of what I have been calling, although he does not describe it as such, the method of Historicism. But he gives it a twist which makes it clear that he is worrying, as I was just now, about the possibility of over-intellectualizing our experience of artworks to the detriment of our emotive involvement. Here is how he states what I am calling the method of Historicism.

Instead of stripping the knight of his armour you can try to put his armour on yourself; instead of seeing how the courtier would look without his lace, you can try to see how you would feel *with* his lace. ... I had much rather know what I should feel like if I adopted the beliefs of Lucretius than how Lucretius would have felt if he had never entertained them. The possible Lucretius in myself interests me more than the possible C. S. Lewis in Lucretius.[7]

Philosophers of art will instantly recognize in this passage a distinct echo of the so-called expression theory of art, which Lewis, Fellow of Magdalen College, Oxford, must surely have known through what is perhaps its most systematic and lucid defense, by R. G. Collingwood, in his *Principles of Art*. As Collingwood puts Lewis's point, the poet works by

thinking in a certain way and then expressing how it feels to think in that way. Thus Dante has fused the Thomistic philosophy into a poem expressing what it feels like to be a Thomist. Shelley, when he made the earth say, "I spin beneath my pyramid of night," expressed what it feels like to be a Copernican.[8]

It is easy to make out what Lewis, and Collingwood before him, were up to here. The goal is to dull the intellectualist edge of the Historicist method by fashioning it to accommodate emotional involvement. Or, put another way, the point of the exercise is to explain how philosophy, a world view, or any other ideational content can be relevant to art and yet prevent art from losing its autonomy: its particular reason for being.

6 Lewis, *A Preface to Paradise Lost* 63.
7 Ibid. 64.
8 R. G. Collingwood, *The Principles of Art* (Oxford: Clarendon Press, 1955), 295. Cf. George Santayana, *Three Philosophical Poets* (Garden City, NY: Doubleday Anchor Books, 1953): "Suppose, however,—and it is a tenable supposition—that Lucretius is quite wrong in his science. ... We could still conceive a world composed as he describes. Fancy what emotions those who lived in such a world would have felt on the day when Democritus or Lucretius revealed to them their actual situation" (p. 39).

If the point of Dante's poem is simply to present the Thomist position, then there seems little point in reading the poem rather than reading the Angelic Doctor himself, or one of the excellent modern textbooks on the subject. But if the point of *The Divine Comedy*, rather, is to make us *feel* like Thomists, to make us feel the Thomist's emotions, as it were, by presenting Thomism in the manner of poetry (whatever that might be), then it has a role that neither Thomas nor his commentators aspired to: a role exclusive to the arts.

Can we not apply this *emotive* Historicist method to the problem at hand? Why not argue that our emotional involvement with the characters in Handelian *opera seria* amounts to our coming to feel, *ourselves*, how it is to feel in a Cartesian way: the way Handel's characters do.

But there is a problem here, and it is that to feel an emotion, I must have the beliefs appropriate to it: if I am angry with my friend, I must *believe* something about him that makes me angry with him; and, as well, I must have a whole set of background beliefs about the nature of emotions, human motivation, and so forth. And part of the belief system that is essential to my emotive life is some set of beliefs, never mind how vague and unsystematic, about how human beings' emotions work. Furthermore, my set of beliefs about the workings of the emotions is, no doubt, radically different from Handel's and his contemporaries' Cartesian beliefs. Consequently, my emotional reactions to other folks, predicated, as they are, on my set of emotional beliefs, not Handel's, are likely to be radically different too; and that goes for fictional folks as well as real ones.

The emotions are not mere gushes of feeling: they are cognitive states. That is the way with emotions. If, however, a requirement for feeling what it is like to be a character in some Cartesian emotional state turns out to be that I must *believe* the Cartesian psychology, then that is an impossibility for me (and for you). For we cannot believe what it suits us to believe merely because it suits us to believe it. Belief is not subject to the will, and to suggest that I can somehow believe the Cartesian theory of the emotions in the opera house, when I do not believe it elsewhere, is to suggest what cannot be done.[9] What I *can* do, of course, is understand the Cartesian theory and hear how perfectly Handel's music represents the emotions, as that theory understands them—which, alas, brings us

---

[9] Interestingly enough, Descartes *was* a "voluntarist" with regard to belief, a position that was conclusively refuted by Spinoza, and is generally repudiated by contemporary philosophers.

right back to an intellectual rather than an emotional involvement and satisfaction.

At this point, I suggest, the method of the Unchanging Human Heart may again begin to seem attractive, not, indeed, as a replacement for the method of Historicism, but certainly as a necessary companion. It may require *both* methods to do the job.

To be sure, the Historicist is right that I must understand the work in its historical context to begin to appreciate it. If, however, the thoughts, feelings, and motivations of the characters in a fictional work are so different, so remote from our own that we have *nothing* in common with them, then, I suggest, though we can understand them, we cannot become emotionally involved with them: we cannot feel with them, or for them. The work may bring us considerable intellectual, and musical, but not emotional satisfaction. And in that respect the doctrine of the Unchanging Human Heart is correct. There must indeed be something emotionally and motivationally unchanging, shared by us and them, something important that lies at the core of an artwork, for us not merely to understand it, but to resonate passionately with it as well. And this thought rings true to our experience that there *are* artworks of the past that are emotionally closed to us.

The question that particularly concerns us here, of course, is whether Handel's operas are such works: works that are intellectually and musically accessible to us, but emotionally closed. It is my hope and expectation that the proceedings of this conference will contribute substantially to answering that question. For, after all, it seems reasonable to believe that the more we come to understand these works, the more likely we are to learn whether and how we can come fully to appreciate them as we do the familiar and accepted masterpieces of the operatic repertory.

But we must not, in the end, come to believe that we are the final arbiters of taste. Whether or not Handel's operas are emotionally closed to us is something no philosophical or musicological argument can answer; nor can such an argument convince an audience, one way or the other. Only direct experience of the works themselves can do that. As Immanuel Kant long ago observed, using his own homey examples, "Whether a dress, a house, or a flower is beautiful is a matter upon which one declines to allow one's judgement to be swayed by any reasons or principles. We want to look at the Object with our own eyes. ... ".[10]

[10] Immanuel Kant, *Critique of Aesthetic Judgement*, trans. James Creed Meredith (Oxford: Clarendon Press, 1911), 56 (§8).

We are currently experiencing a great revival of Handel's operas by companies all over the world. It is the audiences of opera lovers attending these performances, not the arguments of philosophers and musicologists, that will decide the issue. Music, not talk, is going to have the last word. And that certainly sounds like good news to me.

4

Anti-Semitism in *Meistersinger?*

It is no part of my purpose here either to deny Wagner's palpable anti-Semitism or to in any way mitigate its utter repulsiveness. Both are all too apparent. What I do wish to deny is Barry Millington's thesis, expressed recently, that *Die Meistersinger* is an anti-Semitic work, Beckmesser a Jewish caricature.[1] Or, more circumspectly, I am denying that Millington provides any evidence for the thesis, although he provides plenty of evidence for the anti-Semitism of Richard Wagner. Indeed, what Millington does do is to present a brilliant account of how Wagner formed the character of Beckmesser, both literarily and musically, from absolutely despicable caricatures of Jews, his own and those of his contemporaries; and he then goes on to conclude that Beckmesser *is* a Jewish caricature, *Die Meistersinger* an anti-Semitic work, by simply committing the genetic fallacy, which is to say, illicitly inferring from the true premise that the source of Beckmesser's character is a Jewish caricature to the unsubstantiated conclusion that *Beckmesser* is a Jewish caricature.

Let me begin by stating the obvious. It seems wondrous strange that a fictional work in which there are no fictional characters who are Jews should be said to contain in it a caricature of a Jew. For Beckmesser, the character in Wagner's opera *Die Meistersinger* is certainly not Jewish, nor is any other character in the work. (I assume they are all Lutherans.) Shylock is a Jewish caricature, Mr Moses (in *School for Scandal*) is a Jewish caricature, and, to use Millington's quite correct instance, the Pharisees in Richard Strauss's *Salome* are Jewish caricatures (as indeed they already were in the New Testament).[2] No problem here: they are all Jews, in the worlds of their respective fictional works. But how, one wonders, can the Lutheran Beckmesser *be* a Jewish caricature? He isn't even Jewish in the fictional world of Wagner's work.

---

[1] Barry Millington, "Nuremberg Trial: Is there Anti-Semitism in *Die Meistersinger?*", *Cambridge Opera Journal*, 3 (1991), 247–60.
[2] Ibid. 256.

One possible reply might be: well, you are just mistaken. Beckmesser really *is* Jewish. After all, even though no one refers to him as a Jew, it is perfectly obvious from his character as depicted, and his role in the drama, that he is one. We would have certainly known, without a doubt, that Mr Moses, in *School for Scandal,* was Jewish, even if he had not been referred to, just prior to his entrance, as "the honest Israelite". His name is Moses, for goodness sake; and he is a *usurer.* What more do we need to make the all too obvious inference?

But would anyone really want to argue that, in the world of *Die Meistersinger,* Beckmesser is a Jew? If he is, is he a secret one, or what? Do Hans Sachs and the rest know he is Jewish? Or has he wormed his way into their crowd under an assumed name and a forged identity? I don't think I need pursue this line of interpretation any further to convince anyone how preposterous it is.

Here is a second possible reply. Of course, at the surface, manifest level Beckmesser is not a Jew. But *Die Meistersinger* is an allegory: unfortunately, an anti-Semitic one. And while on one level it is a story about the triumph of true art and the creative human spirit over pedantry, plagiarism, and deceit, it is, at a deeper, and more profound, level, really about the triumph of the Aryan over the Jew. At that deeper, more profound level Beckmesser *is* a Jew, or perhaps more accurately, the personification of Jewishness, and, by our lights, a cruel and nasty caricature of it.

I find this allegorical interpretation of *Die Meistersinger* as preposterous as the first. But that is not really the important point. For whether or not either interpretation is preposterous, the fact—which Millington I think conclusively establishes—that the character of Beckmesser was formed by Wagner out of Jewish stereotypes and caricatures is simply no evidence at all for either. There is a logical gap between something's origin and its nature; and that is as true of Beckmesser's character as of anything else. This does not mean, of course, that the source of Beckmesser's character might not provide one with a hypothesis, a bright idea as to what his true character in *Die Meistersinger* might be. But knowledge of the source can only give us the hypothesis, the bright idea: it cannot establish it, verify it, or even provide evidence in its favor. To think otherwise is to commit the genetic fallacy.

But why, then, after reading Millington's account, does it seem so tempting, indeed so *correct,* to say that Beckmesser *is* a Jewish caricature? I suggest that the problem lies in the ambiguity of that innocent-seeming little word "is"—an ambiguity, as it turns out, of rather deep significance for the philosophy of art.

Suppose that two people, call them Bill and Lil, are standing before a portrait in oil. Bill points to a region of the canvas and says: "That is a dab of black paint." And Lil points to the same region and says: "That is a wart on the king's nose." *Both* of them have made *true* statements. But they have used very different senses (or made very different uses) of the word "is". More exactly, Lil has used what Arthur Danto calls *the is of artistic identification*.[3]

Another example will bring this very important distinction of Danto's into the present context. Suppose I write a letter to my friend Ron, who is a novelist, in which I give a graphic description of my Aunt Abigail. Ron likes my description so well that, without my knowledge, he lifts it, verbatim, and puts it into a novel he is writing, where it serves as a description of a character there called "Aunt Betsy". When the novel is published, I read it, and, coming upon Ron's description of Aunt Betsy, I exclaim: "That is Aunt Abigail." Ron corrects me: "That is Aunt Betsy," he says. *Both* of us, of course, are *correct*. But that is because Ron has used the "is" of *artistic identification*, and I have not.

Just this ambiguity is at work in making plausible—indeed *true*—both that Beckmesser *is* a Jewish caricature *and* that he is *not*. He is a Jewish caricature in the very same sense in which that thing Bill points to is a dab of black paint; and he is not a Jewish caricature in the very same sense that it is not a dab of black paint on the king's nose. The artist has been instructed to paint the king "warts and all", not "paint and all". The canvas has paint on *it*. The king does not have paint on *him*. Beckmesser is "constructed" out of a collection of Jewish caricatures as Ron's description of Aunt Betsy is "constructed" out of my description of Aunt Abigail. Certainly, therefore, Beckmesser *is* a Jewish caricature, as Aunt Betsy *is* Aunt Abigail, and the wart *is* black paint. But to say that, in the fictional world of *Die Meistersinger*, Beckmesser *is* a Jewish caricature, is to have failed to "master", as Danto puts it, the "is" of *artistic identification*. It is to mistake the canvas for the king.

I have claimed, then, that the origin of Beckmesser's character in Jewish caricatures provides no evidence that Beckmesser, the character in Wagner's opera, is a Jewish caricature. But I admitted, too, that it might suggest at least a hypothesis to that effect. Does Millington provide any evidence, besides the origin of the character, which I have argued is no

[3] Arthur Danto, "The Artworld", *Journal of Philosophy*, 61 (1964), repr. in Joseph Margolis (ed.), *Philosophy Looks at the Arts*, 3rd edn. (Philadelphia: Temple University Press, 1987), 161–2.

evidence at all, to support the hypothesis that Beckmesser *is*—in the "is" of *artistic identification*—a Jewish caricature? There is indeed another historical claim in Millington's article, again quite convincingly made out, that might *seem*, at least, to be offered as evidence for the hypothesis of Beckmesser's Jewishness. And I want to proceed by briefly considering it. It is also, I think, a fallacy—a fallacy without a name, but one that, I suspect, we are going to see increasingly committed as the days go by.

Millington poses the question towards the end of his essay: "To what extent, we may ask, was the representation of Beckmesser perceived as anti-semitic by German audiences in the nineteenth century?"[4] After adducing briefly, but, to me, quite convincingly, some historical instances, he concludes: "There is some evidence, then, that Jewish contingents in Berlin and Vienna took offence at the representation of Beckmesser."[5] And the offense, it is hardly necessary to add, was (presumably) at what they took to be an anti-Semitic slur.

Now Millington himself, I must caution, does not explicitly present these contemporary reactions to Beckmesser as evidence for the claim that he is a Jewish caricature. But to someone like me, trained to sniff out arguments, it does seem as if that is Millington's intent. However, I have no wish to misrepresent. So I will not ascribe the argument to him, but rather discuss it as an argument that might be advanced by "someone", in support of the hypothesis, and leave it an open question as to whether or not Millington or anyone else has so advanced it. And to begin with, I want to put this argument into a context.

As many of my readers will know, it has become almost axiomatic among historical musicologists that those closest in time to the per-formance practice of any given historical period are the ones in the most favored position to know how best to perform the music of that period. This is the belief, in its most general form, that motivates the so-called historically authentic performance movement. I have begun to notice surfacing what seems to me to be a "corollary" of this "axiom", to the effect that the earliest auditors of a musical work—that is to say, its contemporary audiences—are in the most favored position to understand and appreciate it correctly. Such a belief would be in stark contrast to what I take to be the peculiarly Romantic notion that just the opposite is the case: that the great artist is systematically *misunderstood* by his or her contemporaries, and that only the passage of time can bring understanding and appreciation.

---

[4] Millington, "Nuremberg Trial", 259.   [5] Ibid. 260.

It appears to me that using the violent, aversive reactions of Jews to the early representations of Beckmesser as evidence for his anti-Semitic character requires reliance on the notion that the audience closest in time to the work is always in the favored position to understand it most correctly. For if that is not assumed, the reaction of Jews to early performances of *Die Meistersinger*, although of great historical interest, possesses no particular strength, as evidence, over the reaction of Jews today, or at any other time. The reaction of *anyone*, at *any time*, to a work is some evidence for what is "in" the work, depending, of course, on what the reaction is, and *to what* it is. But to single out the reactions of Wagner's Jewish *contemporaries* to Beckmesser is to single out *their* reactions as having some special evidential status, *qua* contemporaries of Wagner.

But the "Historicist" belief that an artist's contemporaries are necessarily in a favored position to understand correctly his or her work is just false; and so, for that matter, is its opposite, the "Romantic" belief that an artist's contemporaries are necessarily never in such a favored position. *Both*, it is evident, are fallacious, emanating from deep-seated aesthetic and art-theoretical presuppositions. The plain fact is that sometimes an artist's contemporaries do get it right, and later generations don't; and, contrariwise, an artist's contemporaries sometimes get it wrong, and future generations get things straightened out. And in order for us to tell which is the case, in any given instance, we must *first* form an interpretation of our own, and *then* evaluate the early interpretation against it. Thus, that an interpretation was early rather than late is no more evidence of its correctness than that it was late rather than early. By consequence, that Wagner's early Jewish audiences, judging by their expressed aversion to Beckmesser, interpreted him as an anti-Semitic stereotype is simply not relevant to the question of whether he is or not. Perhaps they got it right; perhaps they didn't. Obviously, I think the latter.

Nor is it far to seek an explanation of why Jewish contemporaries of Wagner should have found Beckmesser an offensive caricature of themselves. They were, of course, as present audiences are not, painfully aware, by direct acquaintance, of all Wagner's anti-Semitic sources, including Wagner's own notorious pamphlet, and so must surely have inferred the obvious: that Beckmesser was an amalgamation of these repulsive stereotypes. But just because they were in a favored position to know full well, as present audiences are not, the sources of the Beckmesser character, they were also in a favored position to commit the genetic fallacy and to mistake that other "is" for the "is" of *artistic identification.* Distance and *ignorance* (which in this case is bliss) have put *us* in a far better position, in *this* particular instance, to get things right.

Let me touch on one further point before I close. It may seem as if the argument from the sources of the Beckmesser character to the claim that it is a Jewish caricature has at least this in its favor: it explains *why* Wagner chose, for Beckmesser, the sources he did. For if Wagner did not intend that Beckmesser *be* a Jewish caricature, why in the world did he choose Jewish caricatures with which to form his character? Well, one plausible answer is that he intended Beckmesser as an anti-Semitic Jewish stereotype.

But *that* intention is not borne out by an examination of the work itself. There just is no plausible interpretation of *Die Meistersinger* on which Beckmesser can be so construed—at least, so it seems to me. And that, for me, in the absence of further evidence, overrides the claim that Wagner intended Beckmesser to be read as a Jewish caricature. Wagner was a great enough artist that *if* he had intended so, his intention would have been fulfilled.

So why *did* Wagner choose Jewish caricatures to form his Beckmesser, if he did not intend Beckmesser as a Jewish caricature? Quite simply, I imagine, because he wanted Beckmesser to be a particular kind of nasty character, and the Jewish stereotypes which, alas, he bought into, suited that purpose admirably.

Wagner was a deeply flawed person, his anti-Semitism a case in point. But he was, after all, a great artist. Is it paying the anti-Semite in him too much of a compliment to suggest that, in regard to Beckmesser and *Die Meistersinger*, the better, artistic part prevailed over the worse? Whatever the sources of the Beckmesser character, it seems to me that Wagner did not, in the artistic product, confuse the sources with the result; and we shouldn't either. I think he was aiming at a grander theme than Aryan over Jew would have seemed even to him to be; and I think he succeeded.

I think Barry Millington has done us a service in uncovering Wagner's tracks. But I think we must not forget that the tracks lead *away* from the source, not *to* it. Millington thinks that discovering the anti-Semitic sources of *Die Meistersinger* has "implications for our understanding of the opera [that] are profound".[6] The implications for our understanding of the opera's *origins*, and the workings of the composer's creative process,

---

6 Millington, "Nuremberg Trial", 247.

are indeed profound. Profound too, unfortunately, are the implications for its potential *misunderstanding*. But if the genetic fallacy is still on the books, and it *was* the last time I looked, the implications for its *understanding* are nil, since an invalid argument fails to imply at all. Where *Meistersinger* came from, and what *Meistersinger is*, are, we should be thankful, two separate things.

5

Speech, Song, and the Transparency of Medium: On Operatic Metaphysics

I

When Desdemona sings the "Willow Song" in Verdi's *Otello*, she sings a song in the world of that work, *her* world, just as I sing a song in the real world, *my* world, when I sing "Melancholy Baby" in the shower. But when Desdemona converses with Iago, she also sings, whereas when I converse with my plumber about why my shower won't work, I do not sing: I *speak*.

To distinguish between what Desdemona does when she sings the "Willow Song" and what she does when she converses with Iago, Otello, *et al.*, Edward T. Cone has coined the phrase "realistic song" for the former, "operatic song" for the latter. He then goes on to suggest that frequently in opera the line between realistic song and operatic song becomes blurred, or even tends to break down entirely. This is because, on Cone's view, operatic song and realistic song are frequently so intertwined, one with the other, that it is difficult or impossible to prise them apart and say, with clarity, at any given time, which is which.

What Cone has in mind here can be summed up in three points. First, even when realistic song is going on, the realistic song is usually such an intimate and spontaneous expression of the character's inner states and feelings that it stands to them much more as my own speech to my own inner states and feelings than as a song I might sing by Schubert or Richard Rogers could stand to them. And thus, even where it is clear that realistic song is going on, it seems almost always the case, because of this intimate connection between song and singer, that, in sharp contrast to our world, realistic singers in the world of opera are best seen as composers of their own realistic songs. "In opera, however, a song, whether realistic or operatic, is so intimately connected with the character who sings it that he or she is usually to be accepted as its composer."[1]

Second, the musical themes of realistic song in opera frequently burst their boundaries and transmigrate, as, for example, in the place in Act I of *La Traviata* where Alfredo (on Cone's reading of the scene) is serenading Violetta—so a case of realistic song—but weaves into the tune of his serenade a previously heard theme that we took in the earlier place for operatic song: "his serenade depends on a crucial transformation: the musical motif that we assumed originally to be not realistic but conventional [i.e. operatic] song (representing normal speech) now appears in such a way that it must be taken as 'really' sung—in some sense—the first time, else there would be no actual music for Alfredo to recall and for Violetta to hear." So, "The scene strongly suggests that the rigid distinction between realistic song on the one hand and conventional or operatic song on the other cannot be sustained."[2]

Third, it is a matter of no small significance that the characters in opera are, quite frequently, people who tend to be *singers* in the worlds of their works—that is to say, fictionally singers, beginning, of course, with the very first operatic hero, Orpheus himself, the quintessential singer of songs. Carmen is another. Their number is legion; and this "suggests that Orpheus is not the prototypical operatic hero for historical reasons only: his role as composer-singer symbolizes what it means to be an operatic character".[3] But if what it means to be an operatic character is to be a composer-singer; and if, as is so often the case, expression is achieved by characters singing realistically, as in the case of Orpheus or Carmen, there seems little use left at all in the world of opera for the distinction between operatic and realistic song. Since, in the world of opera, unlike our own world, so much of a character's inner thoughts and feelings is expressed in realistic song, of which the character, therefore, must be thought the composer, it seems only a small next step to the conclusion that, for all intents and purposes, operatic characters just are, all of them, one way or another, composer-singers: creatures whose natural form of expression is music.

This three-faceted blurring of the distinction between realistic and operatic song Cone calls "the fundamental operatic ambiguity (Is speech

---

[1] Edward T. Cone, "The World of Opera and Its Inhabitants", in *idem, Music: A View from Delft: Selected Essays*, ed. Robert P. Morgan (Chicago: University of Chicago Press, 1989), 129.

[2] Ibid. 127–8.   [3] Ibid. 135.

or song being represented?)".[4] Further, he claims that "an adequate comprehension of opera ... rests on appreciation of this ambiguity."[5] Even when the ambiguity is not pressed to its *ultimate* conclusion, its recognition makes clear that "song is the natural medium of expression for operatic characters. ... [I]magine a world in which singing is the norm and speaking the exception: that is the world of opera."[6] But if there really is this ambiguity, if we really always can read operatic song as realistic song, then, truly, all operatic characters are composer-singers. And that, indeed, is the conclusion with which Cone seems to want to leave us, with his parting shot: "When Arnalta, the nurse, hears Poppea exulting after the death of Seneca [in Monteverdi's *L'Incoronazione di Poppea*], she remonstrates, ... 'You're forever going around singing songs about your wedding.' But that is just what characters in opera do: *they go around singing songs all the time.*"[7]

II

Cone's notion that operatic characters might be all imagined in the image of Orpheus, the improvisatory composer-singer, seems to me to be an intriguing and important one, and to capture something palpable about our experience of opera. In a previous essay I attempted to reach Cone's conclusion by a rather different route.[8] In the present one I want to try to carry that project forward. But before I do, I must give a brief idea of how I reached and stated Cone's thesis of the operatic composer-singer. For it is, naturally, on my own version of that thesis that I want to build.

In my previous essay I suggested that there were two reasons to feel uncomfortable, not with Cone's conclusion itself, but with the way it was reached. The first reason was that Cone's method requires obliterating the distinction between realistic and operatic song, since he argues, alternatively, that the intimacy of expression in realistic song makes us want to say that it is really operatic song, and, contrariwise, that the prevalence of realistic singers in opera makes us want to say, in effect: all operatic singing is really realistic singing. This two-pronged attack on the distinction between realistic and operatic song is Cone's

---

[4] Ibid. 131.   [5] Ibid. 129.   [6] Ibid. 134.   [7] Ibid. 138; my italics.
[8] Peter Kivy, "Opera Talk: A Philosophical 'phantasie' ", *Cambridge Opera Journal*, 3 (1991), 385.

pathway to the conclusion of the operatic character as composer-singer. But for those, like myself, who might want to have Cone's conclusion, while hanging on to the distinction between realistic and operatic song, an alternative to Cone's distinction-obliterating argument is an obvious desideratum.

Secondly, in obliterating the distinction between realistic and operatic song, as well as in asking us to imagine operatic characters as all "composers", Cone widens the gap, already difficult for many listeners to tolerate, between the real world and the world of opera. A world in which speech is song is difficult enough for some to accept as an artistic convention. But a world in which all characters are "composers", and in which our ordinary distinction between speaking and singing no longer holds, compounds the felony. Might there not be a way of making out Cone's conclusion while *narrowing*, rather than broadening, the gap between our world and the world of opera which *it*, after all, is meant to represent? That is what I attempted to do in my previous essay.

My argument took off from R. G. Collingwood's thesis that "art", "expression", and "language" are coextensive; and I took as my epigraph his remark: "Every utterance and every gesture that each of us makes is a work of art."[9] I made it clear in my earlier essay, and I want to reaffirm it here as well, that I do not endorse Collingwood's philosophy of art. Rather, I was, and am, making a variation on a Collingwoodian theme. And as I can assume here, as I could not there, that my readers are well acquainted with the details of Collingwood's system, I will not need to dwell at length on the theme, but can move quickly on to the variation.

For Collingwood "expression" (as he used the term) is not a process in which one first determines what it is one wants to express and then casts about for a ready means to express it. It is, rather, always an innovative process, a "creative" process, if you will, in which you feel the need to express you know not what, you know not how, and in the process of coming to know the latter, you at the same time come to know the former: in other words, in finding "expression" for what you vaguely feel you must express, you come to know what it was that you felt. But if "art" ≡ "expression" ≡ "language", then even ordinary speakers of English (or any other natural language), when they succeed in expressing, must have succeeded in making works of art; and that is what Collingwood

---

[9] R. G. Collingwood, *The Principles of Art* (Oxford: Clarendon Press, 1938), 285.

is acknowledging in his paradoxical and dark saying: "Every utterance and every gesture that each one of us makes is a work of art."

Now, of course, Collingwood knew well that this saying had an air of paradox about it. Taken literally, it was not true, even on his own principles, and in order for it to be so, we would have to qualify suitably both "gesture" and "utterance" so as to get the authentic Collingwoodian statement: "Every [successfully expressive] utterance and every [successfully expressive] gesture that each one of us makes is a work of art"—unless, of course, "utterance" and "gesture" are being used in the same Collingwoodian sense as "language": to wit, "language" (properly so-called), "utterance" (properly so-called), "gesture" (properly so-called), already assuming success of expression in the concept (properly so-called). Collingwood, of course, was not saying that "Please pass the salt", when uttered at table, with obvious intent, is a work of art. But nor was he saying that it is "language" (properly so-called). For on Collingwood's view, only when what people ordinarily call "language" is "innovative", is truly "expression" in the proper, Collingwoodian sense, and not merely cliché, language ready-made, and hence by definition not "expression", is it "language" properly so-called. And only when it is "language", properly so-called, is it art.

Without in the least endorsing the philosophical theory, or the dubious philosophical method which produces it, I find Collingwood's remark, that "Every utterance and every gesture that each one of us makes is a work of art", a suggestive metaphor. For it can serve to remind us of a remarkable fact about language: its ability, even in the hands of the minimally competent, to respond on the spot to the novel and the unexpected—in other words, to operate successfully in human conversation, which is, by nature, unpremeditated, spontaneous, "improvisational". Of course we all possess ready-made conversational schemata, and few of us are, like Dr Johnson, linguistic innovators, true conversational artists in our everyday speech. But to a certain extent every conversational situation, when "the ball is in our court", constitutes a novel and unpredicted one. However I expect my conversational partner to respond, I cannot ever know exactly, nor do I usually "plan ahead"; yet, without premeditation, on demand, I respond intelligibly. That is something remarkable about the spoken language that I am not, of course, original in commenting upon. And it is that remarkable "inventiveness", that each one of us must evince in conversation, that makes it true, in even a more extensive way than Collingwood had in view, that our every utterance and gesture is "a work of art", and each of us a linguistic "artist"—the "authors" of our words. This is my variation on Collingwood's theme.

I do not for a moment suggest the above as a philosophical thesis, or a "theory" of language. I suggest it, rather, as an "imaginative exercise". See your world, for now, in this somewhat Collingwoodian way, as one in which you and your co-conversationalists are "authors" of your conversational thrusts and gambits, engaged in the grand "improvisation" of colloquy. We are *all*, in this imaginative, but *not fictional* way of looking at ourselves, minimal linguistic "artists"; for in conversation we have to "make it up for ourselves", as we go along.

But if we see ourselves in this way, then perhaps we will not seem as distant from the denizens of "opera land" as we seemed heretofore. For we share with them the role of "conversational artist": only in their world the "art of conversation" is the art of song, and they are the "composers" of their expression, as in Shakespeare's world the "art of conversation" is poetry, and its conversationalists "poets on demand". This, then, is my way of reaching Cone's conclusion that operatic characters, in the image of Orpheus, invite us to see them as composers and singers of songs. It was this point that I had reached in my previous essay on the subject; and I now want to push it forward, for it will not withstand critical scrutiny without emendation and elaboration.

III

Let me introduce at this point in the argument the hard-nosed operatic "metaphysician", who will not let matters stand as so far stated. Here is his (or her) complaint.

"Your suggestion that we imagine the denizens of 'opera land' as 'composers' of their conversations, as we are the 'authors' of ours, is a pleasing conceit, but a total misrepresentation of the 'metaphysics of fiction'. For if you ask, for example, what Hamlet is doing when he makes his speeches, the answer is not that he is reciting Elizabethan blank verse, of which he is the 'author', but that he is speaking Danish prose, of which he is the 'author'. (He is, after all, a Danish prince.) And if, similarly, you ask what the Countess is doing, when she sings 'Dove sono', the answer is that she is not singing at all but, presumably, speaking seventeenth-century Spanish, of which she is the 'author' (for seventeenth-century Spain is where Mozart and Da Ponte have set *The Marriage of Figaro*)."

The metaphysician's complaint cannot be gainsaid: it is, ontologically speaking, squeaky clean. Yet, one is compelled to ask, what is seventeenth-century Spanish to *me*, when I experience *The Marriage of Figaro*? Or medieval Danish when I experience *Hamlet*, for that matter? If what the metaphysician says is completely irrelevant to my artistic appreciation of these works, then it does not have aught to do with Cone's and my thesis, which is, I take it, about just that very thing: the appreciation of opera as an art.

Well, such a grumpy, high-handed dismissal of the metaphysician's complaint may be appropriate for some others who write about the opera; but it cannot be appropriate for one, like myself, who writes of it as a philosopher of art. For if I am not to heed the arguments of the metaphysician, who is, after all, a card-carrying member of my tribe with considerable seniority, my own philosophical credentials could surely, and with reason, be called in doubt. Answer the metaphysician, I cannot: I have already conceded the correctness of his claim. But accommodate him, I think I can; and to do so I must pursue the metaphysics of operatic utterance a trifle further.

What is the ontological status, then, of the singing in the *Marriage of Figaro*, if what the characters are doing in the fictional world of that work is speaking seventeenth-century Spanish? The obvious, and correct, answer would seem to be that it is the *medium of representation*. That is to say, we must think of seventeenth-century Spanish speech as being represented by eighteenth-century music. The music is the medium. In like manner we must see Elizabethan blank verse as the medium of representation for medieval Danish prose in *Hamlet*, and English with a German accent the medium of representation for German speech in Hollywood war movies of the 1940s.

With that established, we can now introduce the familiar concept of the transparency of the medium. And this is best accomplished by turning, for a moment, to the visual arts. If I set my gaze on Seurat's *Grand Jatte*, I am acutely aware, at all times, of the tiny daubs of paint with which the painter represents his subject; these splotches are Seurat's medium, and it is a singularly *untransparent* medium, because it never ceases to be prominently in the gazer's awareness as he or she experiences the work. At the other end of the spectrum are *trompe-l'oeil* paintings in which the fruit and game are so "realistically" depicted as to tempt one to reach into the "space" of the canvas to touch the objects therein. Here, we are tempted to say, the medium has become *transparent* to perception, is seen through without refraction, to the representational content within. It may indeed be true, as Arthur Danto argues, that "The medium ... is of course never really eliminible. There is always going to be a residuum of matter that cannot be vaporized into pure content."[10] Nevertheless, even though complete transparency is not an achievable (or, for that matter, desirable) goal, that there are works and styles where in the medium is more or less transparent than in others is an important aspect of our aesthetic experience. And that comparative judgment, that perception of degrees of transparency, is all I require for present purposes.

Let us revert, now, with the transparency of medium concept in hand, to more relevant territory. The metaphysician will tell us that in the world of *Hamlet* the melancholy Dane is speaking medieval Danish prose, and that in the world of *Death of a Salesman* Willy Loman is speaking 1940s American-style English. And he will tell us, further, that the medium in which Hamlet's speech is represented is Elizabethan blank verse.

What is the medium of Willy Loman's conversation? Well, that might stump the metaphysician for a moment, because, I want to suggest, the medium in which the dialogue of Arthur Miller's great play is depicted is far more transparent to us than the medium of Shakespearean drama and, therefore, we tend not to notice it, which is to say, we tend not to notice that there is a medium interposed between us and the content at all.

But it is, clearly, a metaphysical impossibility for there not to be an artistic medium of representation of Willy Loman's conversation; for if there were no medium, Willy Loman would not be a fictional character, just as if the "flowers" were not paint, they would be *flowers*, which is, of course, absurd. And a moment's reflection will reveal that the representational medium of Willy Loman's 1940s American-style English just is that very thing: 1940s American-style English—which is why, of course, it is so transparent a medium.

Once, we become aware, however, of the medium in which Willy Loman's speech is represented, and attend to it more closely, we see that it is not *exactly* 1940s American-style English at all. For it has received the impress of the artist's hand. No one succeeds, in life, in expressing his or her thoughts and feelings that perfectly, that powerfully, in their native tongue. Conversation without glitches does not happen in real

---

[10] Arthur C. Danto, *The Transfiguration of the Commonplace: A Philosophy of Art* (Cambridge, Mass.: Harvard University Press, 1981), 159.

salesmen's homes. Emotional climaxes, self-revelations, and insights do not occur at just the right (or just the tragically *wrong*) moments, if, indeed, they occur at all in the ordinary course of human affairs. In other words, the medium, *artistically transformed* 1940s American-style English bears all of the *expressive*, all of the *aesthetic* properties that, as Danto argues, only the medium of representation, not the content itself, can intelligibly be described as having.[11]

Nonetheless, given that the medium in which speech is represented in *Death of a Salesman* has not, as Danto would put it, "vaporized into pure content", which would have been the case if its medium had achieved full and perfect transparency, it surely makes sense to say that this medium is *more* transparent (say) than that of *Hamlet*, in which medieval Danish prose is represented in Elizabethan English blank verse. In a perfectly obvious sense, we will never cease being aware, *strongly aware*, that when we attend a performance of *Hamlet*, we are hearing a *recital of poetry*. To borrow a phrase (if not the concept) from Richard Wollheim, we will never "hear in" the medium of *Hamlet* medieval Danish prose, for all that the metaphysician may say, as we will "hear in" the medium of *Death of a Salesman* ordinary, 1940s American-style English.[12] The medium of *Hamlet* is too thick, too opaque, for that.

That said, it is now time to return to our subject, the opera, and to apply what we have learned. It will be clear, straightaway, that the operatic medium is very far from the transparency end of the spectrum—further, indeed, even than Elizabethan tragedy. For if we cannot "hear in" Shakespearean verse medieval Danish prose, we cannot, *a fortiori*, "hear in" Mozart's music seventeenth-century Spanish prose. Nowhere are we more perceptually aware of medium, and less of content, than in opera and music drama.

Charles Burney called opera "the *completest concert*".[13] He knew full well that it was also *dramma per musica*. But in calling it a concert, he revealed how pervasively *he* thought the medium of opera obtrudes into our experience of it. For as a concert, opera is a recital for voices; and

---

[11] Ibid. 158–9.

[12] Richard Wollheim, *Painting as an Art* (Princeton: Princeton University Press, 1987), 46–7 ff.

[13] Charles Burney, *A General History of Music*, ed. Frank Mercer (New York: Dover, 1957), ii. 676. I have discussed this passage at greater length in *Osmin's Rage: Philosophical Reflections on Opera, Drama and Text* (Princeton: Princeton University Press, 1988), 133–6.

when we hear it thus, we are, of necessity, at the fullest possible remove from the metaphysical center, which is *speech* represented *in* music. We are, in effect, totally involved in the medium: we are listening to *singing*.

Now, of course, opera, even the *opera seria* of Burney's time, which has been charged with being so, is *not* merely a concert in costume. And anyone who experienced it merely as a vocal recital, even when in concert performance, would be seriously misreading it, whether in the obvious case of Wagnerian music drama or in the more "concert-like" case of Handelian *opera seria*. Yet the fact is that, particularly in "number" opera, though not solely there by any means, the "concert attitude", if I may so call it, is very much intermingled with what one might call the "representational attitude". We do, after all, go to the opera to hear beautiful music beautifully (we hope) performed.

What all of this, then, adds up to, it appears, is that when we experience (say) the opening scene of the second act of *The Marriage of Figaro*, we are in a mode of attention that is both—and very *strongly* both—one of attending to a singer giving a "performance" (remember how the action comes to a full stop for the applause!) and attending to a character in a drama making an expressive utterance. Further, both the "concert attitude" and the extreme "opacity" of the representational medium, which, indeed, mutually reinforce each other, make it impossible for us to "hear in" the Countess's "soliloquy" anything like what the metaphysician (quite correctly) tells us is being represented: namely, seventeenth-century Spanish conversation.

What, then, *do* we hear when we hear the Countess as a character, given the opacity of the representational medium and the ever-present "recital attitude"? Well, we hear, I would suggest, a world in which the character is a "composer" of her vocal expression, as, in my world, I am the "author" of mine. And in concluding that, we now have our sought-after accommodation with the hard-nosed operatic metaphysician. The metaphysician has spoken of how things *are*, we of how things *are experienced*. The opacity of the operatic medium, except perhaps in such cases as recitative, *stile rappresentativo*, or a musical fabric like that of *Pelléas et Mélisande*, where we really can hear speech "in" the representational medium, is such that what we hear is characters expressing themselves not in speech represented by the medium of music but in the medium, the *music* itself. That is the truth of Cone's and my conclusion: not an "ontological" truth but an experiential one. Or, to wax metaphorically Kantian in conclusion, the operatic metaphysician has spoken of the operatic *Ding an sich*, we of the operatic "phenomena". And at the operatic end of the spectrum from relative transparency to relative opacity of representational medium, the phenomena are all that we have. The reality—that the Countess is speaking seventeenth-century Spanish, or Elektra ancient Greek—is merely a metaphysical shadow, although, indeed, a metaphysical truth.

6

Music in the Movies: A Philosophical Inquiry

Natura abhorret vacuum

The two major forms of "talked" drama, movies and plays, are sharply distinguished in numerous ways, as artistic practices. But one of the most notable and, I shall argue, most mystifying of these ways is in regard to *music*. For the presence of music in a spoken play is a rare occurrence—although there is a tradition for it—whereas what is rare in the cinema is the *absence* of music. The movies have had, almost from the very beginning, a running musical background. And whereas it is fairly clear what the reason for this was in the silent era, it is by no means obvious, as I shall suggest later on, why music endured in its peculiar relation to the cinema with the advent of the talkies.

What I aim to do in this essay is, first, to show what the roots of movie music are, in the tradition of Western art music: in particular, music for the stage. I shall argue that, in spite of the marked difference in technological resources, the basic aesthetic practices of music in the movies are of a piece with a musical tradition that goes back at least as far as the invention of opera at the close of the sixteenth century.

Second, I aim to show that consideration of the specific musical practice that music in the movies most closely resembles, indeed is a species of—namely, eighteenth-century "melodrama"—suggests to us a puzzle as to *why* the latter was an artistic failure that quickly withered on the vine, and why the former endured after the advent of sound film—after, that is, the condition that made the *raison d'être* of music in the movies *obvious*, no longer obtained; why, in other words, music in cinema outlived the necessity of its apparent function in the silent film.

In the end I shall venture the most tentative conjecture as to why music in the movies has endured, while its analogue in spoken plays—namely, melodrama—was a palpable aesthetic nonstarter. But my conjecture is offered with the utmost diffidence. And anyone is free to offer another. What, I think, cannot be avoided is the question to which my conjecture responds.[1]

SOME HISTORICAL BACKGROUND

For present purposes, the beginning of music for the theater, as we know it, can be located in the "invention" of opera as we know it, at the very close of the sixteenth century. Of course music for the theater does not spring out, fully armed, in 1597—the date of *Daphne*, which tradition calls the "first" opera. There was theater before 1597, and music in it, going back, no doubt, to the ancient Greeks. But this is not the place, nor am I the person to undertake the stupendous task of presenting a history, if such a thing is even possible, of the musical theater. In any case, the musical techniques that developed with startling speed in the first years of the seventeenth century, and the operatic forms they had evolved into by the close of the eighteenth, provide, essentially, the full aesthetic arsenal from which film music has drawn its weapons. So there it is convenient for us to begin.

A group of the Italian nobility, intellectuals, poets, composers—the so-called Camerata—brought what we know as "opera" into the world, in Florence, at the beginning of the seventeenth century. Under the theoretical guidance of Vincenzo Galilei, father of the great Galileo, the composers Jacopo Peri and Giulio Caccini, began composing a kind of musical declamation for solo voice, which they called *stile*

---

[1] A brief word here is in order on the use of the familiar word "melodrama". As musicologists use the term, it refers *specifically* to the genre of drama that consists in spoken words with musical accompaniment, of which Georg Benda's works are the prime (and almost lone) example, and to the technique that survived as a rare occurrence within opera and other sung dramatic works. It should not be confused with the term as used to refer to the popular nineteenth-century vaudeville plays with musical accompaniment, although, needless to say, the latter use of the word must surely have developed from the former. It is the latter use, clearly, that led to the current use of "melodramatic" to mean "sensational", or "overwrought" drama, which these nineteenth-century vaudevilles frequently were. I use the term as musicologists do, my argument being founded on that use and the musical works to which it refers. That music in the movies may have had its origin and model in nineteenth-century melodrama, as Murray Smith has suggested to me, I would not want to deny, for it is hardly part of my argument that the first makers of movies were students of eighteenth-century musical practice, or the art of melodrama as an operatic technique, in Beethoven, Weber, and their ilk.

rappresentativo—the style of the actor—and which was meant to represent in music the emotional tone and cadence of the human speaking voice.

By 1608—the date of the first great operatic masterpiece, Monteverdi's *Orfeo*—the *stile rappresentativo* had evolved into a dramatic representation of human declamation unsurpassed in its sensitivity to the expressive nuances of speech. As a musical rendering of human utterance, it remains still, in Monteverdi, one of the most artistically successful.

Yet, at the very outset, opera (or *dramma per musica*) had built into it a tension that has characterized the operatic enterprise to this day. For as successful as the *stile rappresentativo* was as a dramatic vehicle, it failed to satisfy what might be called our desire for the "pure musical parameters". It was "music", but it wasn't *music*. It does not reward the kind of musical expectations we bring to the "closed" musical forms, either of the seventeenth century or the centuries before and after. The tension between the demands of dramatic declamation and those of the pure musical parameters has defined the driving force of opera and opera "reform", opera theory and opera criticism, from the very beginning to the present moment.[2]

By the end of the seventeenth century, a highly successful "compromise" was reached between the "dramatic" and the "musical" in the form of the so-called number opera. So successful was this compromise that it endured as a going concern past the middle of the nineteenth century, and produced such exemplary operatic achievements as the *opera seria* of Handel, the comic masterpieces of Mozart and Rossini, and, still in fairly recognizable form, the great works of Verdi's early and middle periods.

In its most "unpolluted" form, in the eighteenth century, number opera consists of a chain of separate musical movements, "numbers", each of which displays a closed musical form. These musical numbers, principally aria, duet, trio, larger ensemble, and chorus are separated by "*secco* recitative", which is to say, a rapid, conversational parlando with little or no musical interest—"minimal music", if you will—through which the plot is advanced by "conversation" and "soliloquy", accompanied solely by keyboard, as in Mozartian *opera buffa*, or keyboard and instrumental bass, the "basso continuo", in Baroque *opera seria*.

---

[2] On this see Peter Kivy, *Osmin's Rage: Philosophical Reflections on Opera, Drama and Text* (Princeton: Princeton University Press, 1988), Part I.

What is of special interest to us, and not yet mentioned, is a musical technique somewhere betwixt and between the fully closed operatic "numbers" and the connective tissue of the *secco* recitative, music's limiting case, so to speak. I make reference to what is usually called, in English, "accompanied recitative". In accompanied recitative, the singing voice has full orchestral support, but retains its declamatory, non-melodic character, although with highlighted musical and expressive interest.

The star performer, in accompanied recitative, is the orchestra. And it functions in two ways: both as dramatic and expressive background to the singing voice, and as a musical interlude between appearances of the singing voice, in which it serves as dramatic and expressive commentator on the sentiments of the singer, in whatever character he or she represents. In one kind of accompanied recitative the orchestra is silent while the singer declaims, only entering when the singer falls silent. In another kind, the orchestra provides a running accompaniment to the singing voice. And in a third, the two above-mentioned are combined, the orchestra sometimes being present while the singer declaims, and sometimes silent.

The accompanied recitative, then, is a powerful as well as a flexible medium for musico-dramatic expression. And as such, it endured in clearly recognizable form throughout most of the nineteenth century.

But in addition to its indispensable dramatic role in opera, accompanied recitative gave birth, in 1770, through the fertile brain of Jean Jacques Rousseau, to the strange, short-lived theatrical phenomenon known as "melodrama" (or, sometimes, "monodrama"). In France it was stillborn. In Germany it had a brief, yet noteworthy career, attracting, among the immortals, no less than Mozart, Beethoven, and Carl Maria von Weber. And it surfaces now and again (in Debussy's *Martyrdom of Saint Sebastian*, for example). It yet lives, probably unbeknownst to most of the practitioners, in movie music. To a brief discussion of this "exotic" art form I now turn my attention.

MELODRAMA

Even as late as the eighteenth century, although opera had been a going concern for more than a hundred years, many still thought of it as, in Dr Johnson's famous description, "an irrational entertainment", and still had trouble with dramatis personae who sang rather than spoke. Conversation in musical tones seemed an absurdity, though conversation in blank verse, or even rhymed couplets did not. (I dare say many sophisticated theatergoers today still feel the same way.)

Melodrama was an answer to that difficulty, keeping the music in the pit, speech on the stage. It was, in other words, spoken drama with musical accompaniment. The idea of film music, then, existed fully fledged, some hundred or more years before the invention of moving pictures.

The first such production, *Pygmalion*, words by Rousseau, whose idea it was, music by one Horace Coignet, was performed in Lyon, in 1770. The French let it alone. But in 1772, Anton Schweitzer wrote new music to a German translation of Rousseau's words, and had it performed in Weimar. Goethe loved it. So did Germany. The love affair was brief, however, as we shall see.

Melodrama, as a separate dramatic form, had its first, and only "master" in Georg Benda. Benda was a composer of real talent, if not genius; and his melodramas *Medea* and *Ariadne auf Naxos* so impressed Mozart, in 1778, that he wrote to his father: "I think that most operatic recitatives should be treated in this way—and only sung occasionally, when the words *can be perfectly expressed by the music.*"[3]

It is more than mildly interesting—indeed, prophetic—that Mozart, from the start, did not see melodrama as a separate dramatic entity, but as a dramatic technique: a substitute, *in opera*, for accompanied recitative. And it is also worth noting that Mozart perceived immediately what the origin and nature of melodrama was. Again to his father, in the same letter:

You know, of course, that there is no singing in it, only recitation, to which the music is like a sort of obbligato accompaniment to a recitative. Now and then the words are spoken while the music goes on, and this produces the finest effect.[4]

Thus, as Mozart immediately perceived, melodrama is accompanied recitative with spoken instead of sung declamation. The "opera skeptic" has what he wants: spoken conversation rather than the "absurdity" of conversation in song.

One further point in Mozart's letter to his father deserves special notice. Melodrama, like accompanied recitative, whence it came, made

---

[3] Mozart to his father, 12 Nov. 1778, in *Letters of Mozart and His Family*, trans. Emily Anderson (New York: Macmillan, 1938), ii. 937.
[4] Ibid.

use of *both* declamation without and declamation with accompanying music. That is to say, sometimes the voice declaims between "comments" and "preludes" of the orchestra; and sometimes it declaims with orchestral accompaniment. It was the latter that most charmed Mozart. ("Now and then the words are spoken while the music goes on, and this produces the finest effect.") It is the latter that film music has been able to exploit beyond anything Benda could have attempted. I think that for this reason Mozart would have loved the movies.

Why, then, did melodrama, in spite of captivating the man whom some would argue is the greatest composer the stage has ever known, fail to flourish even in that great composer's hands? Looked at from one point of view, the answer is all too obvious. Looked at as a solution to *the* problem of opera, the problem of reconciling music with drama, melodrama fails. For it fails to *be* music: it fails to give a full-blooded musical experience. Opera is drama-made-music.[5] Melodrama is drama with ... well, with a musical *texture*. It never became, in the hands of Benda or anyone else, drama-made-music. It did endure well beyond the eighteenth century, indeed into the twentieth, as one dramatic technique within opera, as well as within other musical forms, the stirring dungeon scene in Beethoven's *Fidelio* being the best known and perhaps greatest example. But, as a separate "operatic" enterprise, it did not survive beyond its first incarnations.

But why view melodrama as "opera" at all—as, that is, a *musical* form? Why not, rather, view it as a genre of spoken drama, as, in fact, films are viewed—spoken drama with music? Film, after all, is not viewed as a musical form, but as a form of spoken drama, its musical track to the contrary notwithstanding.[6]

But viewed in this way—viewed, that is, as spoken drama with a musical "background"—melodrama becomes deeply puzzling in its rapid demise, because its modern counterpart, the talky, has retained *its* musical "background" beyond its *obvious* purpose, which is to say, to fill the vacuum of silence in the silent film. (More of that in a moment.) So theatrical melodrama withered on the vine, while filmic melodrama

---

[5] As I have argued in *Osmin's Rage*.

[6] Of course, there are exceptions, like *Alexander Nevsky*, where the music is so impressive and so woven into the cinematic fabric, that we are tempted to call them truly "musical" works. But such exceptions are rare, at least in my experience and on my accounting.

flourished (and flourishes). *Why?* That is my puzzle. And to solve it, I must now turn to film music itself.

THE VACUUM OF SILENCE

According to Irwin Bazelon, in a book on music in the movies, "Film music was born illegitimately as a literal-practical child of necessity." In a word, its purpose was to drown out the sound of the moving picture projector. "Sound proofing had not yet been perfected and the leakage of noise from the projector carried over into the auditorium and interfered with the audience's visual enjoyment."[7] Whether or not film music had this ignominious and aesthetically irrelevant origin, I am in no position to say. But what *is* quite obvious is that very early on, even before there was such a thing as music composed specifically for the movies, the piano accompaniment was already serving higher goals than merely that of a pleasant sound to mask an unpleasant one. Indeed, quality aside, it was serving some of the same purposes it presently serves: to provide music dramatically and expressively appropriate to the drama unfolding on the screen. I shall have something more to say about the specifics of this dramatic and expressive function later on. But at this point all I need to say is what I have just said, in these very general terms.

It would be useful, however, to point out that even in its most primitive form, as a more or less improvised piano accompaniment consisting in bits and pieces from the classical and semi-classical reper-toire, music in the movies was doing the same things as it was and had been doing in opera and melodrama from at least the eighteenth century—indeed, was speaking the same dramatic and expressive "lan-guage". And if one should ask the question what the purpose of musical accompaniment was in the silent film *after* it ceased to be that of drowning out the projector's noise (if that ever *was* its purpose), then *one* correct answer would be: to do all of the things for the silent moving picture that it does for sung drama, i.e. opera, or the spoken drama, i.e. melodrama: in general terms, to provide an expressively and dramatically appropriate musical fabric. I am going to call this multiple function of music in the cinema its "aesthetic" function, or, where I

---

[7] Irwin Bazelon. *Knowing the Score: Notes on Film Music* (New York, Cincinnati, Toronto, London, and Melbourne: Van Nostrand Reinhold, 1975), 13.

am more specific, its aesthetic *functions* (in the plural). And the point is that music in the silent cinema shares this aesthetic function, or these aesthetic functions with music in opera and melodrama as well.

There is, however, another sense to the question of music's function in the silent cinema. When asked with this other sense intended, what the questioner wants to know is why music, given its internal function in the silent movie, *is* there in the first place. If its *original raison d'être* really *was* to drown out the projector's noise, why did it remain after that function was no longer necessary? It continued on to provide expressive and dramatic underpinning. But *why* was that expressive and dramatic background wanted, or needed, in the silent film? That is the sense to the question, after the aesthetic function of music within the silent film is given. Call what *this* question is seeking music's "filmic function". What is the filmic function of music in silent cinema?

The answer seems to me obvious enough, and ought to be completely uncontroversial. The filmic function of music in the silent movies is to fill the *vacuum of silence*. It serves *some* of the functions of speech and, marginally, even of the other sounds of the world: storms, battles, and so forth. But principally it serves the function of speech. And if one wonders why *music* was chosen for this role, the answer must be, What else? It was already in place, it was easily assimilable, and it had a 200-year tradition of serving just such dramatic functions in opera and spoken drama.

Were these new or startling ideas, or were they less than perfectly obvious, I might be inclined to dilate upon them at greater length. But they are neither new nor startling, so I need say little to make my point.

In a spoken play, an actor communicates to an audience with sound and visual appearance. And when he speaks, he communicates both with the matter of his speech, and, of course, with the tone and inflection of his voice. In dumb show he has only gesture, countenance, and bodily behavior at his disposal. Speech is denied him. He cannot communicate in sound.

Music can help to make up for that deficit. It not only adds the dimension of sound to the silent screen world, but, more importantly, it adds the dimension of *expressive* sound. It cannot give the silent actress the *matter* of words, but it can give the *emotive expression*. And, indeed, because it comes in company with a visual image of expressive behavior, it can, as Noel Carroll has insightfully pointed out, do so with far greater specificity than it could do as music alone. As Carroll puts it: "Wedding the musical system to the movie system, then, supplies the kind of reference to particularize the broad expressivity of the musical system."[8]

There seems to me, then, to be no very great mystery about what the filmic function of music is in the silent movie. It adds the dimension of sound to a silent world. More importantly, it adds the dimension of sonic *expression* that in a world of sound is the office of human utterance and human speech. But now along comes the talking picture, and at a stroke, the rules of the game are changed forever, the vacuum of silence filled up. The cinema possesses, with the coming of sound, *all* the expressive resources of the spoken theater—and more. For it then possesses not merely the expressive resources of articulate speech and inarticulate utterance—the word and the groan—but all of those sounds, unheard in the theater, that the technique of the sound track can provide: thus, not merely the word and the groan, but the heartbeat and the footstep.[9] (I will say more of this later on.)

My question—the question of this paper—is *why* the music plays on when the sound comes in? If the filmic function of music, in the silent era, is to fill the vacuum left by the total absence of expressive sound, why does it outlast its function when the full resources of expressive sound fill that vacuum in the era of the talking picture?

What's the problem? the skeptical reader may well ask. If pasta substitutes for meat during Lent, that hardly suggests that *after* Lent we will want to give up pasta altogether. Why not have both? Why not meatballs *and* spaghetti? And, by parity of reasoning, why not have speech, sound, *and* music in the movies? The Lent of silence may be over, but there is no reason therefore to give music up, when it makes such a rich aesthetic contribution to the enterprise—richer than ever, indeed, with the added technological resources of the perfectly coordinated music track.

This answer may satisfy some. But anyone who knows the historical roots of film music in eighteenth-century melodrama will remain *un*satisfied by such a facile answer to our question. For the failed promise of Georg Benda's intriguing experiment, even in the hands of the great Mozart himself, whose magic touch in the musical theater has

---

[8] Noel Carroll, *Mystifying Movies: Fads and Fallacies in Contemporary Film Theory* (New York: Columbia University Press, 1988), 220–1.

[9] I omit mention of the stream of consciousness that the over-voice of the sound track can provide, because the drama possesses that (although perhaps less "naturally"?) in the monologue—witness the substitution of over-voice for spoken soliloquy by Orson Welles and Sir Laurence Olivier in *Macbeth* and *Hamlet* respectively.

never been surpassed, leads us to wonder why the selfsame experiment, two centuries later, in the talking picture, should have been such a rousing success.

GHOSTS

Perhaps the best-known, as well as the most bizarre attempt to explain the filmic function of music in the talking film is that of Theodor Adorno and Hanns Eisler in their 1947 book *Composing for the Films*. Adorno and Eisler eschewed the obvious, and, in my view, obviously correct answer to the question of music's role in the silent film: namely, that it is a substitute for human vocal expression, both linguistic and inarticulate. The reason for that seems fairly clear. They wanted an answer to that question that would hold good for the presence of music in the talking film as well; and it is not at all obvious how the expressive role music plays in silent film can possibly also be the reason for its presence in the talky, since what it is a substitute for, *talk*, is no longer absent.

For that reason, I suspect, Adorno and Eisler sought a less obvious role than expression for music in the silent film—a role that they saw as possible for it in the sound film as well. Of music in the silent era, they wrote: "The pure cinema must have had a ghostly effect like that of the shadow play—shadows and ghosts have always been associated. The major function of music … consisted in appeasing the evil spirits unconsciously dreaded." The role of music in the silent film play, then, was "to exorcise fear or help the spectator absorb the shock … ".[10]

Furthermore, according to Adorno and Eisler, the ghosts persisted into the era of sound, although we now had talking ghosts. (An even more frightening prospect, perhaps?) Thus *"the talking picture, too, is mute.* The characters in it are not speaking people but speaking effigies. … Their bodiless mouths utter words in a way that must seem disquieting to anyone uninformed".[11]

So, if the ghosts remain, the need for musical exorcism remains as well. "The sound pictures have changed this original function of music less than might be imagined."[12] The magic is still wanted, and music

---

[10] [Theodore Adorno and] Hanns Eisler, *Composing for the Films* (London: Dennis Dobson, 1947), 75.
[11] Ibid. 76.   [12] Ibid.

is still there to provide it. That, in brief, is the ectoplasmic theory of Adorno and Eisler.

Noel Carroll makes rather quick work of rejecting Adorno and Eisler's proposal; and although there *are* two grains of truth in it (as will become apparent later on), I have no reason to go beyond Carroll's refutation of their proposal as it originally stands. Carroll writes of their account of music in the silent film:

> their theory seems based on pretty flimsy evidence. They claim that film spectators feel discomfort viewing cinematic images *because* we find them ghostly. ... Informal evidence for this might be that audiences are often restless during silent films, unaccompanied by music, and frequently complain about the silence. But perhaps we should take spectators at their word. ... Perhaps it is the *silence* that strikes them and not some putative fear of ghosts.[13]

As for the talky:

> Moreover, pace Adorno and Eisler, one does not encounter comparable complaints with sound films. There is, to my knowledge, no evidence for believing that spectators respond to sound films in the way Eisler and Adorno say they do. ... Adorno and Eisler base their analysis on postulating a state in the spectator that has no basis in the data of film viewing.[14]

Having dismissed the proposal of Adorno and Eisler in this wise, Carroll has a positive proposal of his own to make that merits serious consideration. In his answer to the question of music's function in the cinema, Carroll offers a number of suggestions as to what I have been calling its *aesthetic* function that are, it appears to me, right on the money. But insofar as they are not answers to the question of music's *filmic* function, they need not concern us here.

However, Carroll does offer one suggestion that I *would* characterize as addressing the *filmic* function of music. And I want to turn to that proposal for a moment before I go on to my own.

Carroll writes: "The addition of music gives the filmmaker an especially direct and immediate means for assuring that the audience is matching the correct expressive quality with the action at hand".[15]

I am sure Carroll is right in emphasizing this *expressive* function of music in the movies, and I will make use of it myself when I come to offer my own suggestion concerning music's filmic function in the talking picture. But the question remains to be answered concerning

---

[13] Carroll, *Mystifying Movies*, 215.
[14] Ibid. 216.   [15] Ibid. 222.

why the sound film should require this additional expressive fillip while the legitimate theater does not. Carroll's answer is what might be called a "sociological" one.

Movies are a means of popular expression. They aspire for means of communication that can be grasped almost immediately by untutored audiences. Another way of putting this is to say that moviemakers seek devices that virtually guarantee that the audience will follow the action in the way that the filmmaker deems appropriate.

It being the case, therefore, that movies are for a "popular" audience, the musical track is necessary as an expressive prop to assure a correct expressive reading by the unsophisticated viewer. Thus, "given the almost direct expressive impact of music", its presence in the movies "assures that the untutored spectators of the mass audience will have access to the desired expressive quality and, in turn, will see the given scene under its aegis".[16]

I do not have any doubt at all but that Carroll's conjecture is altogether correct as a partial answer to the question of music's filmic function. I strongly suspect, however, that it cannot be the whole answer, for the following reason. Were the filmic function of the musical track only to give the unsophisticated moviegoer an expressive aid, I believe there would have evolved a genre of cinematic "high art" where the musical track would have been dispensed with, since such a genre would be aimed at a sophisticated audience which, on Carroll's hypothesis, would not require it. Filmmakers, after all, aim at different levels of audience sophistication with different films. And whereas the general run of Hollywood movies was and is aimed at a mass audience, "art films" of various kinds are not, necessarily; yet these films for sophisticates do not lack musical tracks. To the contrary, where one would expect, on Carroll's hypothesis, a decline in the prominence of the music, there is frequently an increase in musical quality and involvement, producing such memorable scores as that for Olivier's *Hamlet*, to name but one outstanding example.

Thus, although I by no means reject Carroll's "sociological" answer to the question of music's filmic function in the talky, I think that it must be amplified with another, which holds not merely for unsophisticated movie audiences, but for movie audiences *tout court*. And to that answer, *my* answer, I now turn my attention.

16 Ibid. 223.

THE VACUUM OF SOUND

I said in my discussion of Adorno and Eisler that there are two grains of truth in their theory, bizarre though it is. They are, I think, first, that what I call the filmic function of music must be more or less the same for both sound and silent film, and second, that this function must have something to do with the way they characterize the personages of the sound film: namely, as "speaking effigies". But it is my view, as we have seen, that the filmic function of music in the silent era was to fill an expressive gap that the vacuum of silence produced. And if, as I also think, it performs the *same* filmic function in the sound film, then it follows that some gap or other must still remain even after the vacuum of silence has been filled up by speech.

So if I am right, that something essential is still missing from cinema, even with all of the resources of the modern sound track in place, that the musical track must be seen as providing, what can that "something" be? I propose a simple answer. Again, as in silent film, it is some aspect of *human expression*, which the "speaking effigies" cannot provide.

There is some evidence for this in the very nature of theater music itself, as it has been constituted at least since the beginning of the seventeenth century, particularly in opera. For although it would be a serious mistake to suggest that music has only one purpose in opera and other forms of musical theater, the dominant one has always been as a medium for the representation and expression of the emotive states of mind of the dramatis personae. This fact is so well known as to require no argument here. Emotive expression on the musical stage is to be found, primarily, in neither word nor gesture, but in *music*. Film music, for the most part, shares this role, as Carroll has pointed out: its primary purpose is always expressive, expressive of the dominant emotion or emotions of character or scene.

But that in itself is not enough to demonstrate *convincingly* that the expressiveness of music in the sound film is there to fill a gap. It may *suggest* that possibility. However, the skeptical reader will naturally want to know exactly *what* the gap in expression is, or *why* one might have reason to believe that there is one, besides the mere presence of *expressive* music.

In silent film the expressive gap is obvious: it is the gap left by the absence of all the emotive expression accomplished by the human voice. But in the talking picture *all* of that emotive expression is restored: for there the actor and actress have ceased to be dumb, have regained all of the expression of which the noise-making human animal is capable.

But *does* the talking filmic *image*, Adorno and Eisler's *speaking effigy*, have *all* of the resources of human expression *tout court*? I suspect that it does not. And although I cannot provide an iron-clad argument for it, I can at least suggest wherein my suspicions lie.

To begin with, let me return again, for a moment, to the hypothesis of Adorno and Eisler. For them the primary motivation for music in the movies is the quelling of what they take, ghosts and goblins notwithstanding, to be genuine fear of the filmic image, whether or not it speaks. How seriously we should take the explanation of this fear in terms of some vestigial trace of fear of the supernatural — they can hardly think film audiences in general consciously believe in spooks — I don't really know. But insofar as the explanation is audience fear, whatever its origin, there seems to be no evidence for it, as Noel Carroll has, I think, convincingly argued.

But there may, perhaps, be at least the suggestion, lurking, of a more reasonable explanation, in Adorno and Eisler's emphasis on the lack, in cinema, of a third dimension. The characters of film, they write, are "endowed with all the features of the pictorial, the photographic two-dimensionality, the lack of spatial depth."[17]

I can't believe, actually, that the two-dimensionality of the screen image can be mined for very much. We scarcely perceive the screen image without depth, any more than we do the picture space of Renaissance painting. But to follow out their theme, perhaps there *is*, metaphorically speaking, a "dimension" lacking in the filmic image that music is there to compensate for, if not substitute for, even when the image speaks. I think that there is; and *what* it is I hope to explain.

Everything that philosophical analysis has revealed to us in recent years, about the concept of human emotive expression, and the reading thereof, testifies to how fragile it really is, when one wants to get beyond the very basic emotions like fear, or anger, or happiness into the more subtle distinctions: how dependent on what the "intentional objects" of the emotions may be.[18] We know how difficult it is to read human

---

[17] [Adorno and] Eisler, *Composing for the Films*, 76.
[18] I refer here to the growing literature on the so-called cognitive theory of the emotions, which emphasizes the role of belief and object in the forming of human

emotive expression, except in the most general terms, out of real context, and in the absence of the emotional setting.

Well, this is nothing to the present purpose, it will doubtless be objected, because in the sound film all of the disambiguating cues are present, as they are in "real life". But *does* it have *all* of them? It *isn't*, after all, "real life".

Of course, it will be replied, but neither is legitimate theater "real life". What does spoken theater have that the talky lacks? *That* is the question.

Well, one thing that spoken theater has that even sound movies do not is the *real presence* of human beings. Does that make a difference? Let me suggest that we have at least some prima facie evidence, and some anecdotal evidence as well, in favor of its really mattering for the communication of emotion whether we confront a talking filmic image, a "speaking effigy", or the real presence: an actor or actress in the flesh. We have *some* reason to think—I do not say it is overwhelming or conclusive reason—that being in the real presence of the speaker, even in the public ambiance of the legitimate stage, provides a more intimate expressive connection and more subtle expressive cues than can be had in the movies, isolated in darkness, from a talking image. And the reason for that reduction in power and connection seems to me completely *un*mysterious, even if the nuts and bolts are not well understood. Nor does it have aught to do with ghostly metaphysics, but with the perfectly reasonable conjecture that a physically present human being offers more expressive cues than a moving photographic image, even though it talks.

But what *are* these additional expressive cues, it will fairly be asked, that the real presence exhibits and the film lacks? My altogether disappointing answer is that I do not know, though I hope to amplify that answer somewhat in some of the following remarks. So I must allow, at this point in the argument, that the skeptical reader may well say of my conjecture what Noel Carroll said of the theory of Adorno and Eisler: "based on pretty flimsy evidence". Yes, that is so. Yet it is not based on no evidence at all. And it is, I submit, an eminently sensible conjecture that accords well with our ordinary experience of human expression and interpersonal transactions. Who does not feel

emotions. A useful bibliography of this and other work on the emotions can be found in Amélie Oksenberg Rorty (ed.), *Explaining Emotions* (Berkeley, Los Angeles, and London: University of California Press, 1980).

the relative remoteness of the electronic or filmic image, as compared to the real presence of a human being, where emotive communication is concerned? Doubtless, many of the emotive cues are experienced but semi-consciously, if consciously at all. (More of that anon.) But who doubts that they are there?

Well, perhaps that last rhetorical question is the result of a quite unjustified confidence. Doubtless there are doubters. What more can I say to dispel their doubts?

A SECOND OPINION

As I have said, I offer my hypothesis with regard to the filmic function of music tentatively, and probably with as many misgivings as the reader who receives it. And perhaps one way to remove at least *some* of the misgivings (I doubt if I can remove them all) would be to present an alternative hypothesis, a second opinion that may seem inviting at first, but turns out to be not as attractive as it first appears. Here, then, is another proposal for the filmic function of music in the talking film. It is less "elegant", more complex than the first, but, maybe because of that, more convincing to those who do not share my intuition of a remaining expressive vacuum in the talky. I shall argue, however, that it has problems of its own that render it, at least as I perceive things, less plausible than the simpler and more elegant one it is meant to replace.

Assume, for starters, that my account of the filmic function of music in the silent era is, on the whole, correct, that, in other words, music is filling the expressive vacuum that the absence of human, emotively expressive speech creates. Assume further, if you like, although I do not think it is essential to the proposal, what might be called a principle of musical "squatter's rights". Once music was firmly in place in the movies, it would have tended to stick, unless there were some powerful force to evict it after the advent of sound. It was solidly entrenched, and therefore a familiar element in the motion picture, whose removal would have itself caused feelings of *angst*, dislocation, and deprivation of an expressive element the viewer had come to expect.

Furthermore, in suggesting the analogy between talking film and spoken theater, it may well be objected that I have ignored another analogy, every bit as obvious and valid, between talking film and silent film. For, after all, the talking film, unlike spoken theater, provides opportunities for what might be called "scenic intervals", which will be empty of people, and therefore empty of speech—perhaps, indeed, empty of sound altogether. Music, so the argument might go, is needed to fill the sound vacuum that remains in the gaps between talking—gaps that hardly ever exist in legitimate theater.[19]

The problem I have with this suggested alternative explanation is that it provides no reason for why the music is not reserved solely for the gaps: why, that is, it accompanies speech as well, which it manifestly does in so many sound films. Nor, it turns out, does it even explain, really, why it should accompany the scenic gaps either.

The problem we began with, remember, was why melodrama did not survive as an autonomous artistic practice where as its twentieth-century descendant, the sound movie with music, did. Melodrama is a form of drama in which words are spoken, with musical accompaniment, opera a form of drama in which the words are sung and musically accompanied, theatre a form of drama from which music is all but absent, sound cinema a form of drama in which the words are spoken with musical accompaniment a good deal of the time. Opera, theater, and sound cinema have survived and flourished, melodrama has not, apparently because spoken words with musical accompaniment did not constitute an artistically viable enterprise. *Why*, then, is it an artistically viable enterprise in sound cinema? That is our question, and it remains, whether or not music *does* have the filmic function of filling the gaps of silence between the episodes of talking: filling, that is, as it does in silent cinema, the vacuum of silence.

But, furthermore, it turns out to be false that even as a filler of the gaps between episodes of dialogue, music has the filmic function, as it does in silent cinema, of filling the vacuum of silence left by the absence of speech. For the scenic gaps between episodes of dialogue are either, in life, themselves silent—for example, a city asleep or a quiet landscape—or they are noisy in life—for example, a city awake with traffic or a prairie alive with cattle. If the latter, then the sound track provides the appropriate sonic background; if the former, the absence of sound is not what I have been calling the vacuum of silence at all, because there was no sound to begin with. The vacuum of silence is a sonic space with the sound sucked out, as in silent cinema. But the silence of the world is truly represented by the silence of the

[19] The alternative that I am presenting and criticizing here was suggested by Richard Allen.

screen; and there should be no felt need for music to fill *that* silence at all.

Is there a felt need for music to fill the silence of a silent world? If so, and it seems that there is, since music obtrudes even there, then even *there* there must be a vacuum. But what does a filmic representation of a silent city or a silent landscape lack that its real-life counterparts possess? Could it be that some subtle expressiveness, in some way analogous to the expressiveness that, on my hypothesis, is lost in the transfer from the real human presence to the filmic image, is also lost in the transference of in-life silent scenes to their filmic representations? Well, after all, our non-peopled world—the world of mountains and fields, animals and plants, machines and artifacts—has expressive properties of its own, does it not? Or is that too improbable a hypothesis to entertain? And does the filmic image of these creatures and things also lack a subtle essence that music has come to restore?

Even more puzzling still, music is present, more often than not, in gaps that are full of noise—that is to say, in noisy landscapes. So even where the city is awake with traffic, or the prairie alive with cattle, the sounds of traffic and cattle seem not to suffice. Even *here* the sound of music is felt to be required. Even *here*, where sight *and* sound are made present, with all of the technical resources of the cinematographer and sound engineer at our command, the expressiveness of music seems to be wanted. What else can it be wanted for but some subtle essence of expressiveness that these impressive resources lack? The chase without the *music* of the chase? Unthinkable!

In any event, far from solving the problem of music's filmic function in sound cinema, the theory of the gaps (if I may so call it) raises a problem just as puzzling, if not more so, than the one it fails to solve. And so I will leave it for someone else, perhaps, to make more of than I have been able to do, returning to my original hypothesis, for the purpose of further elucidation.

A REFINEMENT

Now I am not, of course, saying that emotive expression, *tout court*, fails to be captured by the filmic or photographic image. Indeed, there is strong evidence that facial configurations, in particular, are universal in the species, and, clearly, transfer quite adequately from the real presence to the photographic or even painterly image. The research of Paul

Ekman, for example, has made this quite apparent. But it has *also* made quite apparent how limited the *universal* emotive repertory is. Ekman writes in this regard:

The evidence of universality in emotional expression is limited to the emotions of happiness, surprise, fear, anger, disgust, and sadness. We expect that there are also universal facial expressions for interest and, perhaps, shame. There may be other emotions for which there is also a universal facial expression, but probably not many.[20]

Thus, to the extent that the filmic image relies on facial expression, it is limited to a rather small and unsubtle repertory of emotions. Indeed, beyond this, even speech does not seem to be the major, or at least the sole, means of divining human emotion. For human beings, generally, do not, so to speak, wear their hearts on their sleeves, and tend to "manage" their emotive expressions, as Ekman puts it—which is to say, they, to a certain extent, mask or control the revelation of their inner states. Nevertheless, emotive expression tends to "leak" through the control system; and, Ekman has concluded, "there is more leakage in body movements than in either words or facial movement … ".[21] But even body language, apparently, is not of itself the basic key to the reading of human emotions. Indeed, the key turns out to be very complex. Ekman writes:

The estimate that emotion is present is more likely to be correct when [among other things]

— The response system changes are complex, when it is not just a facial, or skeletal, or vocal, or coping response, but a combination;

— the changes are organized, in the sense of being interrelated and distinctive for one or a combination of emotions. …[22]

What emerges from Ekman's work, then, is that recognition of the human emotions, in any of their subtlety, is a matter of recognition of extremely subtle cues, well beyond the obvious ones of facial expression, body movement, or even speech. We are, either by nature or nurture, or both, finely tuned to these cues; and if they are absent, our ability to recognize emotions in others will be dislocated.

---

[20] Paul Ekman, "Biological and Cultural Contributions to Body and Facial Movement in the Expression of Emotions", in Rorty (ed.), *Explaining Emotions*, 97. In adducing the work of Ekman, I am responding to a suggestion of Murray Smith's, although I am drawing a favorable conclusion for my hypothesis, whereas, I think, he expected the opposite.
[21] Ibid. 89.   [22] Ibid. 87.

Now it is clear that the sound film captures all of the gross parameters of emotive expression—notably, facial configuration and speech—that convey, when unmasked, the basic repertory of human emotions. What Ekman's work suggests, though, is that human beings, because of the dual phenomena of management and leakage, are attuned to far more subtle cues than those. I hypothesize that it is these more subtle cues that may be lost in the filmic image, even when it speaks, and the absence of which the audience "feels", "senses", "intuits" as an emotive vacuum, a vacuum that, I have been arguing, music helps to fill. Or, perhaps another way of putting it, it warms the emotional climate, even though it cannot substitute for the emotive cues that are lost.

Of course, the legitimate theater cannot, no more than can the cinema, present to its audience *all* of the subtle emotive cues of which I speak. For the stage actor, no more than the movie actor, is really angry when he "expresses" anger, in love when he "expresses" love, *pace* the "method" (and other such myths, which may be true in theory but impossible in practice). Many of the cues that evade our management may be unknown to us, and some that are not beyond conscious control. But those that the actor can reproduce, either by "art" or by "instinct", are going to be harder to pick up, so I am suggesting, out of the real presence. Thus the cinema will, to appropriate Plato's image, be at two removes from emotive reality, an image of a pretense. And it is the image of the pretense that, so I am arguing, is most in need of the emotive enhancement of which music is so eminently capable.

That last remark merits amplification. It is certainly *not* in music's power to fine-tune emotive expression beyond the offices of human language. Indeed, the shoe is on the other foot, as I have argued elsewhere: language, in vocal music, fine-tunes musical expression, for music's expressive repertory, without the assistance of linguistic props, not coincidentally, in my view, is pretty much that of Ekman's catalogue of facial expressions.[23] Thus, what music adds to the emotive pot is not a functional equivalent for what expression the talking filmic image may lose, but provides expressive oomph for that expression that remains: the sadness is sadder, the happiness happier. To adduce an analogy, the uncle cannot replace the mother, but he can become an additional father, if you will, strengthening the father that is already there. The

---

[23] On this see, Peter Kivy, *The Corded Shell: Reflections on Musical Expression* (Princeton: Princeton University Press, 1980).

loss remains, but is less keenly felt because what remains has been amplified.

Now at this point in the argument a comment is perhaps in order concerning not what might be lost to expression when we go from the real presence to the filmic sound image, but what might be *gained*, both through cinematographic techniques of all kinds and the techniques of the sound track, which is not, of course, or need not be, just a recording of the same sounds that would be heard in the theater, or even in life, but sounds that we could not hear although there nevertheless, and perhaps of expressive use.[24]

Let me adduce an example of each. Perhaps the most obvious example of visual advantage that cinema has over the theater is the close-up. And since so much expression of the grosser variety, of the basic emotions, is displayed in the face, the expressive contribution of the close-up is obvious. I can get closer to a person's face in the filmic image than I can ever get either in the theater or in life.

As for sound, let me just mention an old chestnut: the beating heart. The sound of another's heartbeat is something of course that one almost never hears in life, under usual circumstances, or in the theater at all. But it is easy enough to do, and has been done more than once, to give the impression, through the sound track, of hearing a person's heartbeat. And a fast, loud heartbeat, when other cues are in place, is a dead giveaway to, and a standard cinematic icon for, *fear.*

Now, both the visual close-up and the sound close-up (if I may so call it) can be, then, expression-enhancers. But the question is whether they help to fill the expressive vacuum of which I have been speaking: the vacuum occupied in life, and, at least partially in the theater, I have been arguing, by those subtle cues alluded to by Ekman and others. The answer seems to me to be negative. Here is why.

The visual and sound close-up are, of course, artistic devices. But the subtle emotive cues are "in-life" occurrences; and our emotive sensibilities are tuned, either by nurture or nature, or both, to those in-life occurrences. Few get within three inches of another's nose, in life; no one lays her ear on his chest, unless one is a doctor or a lover. No: the subtle cues of which Ekman and others have written are perceived in everyday human encounters and situations. Thus the cues they may

---

[24] I am responding here to a suggestion by Murray Smith with regard to both visual and sound techniques, and to a request for more about sound techniques from Peter Sacks.

fail to encounter in the movies cannot be substituted by the visual and sonic close-up; nor will their feeling of lack, of something missing in the expressive canvas, be assuaged by them.

In short, the visual and sonic close-up, and other cinematic and sonic techniques of the movie, perform much the same function when they are being used *expressively* as music does. They reinforce the gross emotive cues that are already there: they do not—cannot—replace the ones that are, on my hypothesis, absent.

But this prompts the objection that if the expressive function of these cinematic and sonic techniques *duplicates* this same expressive function of music, then that expressive function cannot be the explanation for why music should be there. Music would seem to be distinctly *de trop*. Who needs it?

Well, although I think it is perfectly true that the filmic function of music is, to a certain extent, reinforced by other cinematic techniques, both visual and sonic, the ubiquitousness of the musical medium, its ability to be present always and everywhere, and to seep into every crevice, makes it the prime mover in the enterprise of filling the expressive vacuum. Close-ups come and go; music endures. Indeed, the overwhelming presence of music, almost everywhere, almost all the time, speaks of its pride of place *in this particular regard*.

This, of course, is emphatically *not* to say that music has pride of place in the cinema *tout court*. If *that* were the case, cinema would be recognized, like opera, as a basically *musical* art, which, needless to say, it is not. All I am saying is that in this particular filmic function of filling what I have been calling the expressive vacuum, music has pride of place. In narrative, of course, cinematic technique, both visual and auditory, is the basic machinery, and music almost impotent to help. Its peculiar genius here, as in opera, song, and liturgy, is *expressive*. What *else* it can do is a matter of perennially unresolved controversy, on which I am on the side of the "minimalists".

Thus, to sum up this part of the argument, I have been urging that although other elements of cinematic technique, both visual and aural, can, to a certain extent, perform the filmic function of music—namely, to fill the expressive vacuum by reinforcing those expressive cues that are in place—they are far less suited to this task than music, which, *in this particular respect*, has the lion's share, by natural right. That, in any case, is my conjecture, which I offer as I have said before, in the spirit of conjecture alone.

WHEN THE MUSIC STOPS

I have, so far, been talking about the *musical presence* in both silent and sound cinema. But at least a brief comment is in order, perhaps, about those rare occasions in the talking picture where music is *absent* altogether. What might the significance be of *that*? In particular, what might the significance be, for my argument, of films in which music is intentionally omitted completely, for *expressive* purposes, as surely is done from time to time?

Two films of recent memory, *The China Syndrome* and *The Birds*, have been suggested to me as examples of films that "do not possess a musical score, and yet … are not expressively underpowered".[25] Indeed, one might make the even stronger claim that far from the lack of a score rendering them "expressively underpowered", it renders them expressively *supercharged*, beyond what even an expressive musical score might provide. For the perceived absence of music *itself* has an expressive power uniquely its own.

This is perfectly true, and *The Birds*, it seems to me, exemplifies the expressive impact of musical absence in a really quite stunning way, in that the naked sound of the birds, without musical accompaniment, is rendered all the *more* ominous. But worthy of note though the absence of a musical score is, as an expressive (and dramatic) technique, it is something of a red herring here, if, at least, it is intended as a criticism of the view that music's filmic function is to fill an expressive vacuum, *The Birds* and its ilk being incontrovertible instances of film's impressive expressiveness in the complete absence of a musical accompaniment.

The reason why such an argument fails is that the expressive effect of music's occasional *absence* from film is parasitic on its almost universal *presence*. Only when the presence of music is so familiar as to be completely taken for granted can withholding it from all (or part) of a film produce the stark expressive effect that Hitchcock attains in his avian horror story. The great opera composers well knew this, which was why melodrama could be used, *but sparingly*, as an occasional dramatic technique in a sung work, where the disappearance of music altogether and the sudden intrusion of the speaking voice, could produce such expressive effects as Beethoven accomplished in the dungeon scene of

---

[25] Murray Smith, in a private communication.

Fidelio, the emptiness of the spoken voices underscoring the emptiness of the subterranean galleries through which Rocco and Leonore descend.

But from the expressiveness of music withheld, one can scarcely argue for the expressiveness of film without music altogether. For only against the canvas of music as a ubiquitous expressive part of film generally, can the silencing of music have what expressive effect it does. If all cinema were without music, the absence of it in *The Birds* would neither be noticed nor have any expressive effect at all.

AN EXPERIMENT AND A CONCLUSION

Before I come to my conclusion, one other feature of my hypothesis that, it seems to me, might make it more attractive to the skeptic, and that perhaps deserves mention, is that it might very well be verifiable in experience—a characteristic perhaps unexpected in a conjecture offered as part of a *"Philosophical* Inquiry". It is not difficult to imagine different audiences confronting the same film or film excerpt with and without the musical track, or a filmed scene and the same scene "in the flesh". Nor is it difficult to imagine ways of canvassing such audiences as regards their respective "readings" of expressive content or their emotional reactions towards it. My expectation is that there would be significant differences in these readings and reactions bearing out my hypothesis.

But perhaps a more complex, and aesthetically interesting, set of "experiments", at least in the broad sense of that word—that is to say, "experiences"—might be considered here. There are two ways in which one might think of a preexistent play—say, a Shakespearean tragedy—being "transferred" to cinema. In one version, the camera would "sit", as a member of the theater audience, so to speak, and register what goes on before it on the stage. And such movies, minus music track, have certainly been made. In a more interesting version, however, the play would be "adapted" for the screen, utilizing all of the visual and aural techniques of the medium, with only the absence of music to distinguish it from other films. And that too has been done.[26]

The skeptic might now suggest that, *of course*, the first version of the "experiment" will support my hypothesis, because it proposes a

---

[26] I am responding here to a query of Murray Smith's.

hopelessly dessicated, emasculated filmic artifact. *Of course* there will be a felt expressive vacuum in the first kind of music-less cinematic play, because none of the special expressive resources of the cinema have been utilized. I have, so the objection will go, stacked the deck in favor of my hypothesis. But if the experiment is performed in the second version, with all of the expressive techniques of the modern cinema in place, the lack of music will not create any feeling of expressive vacuum, for the cinema's non-musical expressive arsenal will fill the expressive void. Thus there is no reason why the experiment, in its second, more sophisticated version, will support my hypothesis in the least.

Now to begin with, *if* the first version of the experiment *does* produce a feeling of expressive vacuum in the filmic version of the play without musical track, it will show that at least part of my hypothesis is correct: namely, the claim that some expressive quality is lost by the direct transfer from the real presence to the unadorned filmic image, from the live play to the play "literally" reproduced on film, without the addition of music or special cinematic technique.

But, of course, the second version of the experiment puts my hypothesis to a severer test. For if sophisticated cinematic techniques, both visual and aural, are brought to bear in the transference from theater to movie house, from the real presence to the filmic image, and, in particular, those that are expressive, then, presumably, the objector might opine, it would be highly unlikely that any expressive vacuum would be felt. Whatever was lost in the transfer from the real presence to the filmic sound image would have been made up for (although not replaced) by all of the expressive resources of the cinematographer's art. So, although my hypothesis might explain why music might have continued in sound cinema at a technically primitive stage of its development, it cannot explain why it should remain when all of the sophisticated techniques were in place. It should have withered on the vine like the melodrama of old.

For reasons already adduced above, it does not seem to me that the expressive power of cinematic techniques alone, whether visual or sonic, remove the sense of expressive vacuum that departure from the real presence engenders, without the aid of the musical track. But that argument is irrelevant here. For what is being proposed is in the spirit of a "crucial experiment". And whatever results I, or anyone else, may *expect* from it, prior to its being carried out cannot substitute for its *being* carried out. Many is the expectation that *experience* has dashed.

In any event, all I wish to suggest is that my hypothesis has empirical content. Whether that content can really cash out in experimental terms remains an open question.

Of course my hypothesis might be defeated; if it were, though, another would be needed. For it seems to me that the question which this hypothesis is meant to address will not dissolve; nor will it be answered by the quite reasonable task of investigating further the aesthetic functions of music in the sound film. Its *filmic* function will yet remain mysterious to anyone who gives serious thought to the history of eighteenth-century melodrama, and to the history of the cinema which, whether for the reason suggested, or some other, has not recapitulated it but evolved into the most popular combination of music and spoken drama in the history of either.

I offer my conjecture with not a little diffidence, and have said it often enough to have begun to sound like Uriah Heep. But I press my *question* in the strongest possible terms. Until we understand not merely the aesthetic functions of music in the movies, many of which we do already, but its filmic function as well, we will fail *in essence* to understand what is arguably the most important artistic event and practice for our century—certainly the most widely influential, for better and for worse. And music, I emphasize, *is* of the *essence* of the modern cinema—not merely an inessential accompaniment. That, its continued presence has amply demonstrated. If we do not understand music's filmic function in cinema, we do not understand cinema itself.[27]

[27] I am extremely grateful to Richard Allen, Noel Carroll, Peter Sacks, Alex Sesonske, and Murray Smith, who have all read earlier versions of this paper, and provided useful and generous comments. They have tried as hard as they could to save me from my ignorance and folly. Where they have failed, the blame is entirely mine.

PART III

PERFORMANCE

7

On the Historically Informed Performance

I

After my book *Authenticities* was published in 1995,[1] various people told me that I was, in effect, beating a dead horse; for the book was an extended analysis and critique of what had come to be known as the "historically authentic performance", which was supposed to be—at least as I understood it—the performance of a musical work in strict compliance with the way that work would have been performed in its own historical period and no other; or, if it didn't come to the same thing, in strict compliance with the performing intentions of the composer. But, so I was told, no one was pedantic or dogmatic enough any longer to endorse or pursue that sort of thing. Rather, what was now endorsed and pursued in its stead was something much more reasonable, yet, I presume, still in the historicist spirit: it was called the "historically *informed* performance". And none of the critical or analytical things I said in *Authenticities*, so these folks admonished me, had anything to do with *that* project at all.

When these things were said to me, I immediately became suspicious. And over the years since, I have often found myself wondering just what a historically *informed* performance might be, and how it might differ from a historically *authentic* one. What was particularly on my mind, what bothered me and made me suspicious, can best be explained with an example.

There recently took place in the United States a dispute between those who want us to pay less income tax than we have been paying and those who want us to pay about the same amount of income tax we

[1] Peter Kivy, *Authenticities: Philosophical Reflections on Musical Performance* (Ithaca, NY: Cornell University Press, 1995).

have been paying. But that is not exactly how the disputants put it. The former group, the little-endians, said they were in favor of what they described as "tax relief", whereas the latter group, the big-endians, said they were against what *they* described as a "tax cut".

Well you know, and I know, that "tax relief" and "tax cut" are names of the same thing: as logicians would put it, both descriptions have the same extension, the same reference. So why are the little-endians and the big-endians so intent on each sticking tenaciously to their own way of putting it?

Clearly, the answer is that the little-endians are trying to cash in on the positive connotation that attaches to the word "relief", and the big-endians are trying just as hard to block this maneuver. They are all involved in what R. G. Collingwood described as a "courtesy definition",[2] or, as Charles Stevenson described the same thing a few years later, a "persuasive definition".[3] The general idea is this: to redefine a word or phrase that may have negative connotations in a positive way, or vice versa, depending upon whether you are for or against the referent of the phrase. Thus the little-endians redefine "tax cut" as "tax relief", to suggest that they are relieving you of a burden—easing your pain. The old phrase, "tax cut", has no such connotation, and hence, for rhetorical effect, is discarded by the little-endians, but tenaciously held onto by the big-endians, if not for its negative connotation, at least for its neutrality. But the important point is that both the little-endians and the big-endians are *talking about the same thing*, while trying to convince you that they are talking about different things, so that if you are against a tax cut, maybe you will be in favor of something as attractive-sounding as tax relief, or if you are in favor of tax relief, perhaps you will be teased into being against a tax cut. It sounds pretty silly; but it's suprising how much of this kind of thing goes on anyway.

Given that the late Charles Stevenson was one of my teachers, and R. G. Collingwood's *Principles of Art* a book I teach regularly and know pretty thoroughly, I suppose it is not very surprising that when I was told that "historically authentic performance" was out, and "historically informed performance" in, my first thought and nagging suspicion, was that I might be being confronted with a courtesy or persuasive definition. The word "authentic", in the phrase "historically authentic

---

[2] R. G. Collingwood, *The Principles of Art* (Oxford: Clarendon Press, 1938), 8–9.
[3] Charles L. Stevenson, *Ethics and Language* (New Haven: Yale University Press, 1941), 210–24.

performance", had, over the years, taken on a somewhat negative connotation, due to the dissatisfaction that some people felt with the performances that went by that name, as well as criticism that some musicologists and philosophers had leveled against the underlying theoretical assumptions of the enterprise. The word "informed", substituted for "authentic", removed all the negative accretions: it certainly sounds nice to be "informed". Who could object to that?

But the question that nagged at me was: Do "historically authentic performance" and "historically informed performance" name the same thing or not? Was I being offered tax relief rather than a tax cut, in other words, the same thing under a different description? Or was there a substantive difference between them that would enable the latter to evade my critique, yet still retain some of the Historicist spirit of the former? That is the question I want now to tackle. I have not reached a conclusive answer. But I have reached some tentative conclusions. And if all I do, right now, is stir the pot to see what surfaces, I will be content.

II

So, now to begin, what might it mean for a performance to be historically informed? The first thought likely to occur to the inquirer is that it must mean a performance by a historically informed *performer*. In other words, it is the performer who is informed, not the performance. For, after all, to be informed seems to be a mental state; and a performance, needless to say, cannot be in a mental state. So it can't be the performance that is historically informed; it must be the performer. "Historically informed performance", then, turns out to be short for "performance by a historically informed performer".

Now I assume that when we talk about a historically informed performer, we mean a performer informed with regard to whatever aspects of music history might be relevant to the performance of musical works. A historically informed performance will be, then, a performance by such a performer. A historically informed performance of Bach's Italian Concerto, for instance, will be a performance by a keyboard player who knows how the work was performed in Bach's time, what Bach's performing intentions were for the work, and so forth.

The obvious problem with this analysis of what might be meant by a historically informed performance is that it allows *any* actual performance to be historically informed just so long as the performer is historically informed. Charles Rosen, for example, is an historically informed performer, if ever there was one. But he performs on a modern Steinway piano, and, in many other ways as well, conforms to our idea of what is just the opposite of a "historical" player: namely, a mainstream one. Indeed, just so long as the performer was historically knowledgeable, her performance of the Italian Concerto would be historically informed *any* way she played. *That* surely could not be what people were telling me when they explained that the historically authentic performance was out and the historically informed performance in. Presumably, when you substitute one thing for another, the thing substituted must retain at least *some* of the important features—the desirable ones, one would assume—of the thing substituted for. And if a performance qualified as historically informed *merely* on account of the performer's being historically informed, that would not be the case. Vladimir Horowitz once said that he played Mozart like Chopin and Chopin like Mozart. If he meant that he played Chopin the way he knew Mozart played Mozart, and played Mozart the way he knew Chopin played Chopin, then his performances of both Mozart and Chopin were, on this construal, historically informed. That clearly won't do. Merely having a historically informed performer is just too weak a condition for being an historically informed performance. Something more or different is required.

What is missing, of course, from the above characterization of the historically informed performance is some *connection* between the performance and the fact of the performer's being historically informed; and it must, in addition, be a *relevant* connection. We are driven to ask, in other words, *why* the performer should be historically informed. And this begins to look like a special case of the age-old question, Why study history? Does the study of history have any practical value, beyond the mere satisfaction of our natural curiosity about the past? And, in particular, does the study of performance history have any practical value beyond the mere satisfaction of our natural curiosity about the musical past? Let's worry these questions awhile.

III

I will begin on a slightly humorous note. One of the most familiar answers to the general question, Why study history? is summed up in the old adage, Those who do not know history are doomed to repeat it. The idea, of course, is that history is a series of mistakes, and the purpose of learning history is to familiarize yourself with these mistakes so that, when placed in similar circumstances, you will avoid making them yourself.

Proponents of the historically informed performance will, no doubt, find this ludicrous as a defense of their project. For it is not to avoid mistakes of the past, presumably, that they think the performer should be historically informed; rather, quite the opposite, she is to be historically informed so as to be enabled to *emulate* the past, because in the past performers had things right. That is the essence of the Historicist spirit that the historically informed performance is supposed, I assume, to have in common with the now abandoned historically authentic performance.

However, there is a point liable to be missed here: it is that it may not be *so* ludicrous, after all, for the historically informed performer to mind the adage that those who do not know history are doomed to repeat it. For the total performance history of a work includes not merely performances by the composer and his contemporaries, who presumably had it right, but all of the performances since, by performers who got it wrong because *they* were not historically informed. (Presumably we do *not* want to perform Handel's oratorios the way Baron van Swieten did.) So it makes a good deal of sense to suggest that the historically informed performer, like the the historically informed general, or the historically informed financial advisor, can indeed learn from the mistakes of her predecessors at least what to *avoid*.

But these considerations now lead to a problem. If the proponent of the historically informed performance accepts that there are many mistakes in the performance history of any given work of the past, subsequent to the period of its original performances, why should she think that that one period is immune from the "mistakes of history"? Why is it "ludicrous" to think that we can learn from the mistakes of Handel's contemporaries, as well, even, from the mistakes of Handel himself?

Now at this point in the argument the proponent of the historically informed performance has, it seems to me, two ways to go. She can make the familiar claim, for the familiar reasons, that the performances of the composer, and those of his contemporaries who share his culture and performance practice, are the optimal performances, and those that should be emulated by the historically informed performer. *Or* she may make the more moderate claim that *sometimes* the composer and his contemporaries got it right, sometimes wrong, and it behooves us to know how they did things so that we can emulate their successes and shun their failures.

I shall discuss both options in the following remarks. But first I want to go back to considering the very basic question I began with. What does it mean for a performance to be historically informed?

IV

Let me remind you how I dealt with this question. I remarked, to begin with, that it seems as if the historically informed performance is a *performance* that is historically informed. But that sounds absurd. To be informed is to be in a certain mental state. And performances are not the kind of entities that can be in mental states. So the obvious alternative is to say that it is the *performer* who is to be historically informed, and a historically informed performance can, then, simply be defined as a performance by a historically informed performer.

The problem that this definition immediately raised was that a performer might well be historically informed, and her performance completely uninfluenced by that knowledge. One could be as historically informed as you like, but completely reject that historical knowledge as a guide to performance. But surely this would be a *reductio ad absurdum* of what the historically informed performance is supposed to be. And to avoid this *reductio*, some kind of stipulation must be made to the effect that the performer not only be historically informed but that her *performance* be influenced by that knowledge in some appropriate way. *What* the appropriate way might be, we will have to consider more closely in a little while. What I would like to point out here and now is that we are at a place where it would be well for us to reconsider the initial decision to rule out the possibility of it really being as the phrase "historically informed performance" seems to imply: it is the *performance* that is informed, after all. How can that be?

Well, a quick trip to the philosopher's friend, the *Oxford English Dictionary*, can answer that question straightaway. For the second definition given there, of "to inform", after the obvious one, is: "To give 'form' or formative principle to: hence to stamp, impress, or imbue with some specific quality or attribute. ... " So it now becomes clear that what the proponent of the historically informed performance should say is that a historically informed performance is one that has been formed or stamped or impressed or imbued with history: with, that is to say, performance history. This is not to say that the performer should not be historically informed in the first sense of "to inform". On the contrary, the performer being historically informed (in the first sense) is the *means* to the *performance* being historically informed (in the second sense). And now we must investigate just what it would mean for the performance of a musical work to be historically informed: for it to be formed, stamped, impressed, imbued with or by history.

V

Recall, to begin with, why we are interested in asking and answering this question: the question of what a historically informed performance might be. It is because, at least in my own case, I had thrown up to me that what I and others were calling the historically authentic performance had been supplanted by something else, the historically informed performance, which, one presumes, fulfilled many or all of the goals of the historically authentic performance, preserved its historical "spirit", while avoiding its pitfalls, and so, in effect, avoiding my analysis and critique of the kind of historical performance it had supplanted. And what I was suspicious of was whether there was a real difference of substance here at all, or whether what I was being offered was merely a persuasive definition: historically informed for historically authentic; tax relief rather than a tax cut; in other words, a rhetorical flourish.

But this issue cannot be resolved, obviously, until we have before us a clear idea of just what a historically authentic performance is. For unless we know that, we cannot know whether the historically informed performance, whatever we determine *it* to be, differs in substance from the other. So for the next few minutes I will concern myself with outlining what, in my book *Authenticities*, I took the historically authentic performance to be.

In *Authenticities* I distinguished four ways in which I thought a musical performance might plausibly be described as "authentic"; and the first three, which I called "authenticity of intention", "authenticity of sound", and "authenticity of practice", I singled out as being most obviously connected to the concept of *historical* authenticity, the way I understood it. The fourth, what I called "personal authenticity", seems, however, on first reflection, to be inimical to the historical authenticity concept. But, as it turns out, it is also connected to historical authenticity, although certainly in a less than obvious or intuitive way.

Authenticity of intention is, quite simply, the historical authenticity of performance one achieves when following as closely as possible the performing intentions of the composer. Authenticity of sound is the historical authenticity one achieves in duplicating as closely as possible the way a performance of the work in its own time would have sounded. Authenticity of practice is the historical authenticity one achieves in reproducing as closely as possible the performance practice prevailing in the historical period of the composition being performed. And the reason why the three must be distinguished, even though they seem to be part and parcel of the same enterprise, is that there is no reason to believe that they will necessarily converge on the *same* performance.

It also turns out that none of these concepts of authenticity is quite as simple and unproblematic as it first appears. Each one has a hidden complication—or, rather, *at least one*.

The complication in authenticity of intention is that as the concept of intention is applied in human affairs, allowance is made for what I call "counterfactual intentions". The question of what the Founding Fathers intended in the US Constitution is not only the question of what they intended when they framed it, but what, given those intentions, they would have intended, here and now, given the new circumstances in which we find ourselves, but which they could not possibly have anticipated. And so also with the performing intentions of composers. What Bach's performing intentions would be today, given the circumstances in which we make music today, are *part* of what his performing intentions *were*, when he was alive, even though he could not possibly have anticipated what musical life would be like in the twenty-first century.

What complicates the authenticity of sound is that there are two possible, and sometimes incompatible, goals of the quest for such authenticity. When I say that I want to produce musical sounds as close as possible to those produced by a performance contemporary with the work, do I mean the musical sounds as perturbations of the air, or the sounds as heard by a contemporary audience? For if I mean the latter, this might well be achieved by *not* doing the former. To take the simplest of examples, a performing force that might have seemed massive to Bach's audience seems intimate chamber music to our Wagnerian ears, which means that we might need twice or more the number of performers that Bach used to produce the same effect on us that his forces produced on his contemporaries.

Duplicating a past performance practice raises the intriguing issue of which aspects of that practice are artistically relevant and which are not. In *Authenticities*, apropos of this, I asked the particular question of whether the visual aspects and audience attitude of a performance—its physical setting, ritualistic or social function, and so forth—were artistically relevant, and therefore essential to the project of reproducing a past performance practice. I referred to this as the music's "choreography," or *mise-en-scène*, and presented some considerations pro and con.

The purpose of pointing out all of these "complications" pertaining to the concept of the historically authentic performance was to make the point that in some surprising ways what is customarily taken to be historically *inauthentic* may be more historically *authentic*, after all, and vice versa. And this applies in spades to the fourth of my authenticities, personal authenticity, which I want to mention briefly now before moving on.

By the personal authenticity of a musical performance I meant something close, I suppose, to originality. Musical performers are, I take it, artists—"performing artists" is what they are called. And musical performances, I take it, are works of art. Furthermore, *one* of the things that artworks are customarily praised for is their originality, *one* of their demerits is customarily taken to be their derivative nature. An artwork that stays too close to its models is not personally authentic, not original, in that it is not a product of the artist's own personality, but derivative from the artistic personalities of others. This is true of musical performances as of other artworks. Great performers usually have styles all their own: styles that emanate from *them*, and, therefore, their performances are correctly characterized as "personally authentic".

But does it not seem obvious, then, that personal authenticity is completely inimical to the historical authenticity project? For, ideally, the point of the historically authentic performance is to duplicate, as closely as possible, someone else's performance, even if it is not an identifiable person's performance but some idealized historical artifact, constructed on the basis of whatever historical knowledge the musicologists can muster at this particular point in time. However, the personally authentic performance is supposed to be an original, imaginative creation, like any other work of art, bearing the personal stamp of the performing artist, and although not uninfluenced by the performances of others, nevertheless independent of them, and certainly never in imitation of them.

But even here, in this seemingly obvious point, a complication lurks. For if it is the composer's intention that, at least within certain constraints, the performer is to be original, is to be personally authentic; if originality, personal authenticity, is a working aspect of the performing practices of past periods; if it is part of period sound; then, it would seem, to achieve true authenticity of intention and practice and sound, the performer must achieve personal authenticity as well. It is part of what I call the "original contract" between composer and performer (of which more anon).

Now, having laid out some of the vagaries and complexities of the concept of the historically authentic performance, at least as I see it, I am going to ask you, perversely enough, to put them aside; to put them out of your minds. Or, perhaps a better way of saying it, I would like you to keep them in the back of your minds while I go on now to give a very general characterization of the historically authentic performance that will serve as the idealized model against which we can measure possible candidates for the historically informed performance, to the end of determining what the difference or differences between them might be.

VI

Ever since there has been a recognizable musical notation in the West, *and* a clearly distinguishable division of labor between composer and performer, even when they are embodied in the same person, there has been what I called just now the "original contract" between the composer and the performer; and I shall refer to it, from now on, specifically as the "old contract", for reasons that will become apparent in a moment. According to the terms of the old contract, there is a gap, an intended, an approved gap, between notation, which is to say work, and performance. The notation does not fully determine the sound occurrence which is the performance, and it is the performer's task to fill this gap.

Of course the first duty of the performer, under the old contract, is to comply with the notation; and "score compliance", as this has been called since the publication of Nelson Goodman's *Languages of Art* in 1968, is a very complicated and notation-relative concept.[4] It will suffice to say, in this regard, that whatever the nature of score compliance is in

⁴ Nelson Goodman, *Languages of Art: An Approach to a Theory of Symbols* (Indianapolis: Bobbs-Merrill, 1968), 143–8, 179–92.

any given period in which there is both a work–performance distinction and a composer–performer distinction, score compliance is a necessary condition for an acceptable performance, as well as the performer's initial obligation.

But once the primary obligation to score compliance is discharged, there remains a large area of indeterminacy in which the performer is free, at least within the limits of her performance practice, to exercise her taste, musical judgment, and creativity. And if she is one of the gifted few, she may achieve personal authenticity as well. To appropriate a phrase of Collingwood's, the performer, under the old contract, is the composer's collaborator—quite literally, an artistic collaborator in the production of the work.[5]

Of course, it would make no sense to talk about the *old* contract between composer and performer if I didn't think that there was a *new* contract too. And so I do: it is the contract implied by the project of the historically authentic performance.

What I suggested in *Authenticities* is that the project of the historically authentic performance is akin to an archeological project: it is an attempt to reconstruct, as accurately as historical knowledge allows, a musical artifact of the past: in a word, a past musical performance. And what it in essence does, what its ultimate goal is, is to close the gap between score and performance. To understand what I mean by this, we must reflect briefly on what a score or notation does, what its function is, when it operates with the composer–performer and score–performance distinctions at least roughly in place. It is, in effect, from the performer's point of view, a set of instructions for producing a performance of the work.

Some of the instructions are totally obvious: in black and white, so to say. If the score notates concert A for the second oboe, then concert A is what the second oboe must play. But should the second oboe play with vibrato? If he likes, you would think; one oboe player might, another not; *that* is according to their individual taste as performers. This is a "gap" between notation and performance—under the old contract, that is.

But under the new contract, whether the second oboe vibrates is *not* a matter of choice if the work he is performing was composed in a period in which the historian has determined that vibrato was not known, or was used very infrequently. Vibrato-less sound, in that case,

5 Collingwood, *Principles of Art*, 320–1.

even though not explicitly mandated, like the concert A in the second oboe, is *implied* by the score, given the historical circumstances; and what is implied by the score is part of the score, and therefore part of the performer's primary obligation to comply with. Under the old contract, vibrato or lack thereof is in the gap between score and performance, which is the prerogative of the performer; under the new contract the absence of vibrato has become part of the score, albeit an implied part, and is nonnegotiable. Multiply this example over and over again for other of the parameters of performance, and you will get the idea of what I mean when I say that under the new contract, under the discipline of the historically authentic performance, the ultimate goal is to close the gap between notation and performance.

Now there is an important caveat to enter at this point. *Of course* I am not saying that the characterization of the historical performance project is a characterization of any *existent* performance practice or any performance that has ever or will ever be given. For that would make the assumption of *complete* historical knowledge, and all of us know that that is an ideal that can never be realized, any more than can the ideal of complete scientific knowledge. And where historical knowledge of performance leaves gaps, which it *always* will, the performer under the second contract will, just as the performer under the first contract, have to fill the gap with performance decisions based on her taste, musical judgment, and creativity.

What this all goes to show, it may now be retorted, is that there is no crucial difference between the old contract and the new. Both acknowledge that in practice the score can never fully determine performance sound; and where it does not, in what I have been calling the gap between score and performance, the performer is as free under the new contract as under the old, to exercise her taste, musical judgment, and creativity.

Of course, in practice that is *in general* true. But it is clearly not true in *particular cases*. For if one has signed the new contract, and means to abide by it, then, in practice, historical knowledge, when it becomes available, always trumps musical taste, musical judgment and performance creativity, if they conflict. Whereas if you sign the old contract and mean to abide by it, historical knowledge is just one of your options. You may play it the way the composer intended, or the way his contemporaries played it, or the way it may have sounded back when, if your taste and judgment incline that way. But you are perfectly free to play it another way, if that way sounds good and right to you, historical evidence to the contrary notwithstanding. Under the new contract, "But I like it better the other way" never trumps "This is the historically authentic way". If you let it, then you are open to the charge of breach of contract.

Furthermore, the gap between score and performance holds a very different aesthetic significance under the new contract from what it does under the old. To put the point bluntly: under the old contract the gap between score and performance, which the performer is supposed to fill with her musical taste, judgement, and creativity, is an aesthetically desirable and desired feature which we cherish. But under the new contract the gap between score and performance is an unwanted gap: it is the gap between ignorance and knowledge. The ideal of the historically authentic performance, if you take the concept seriously, and strictly, is to fill the gap: to have performance totally determined by whatever historical parameters you take to be the relevant ones: whether those of intention, or sound, or practice, or some mixture of them all.

I think there is another, really neat, elegant way of expressing my thought here. It is this. The historically authentic performance is the performance that, to the fullest extent possible, is historically informed: to the fullest extent possible, formed, stamped, impressed, imbued with performance history.

You will of course perceive right away that I have engineered this conclusion very carefully. It has been my intent all along to show that one way, for me a very convincing way, of understanding the concepts of the historically authentic and historically informed musical performance leads to the conclusion that they are simply names for the same thing: it's the difference between a tax cut and tax relief, which is to say, no difference at all.

Understood in this way, the substitution of the historically informed performance for the historically authentic performance is a classic case of a persuasive or courtesy definition. And I think it might be worth a moment to contemplate what might be at work here.

VII

As I suggested earlier, the term "authentic" began to take on a negative connotation as performances under that name came under criticism by those who were, for one reason or other, either in principle or in practice, dissatisfied with them. In particular, it came to have associated with it a kind of rigid dogmatism suggesting there was one and only one correct way, or small range of correct ways, to perform a piece, and all other ways were either bad or just plain incorrect: not *bona fide* instances of the work; not, in a word, "authentic". I think it was something like this train of thought that must have been behind a remark of Richard Taruskin's, with which I am certainly in sympathy, that "The word ['authentic'] needs either to be rescued from its purveyors or to be dropped by those who would aspire to the values it properly signifies."[6]

But has it not been just what Taruskin was recommending that those who have wanted to talk about the historically *informed* rather than the historically *authentic* performance have done? They have not indeed "rescued" the word "authentic" from its purveyors. As a matter of fact, that is what I tried to do in *Authenticities*. However, they *have* followed the other alternative Taruskin gave: they have chosen to replace it with the word "informed".

What does that accomplish? Well, if it turns out, as my previous argument has tried to show, that at least according to one quite plausible interpretation of the two concepts, the historically authentic performance and the historically informed performance are one and the same thing, then, substantively, absolutely nothing has been accomplished. But rhetorically, so to speak, something has: and it is not, to be perfectly blunt, all that intellectually respectable. Here is what I think is going on. "Historically *authentic*" has come to sound dogmatic and inflexible; "historically *informed*" sounds much more pliable, less dogmatic and more open to alternatives. That is because the word "informed" suggests a wide latitude in performance, whereas "authentic" came to be associated with a monistic, rigid mind-set. I think this is because people mouthed the phrase "historically informed performance" without carefully distinguishing in their own minds between the sense of "informed" in "historically informed performer" and that in "historically informed *performance*", thus unconsciously drawing on both senses, without making it clear to others which notion was operative. The concept of the historically informed *performer* contributes that sense of non-dogmatic flexibility that was to be an antidote to the rigidity of authenticity, while the concept of the historically informed *performance* expressed, to appropriate Taruskin's well-chosen phrase, the values to which its proponents aspired, historical performance values, that the historically

---

[6] Richard Taruskin *et al.*, "The Limits of Authenticity: A Discussion", *Early Music*, 12 (1984), 3. Cf. Kivy, *New Essays on Musical Understanding* (Oxford: Clarendon Press, 2001), ch. 1.

authentic performance concept embodied. But the strategy is not quite intellectually respectable, because it dupes the unwary into thinking that they can have the flexibility that the historically informed performer allows *as well as* the historical spirit that is implied by the historically informed performance.

Now I do not for one moment suggest that anyone who threw the historically informed performance up to me, or anyone who uses that description these days, was, or is, intellectually dishonest or in bad faith. Unlike the purveyors of tax cuts and tax relief who know exactly, with premeditation, who they are trying to dupe, and how, those who advocated and advocate the historically informed performance are convinced, I am sure, that they were, and are, advocating a real alternative. All I am saying, to repeat it once again, is that there is *one* very plausible construal of the historically authentic performance, and one very plausible construal of the historically informed performance, such that there is no difference of substance between the two. And in that circumstance the argument between the two parties is no argument at all.

But here the purveyors of the historically informed performance will, quite rightly, respond that I have admitted that this is only *one* way to construe the two things. There may well be *another* way, they will say, to reasonably construe the historically informed performance such that it is substantively different from the historically authentic one. Furthermore, they will continue, that *other* way might succeed in preserving the historical performance values of the historically authentic performance people while avoiding the dogmatic rigidity their project seems to imply. This proposal I want to consider in the closing section of my paper.

VIII

The concept of authenticity seems to imply, in the context of prototype and something that is modeled on it, an exact matching of the "authentic" model and the prototype that it is intended to model. Thus, a completely "authentic" reproduction of a 1938 Buick sedan would have to be exactly like the original in every perceivable physical characteristic. And it is this sense of exact compliance with, exact modeling of a prototype, that the concept of the historically authentic performance carries with it. It is that implication of point-for-point correspondence that the defender of the historically informed performance, whom I have imagined above, would like to evade.

Well, what's the problem? What's the big deal? The notion of historical authenticity may bring with it the implication of exact, point-for-point similitude. But why should the concept of being historically *informed* do so? If you define a historically informed performance as one by a historically informed performer, there is no implication that the performance must be like a past performance in any respect at all (except, of course, compliance with the score). And if you define it as a performance informed by history, in the sense of being formed, stamped, impressed by history, there does not seem to be any implication at all that it needs to be *totally* informed by history, merely that it be informed in *some* respects.

Let's take the first suggestion, that the performer must be historically informed. The first question the skeptic will ask is, *Why?* Why should it be a good thing or a required thing that a performer be historically informed?

Don't say that it is just obviously a good thing to know the history of the activity in which you are engaged. Sometimes it will be relevant, sometimes irrelevant, and sometimes, I dare say, it is a bad thing, and impedes progress with the solution of a problem.

So the supporter of the view that a musical performer should be historically informed must give us some particular reason or reasons why it is a good or necessary thing *in this particular practice*. One very obvious answer is that if you know, say, how Bach and his disciples performed the Italian Concerto, or how Mozart performed his piano sonatas, then you may acquire new ideas about how to perform these compositions that you would not have obtained otherwise, and these ideas may turn out to work really well for you. But the problem with that response is that it is just too open. It would not distinguish the historically informed performance from any other. *No* performer would reject the proposal that one might get good ideas about how to perform a work by finding out how it was performed in the composer's lifetime, or what the composer's performing intentions were. Certainly the so-called mainstream performer would not reject it, and many mainstream performers *do* perform works of the past in *some* of the ways they were performed in their respective historical periods. However, if the only reason for the performer's having historical knowledge is that it is a possible source of performance ideas, this does not in any way make historical knowledge a *favored* source. It is just one of many possible sources of performance ideas, *all* of which are evaluated on the basis of the performer's musical judgment, taste, and creative intuitions. Being *historical* carries no weight in itself. Such an attitude towards the performer's historical knowledge preserves none of the values of the historically authentic performance movement.

In any case, this is a conclusion we already reached a while ago, when we rejected altogether the suggestion that the historically informed performance could be understood as the performance of a historically informed performer. So we must move on to the more promising suggestion that the historically informed performance is a *performance* informed by history. And we must avoid, somehow, the collapsing of this into the historically authentic performance, making them just two descriptions of the same practice.

Well, again, what's the problem? What's the big deal? Why not just say that a performance is historically informed just so long as *some* of its aspects are formed or impressed or stamped by historical sound, historical performance practice, or the composer's performing intentions, or, perhaps, a judicious mixture of the three? Why should we need to say any more than that? And in particular, why should we have to say that every single aspect of a performance must be historically informed for it to be a historically informed performance? A historically *authentic* performance must fit that description. But there is no need for a historically informed performance to—so, at least, its defenders can say. That way the rigid Historicism of the historically authentic performance can easily be evaded, while still preserving the "historical spirit" of the historically authentic performance project.

Alas, things are not as simple as that. For here, as formerly, we must ask the defender of the historically informed performance *why* a performance *should* be historically informed? And the defender will have to be very careful about the answer he gives. There are snares for his feet.

Suppose the defender of the historically informed performance says the following. "Those aspects of a performance that work better, in the performer's opinion, if historically informed, should be rendered in a historically informed manner. Those that do not work better should be played in ways the performer does think work better, even though not historically informed."

That's fine. Who would quarrel with it? Certainly not the mainstream performer. Of course the performer should play the music in ways she thinks work well. And if some of those ways are historically informed ways, then in those ways of course her performance should be historically informed. But if she thinks that *none* of the historically informed ways work better than other, non-historical ways, she ought, clearly, to perform the work through and through in ways *not* historically informed. And that clearly goes against the grain of the historical performance project in any of its forms.

Again, the concept of the historically informed performance offered here is far too liberal. It evades the inflexible dogmatism of the historically authentic performance; but it evades as well the historical spirit and values it was supposed to pursue. It will not do.

What is needed, it seems clear, is a strong historicist premise to the effect that the historically informed way to render *any* aspect of a musical work in performance is *always* the better way. Needed, as well, are rational grounds for believing that the premise is true.

I do not have the time here to go into the arguments usually adduced in favor of this kind of historicist premise. Some of the familiar ones are, I am certain, known to most members of my audience, and I investigated two of them in some detail in *Authenticities*. These were the argument that the composer's performing intentions are always to be preferred, when known, because the composer always knows best, having an intimate acquaintance with his work, *his* creation, that no one else can ever achieve; and the argument that since the composer had in mind, when he composed the work, just those performance means and performance practices available in his time, the work is ideally suited, perfectly adjusted, to these and no others. Both, I argued in *Authenticities*, are indefensible.

But that is not the relevant issue here. Here, the relevant issue is whether, if the strong historicist premise can be rationally defended, it will give us a concept of the historically informed performance that is *both* more flexible than the concept of the historically authentic performance and at the same time preserve the historicist spirit that the historically authentic performance concept embodies. The answer is that it will not, because it will result in making "the historically informed performance" just another name for "the historically authentic performance" — the very conclusion we reached earlier that we are now trying to avoid. Here is why.

Take any musical work of the past that you like. It will have two kinds of features. There will be those that we have historical knowledge about, with regard to how they were performed in the historical period of the work, how the composer intended them to be performed, how they may have sounded in the historical period of the work, and so on, and there will be those features about which we have no such historical knowledge.

Following the strong historicist premise, that the historical way is always the best way, the performer is clearly obliged to inform her readings historically of those features of the work about which we have historical performance knowledge. Those features about which we have no such knowledge she is free to render as she thinks best. But each time historical performance knowledge becomes available to her about one of these latter features, she is obliged, then, if she continues to follow the strong historicist premise, to give up her way of performing it, if it differs from the historical way, and render it, rather, in a historically informed manner, because the strong historicist premise says: the historically informed way is *always* the best way.

It should now be becoming clear that *if* the strong historicist premise is adopted, the performer who devotes herself to historically informed performance will have exactly the same attitude towards features of the work that we have no historical performance knowledge about as the devotee of the historically authentic performance. She may play them as she thinks best, in accordance with her musical judgment and taste. But it will always be second best to the historically informed performance (unless, of course, she accidentally discovers ways of performing that turn out, in the event, to be the historically correct ways). Exactly as in the case of the historically authentic performance, the space in which she can exercise her own taste and musical judgment will be an unwanted, undesirable gap, because the strong historicist premise states, unequivocally, that the historically informed performance is always best; so if, out of historical ignorance, she renders some aspects of the work according to her own lights, no matter how good these renderings may be, they will not be the best renderings. In other words, if the strong historicist premise is accepted, the ultimate goal of the historically informed performance turns out to be the very same goal as that of the historically authentic performance: which is to say, to fully determine performance through historical knowledge, to close the gap between performance and score (broadly conceived).

At this point we, or at least *I*, am at an impasse. It appears that there is no way to steer between Scylla and Charybdis. If we make the historically informed performance too liberal, then it becomes a trivial notion; it embodies no principle that would be rejected by any sensible performer. All it says is that if a historically informed performance seems better to the performer than the alternatives in regard to any musical feature, then the performer should adopt it. No one would quarrel with that. But it fails to capture the historicist spirit of the historically authentic performance project.

On the other hand, if we adopt the strong historicist premise, that the historically informed performance is always the best, then the historically informed performance collapses into the historically authentic performance. There ceases to be any discernible difference between them, either in practice or in principle.

Tax cut or tax relief? No difference! Historically authentic or historically informed? No difference? You tell *me*. I am open to suggestions.

8

Ars perfecta: Toward Perfection in Musical Performance?

PERFORMANCE AS ART

The major purpose of this paper is to explore the question, Is there such a thing as the perfect performance of a musical work? Its major thesis is that there is not. That thesis, however, is not advanced *de novo*, but as the implication or, if not that, then the not unwarranted concomitant of an already developed view concerning the nature of performance in the Western classical music tradition.[1] So, before I get to the examination and defense of that thesis, I must acquaint the reader with the theory of musical performance that it has at its heart.

I practice the kind of philosophy of art that might with some justification be termed "Aristotelian". I follow the method that, according to Stuart Hampshire, characterizes Aristotle's moral theory, and which he describes as follows: "Aristotle states clearly that moral theory must be in accord with established opinions and must explain those opinions as specifications of more general principles. ... Acceptable theory will not undermine established moral opinions nor bring about a systematic moral conversion."[2]

Similarly, I make the assumption that a theory in the philosophy of art must be in accord with established relevant opinions and must explain those opinions as specifications of more general principles. As well, acceptable theory in the philosophy of art must not, as I practice it, undercut established aesthetic opinions or bring about a systematic aesthetic conversion.

[1] Peter Kivy, *Authenticities: Philosophical Reflections on Musical Performance* (Ithaca, NY: Cornell University Press, 1995), ch. 5.

[2] Stuart Hampshire, *Two Theories of Morality* (Oxford: Oxford University Press, 1977), 1.

With this statement of methodological principle on the table, I can now go on to lay down some of the established opinions concerning musical performance that I want my theory to be in accordance with.

I begin with perhaps the most obvious point. A performance is *of* a work. It is, as a recent writer, whom I will be discussing later on puts it, *intentional*: which is to say, it takes an intentional object, i.e. the work of which it is the performance.[3]

Second, performers are customarily thought of, and described, both by fellow musicians and lay audiences as "artists": "performing artists".

Third, I take it as a valid inference from the description of performers as performing *artists* that their performances are artworks. Indeed, that is the very heart of my proposal.

Finally, it is common parlance, particularly among reviewers of concerts, to describe performances as "interpretations" or (sometimes) "readings" of musical works. I take the former literally and the latter metaphorically; which is to say, I take it that performances of musical works are interpretations of them in the same sense in which works of literary criticism are interpretations of literary works. But, I take it, "readings" of literary works are a particular kind of interpretation, namely, an interpretation of their meaning; and since I take absolute music, which is the only kind of music whose performances I am considering here, not to possess meaning, I take the phrase "so-and-so's reading" of Beethoven's First Piano Sonata to be a metaphor for "so-and-so's interpretation" of same.

So, to sum up, I take it that a musical performance of the kind I am discussing here is always a performance *of* some preexisting musical work, executed by one or more performing *artists*, (therefore) a work of art in its own right, and, finally, an *interpretation* of the work performed, in the same sense in which what a literary critic does is "interpretation", although without the dimension of "meaning", interpretation that so often is a major part of the literary critic's work.

Given, then, that the central claim I am making about musical performances is that they are executed by performing artists, and are, therefore, works of art, the central questions I must ask are, What kind of artist is a performing artist? And, if it does not amount to the same thing, What kind of artwork does she or he execute? In my book *Authenticities* I suggested that the art of performing might best

---

[3] Gilead Bar-Elli, "Ideal Performance", *British Journal of Aesthetics*, 42 (2002), 226 *et passim*.

be understood as part of the craft of musical composition known as "arranging". Let us see, briefly, how this suggestion plays out.

Being an oboe player, I am perhaps more appreciative of, and sensitive to, the art of musical arranging than other music lovers. Woodwind players, because of the paucity of their recital and chamber music literature, must, of necessity, include in their repertoires various arrangements of works originally written for other instruments, frequently strings. When you play such arrangements, you become acutely aware of the artistry that is displayed and required to execute the really good ones. They are, I urge, works of the musical art.

But, of course, an arrangement is an arrangement *of* ... . It does not come into being on its own, so to speak; it is beholden to the work of which *it* is a *version*. In ordinary musical parlance, there are not two works: the work and its arrangement (say) for woodwind quintet. The arrangement *is* a version of the work. Of course, there are folks with metaphysical or logical axes to grind who would insist that any change whatever makes a "version" of the work a different work. For an "Aristotelian" in these matters, such as myself, that smacks of theory disregarding the data it is supposed to be the theory *of*, a point to which I shall return later on.

My suggestion, then, is that performances of musical works are "versions" of them, their closest relatives being musical arrangements. Musical performing artists are "arrangers" of the music they perform. They execute "versions" of the works they are performances of; and just as we admire and appreciate one arrangement of a work for some features, another arrangement for others, so we admire one performance of a work for some features, another performance for others. In each case we assume that there can be more than one version of a work, whether arrangement or performance, that is admirable and worthy of appreciation. Indeed, that assumption seems to be part of the very fabric of our musical world.

Performances, particularly great performances, are admired and appreciated as works of art in their own right, always with the rider that they are not "free-standing" works of art, but versions of pre-existing works of art of which they are the performances. The working out of the metaphysical and logical details of what goes on when we appreciate a performance of (say) Beethoven's First Piano Sonata both as the artwork, performance of op. 2, no. 1, and the artwork, op. 2, no. 1, is a tricky business. I have tried to work out some of them in *Authenticities*. But that is not my main topic in this paper. Rather, it is what I take to be the at least apparent implication of the view that there are many separate performance artworks, all performances of, versions of, op. 2, no. 1, admired and appreciated as artworks in their own right: namely, the implication that there cannot be one, and only one, perfect (or ideal) performance of op. 2, no. 1, but there must be many beautiful, successful, admirable performances of it, some better than others, some of equal merit, in their own special ways. Just as it does not make sense to say that there is only one perfect or ideal painting of a given landscape, for example, so it does not make sense to say that there is only one perfect or ideal performance of op. 2, no. 1. Just as each painter of the landscape is an artist with a personal style of his own, so each performer of op. 2, no. 1, is an artist, a performing artist with a personal style all her own. If painters are great artists, they may produce equally great, though artistically distinct painting artworks. Similarly, if the performers are great artists, they may produce equally great, though artistically distinct performance artworks. That is the implication I wish to examine and, in part, defend.

In fact, I intend to examine two possible reasons for denying what I shall call "the plurality view" of musical performance, in favor of what I shall call "the unitary or monistic view", emanating, respectively, from the thesis that musical performances are *interpretations*, and the thesis that musical performances are *intentional*, two of the four notions about musical performance that I took to be part of musical common sense. What I call the plurality view of musical performance is, of course, the view I have just been outlining above, that there can be many equally good, equally admirable, equally successful performances of the same musical composition, but no single perfect or ideal performance. What I call the unitary or monistic view is, naturally, the view that denies this: the view that, for any given work, there can be, perhaps, many equally good, equally admirable, equally successful performances, but only one perfect or ideal performance, that is supremely good, supremely admirable, supremely successful, whether or not it in fact is ever achieved or known.

I will begin with the objection to the plurality view of musical performance that seems to me to emanate from the thesis that musical performances are interpretations of musical works. I will go on from there to the objection predicated on the intentionality thesis. My conclusion, a tentative one, will be that, these objections to the contrary notwithstanding, the plurality view of musical performance remains the more plausible one. First, then, performance and interpretation.

PERFORMANCE AS INTERPRETATION

It has sometimes been maintained that when musical performers are referred to as "interpreters", we should take this description metaphorically. But if we are to take the description metaphorically, which I do not, what exactly is the *literal* sense that we are to eschew? I think it fairly obvious that the literal sense of "interpretation" that we all have in mind in these contexts has its most prominent exemplar in literary interpretation; in particular, in the interpretation of literary fiction. Furthermore, I take it that the aspect of literary interpretation that we mainly have in mind, as providing the literal sense of "interpretation", is the interpretation of *meaning*. (I put aside the worry that literary critics say or write their interpretations, whereas musical performers do not say or write anything, *qua* performers. For interpretations can be shown, as well as said or told, and showing their interpretations is exactly what performers do, *qua* performers.) The assumption of the literary critic is that, at least in many cases, the writer of literary fiction wishes to express something important through her novel, or poem, or play, and that it is one of the literary critic's major tasks, perhaps *the* major task, to reveal to us, through his interpretations, what it is that the novelist, or poet, or playwright wished to convey.

Now literary works of art are, perhaps as part of their very nature, not "out front" with their moral, or political, or philosophical messages, if indeed they have any. They do not wear their meanings on their sleeves, except when they are aesthetically defective and deserve the charge of being "didactic", in the pejorative sense of that term. That, of course, is why they require interpreters, whose job it is to make their meanings clear to us.

But, needless to say, literary artworks are not the only texts that require interpretation. Philosophical texts, for example, are notoriously opaque, and in need of expert explication. Furthermore, it is quite natural—even, most would say, essential—for the philosophical interpreter to work on the assumption that, for any given philosophical text, there is one and only one optimal, true interpretation. Interpreters will, no doubt, never agree on what that optimal, true interpretation is. However, each will advance his or her own interpretation as the true one. And if the philosophical text under scrutiny is vague or ambiguous on any point, the one true, optimal interpretation will correctly locate the vagueness or ambiguity. Those are the rules of engagement for the explication of philosophical texts, at least among a large community of scholars in the Western philosophical tradition.

The point, for our purposes, is that if it is axiomatic that there is one, and only one correct meaning–interpretation of a given philosophical text, it seems entirely reasonable to assume the same for the meaning-interpretation of any given literary text, if, that is, it is a literary text in which the author intends to convey philosophical views, or political views, or anything else like that. Literary critics are, no doubt, unlikely to agree on what a complex literary text like *Faust* or *The Divine Comedy* is saying. But if it is part of the author's purpose to "say" things, then there ought to be one, and only one correct interpretation of what he or she has said.

In our own time, the most famous and distinguished philosophical defender of this unitary view of literary interpretation was the late Monroe Beardsley; and we would do well to look at what he says in its defense. Beardsley writes, in his classic monograph *The Possibility of Criticism*:

some critical theorists have recently emphasized the element of creativity in interpretation. By comparing literary interpretation with the performing artist's interpretation of score or script ... they have suggested that the literary interpreter too has a certain leeway, and does not merely "report" or "discover meaning" ... but puts something of his own into the work; so that different critics may produce different but equally legitimate interpretations, like two sopranos or two ingenues working from the same notations. I find myself rather severe with this line of thought. There is plenty of room for creativity in literary interpretation, if that means thinking of new ways of reading the work, if it means exercising sensitivity and imagination. But the moment the critic begins to use the work as an occasion for promoting his own ideas, he has abandoned the task of interpretation.[4]

A little later on Beardsley draws the conclusion—what I would call the unitary or monistic view of literary interpretation—in this way:

I hold that there are a great many interpretations that obey what might be called the principle of "the Intolerability of Incompatibles," i.e., if two of them are logically incompatible, they cannot both be true. Indeed, I hold that *all* of the literary interpretations that deserve the name obey this principle.[5]

---

[4] Monroe C. Beardsley, *The Possibility of Criticism* (Detroit: Wayne State University Press, 1970), 39–40.

[5] Ibid. 44.

In other words, what Beardsley is saying is this. In contrast to performance, where plurality is to be expected, the literary critic's job is merely to "'report' on 'discovered meaning'". Note well that it is *meaning* that is on Beardsley's mind, because it is the interpreter's search for *meaning* that makes the unitary theory of interpretation seem the most plausible one, at least to many people. Why is that?

In qualifying his view, Beardsley writes: "But of course I do not wish to deny that there are cases of ambiguity where *no* interpretation can be established over its rivals; nor do I wish to deny that there are many cases where we cannot be sure that we have the correct interpretation."[6] Beardsley's point is that we easily confuse the existence of conflicting interpretations, unresolvable in practice, with conflicting interpretations unresolvable in principle, and therefore equally valid, acceptable, or true. John Burnet said of the extant writings of Heraclitus, "Some of these fragments are far from clear, and there are probably not a few of which the meaning will never be recovered."[7] Burnet is one of many interpreters of the fragments of Heraclitus, and was under no illusion that his interpretation would ever prevail over all the others. He did not, however, express this skepticism in terms of a plurality of correct interpretations. On the contrary, he was skeptical that *the* meanings of many of the fragments had been or ever would be understood; as he put it, "there are probably not a few of which the meaning will never be recovered." The assumption, nevertheless, and it seems a reasonable assumption, is that *the* meaning is there, to be recovered, even though it never will be. With regard to *meaning*, then, the unitary or monistic theory of interpretation seems to press itself upon us as almost a necessary assumption of the enterprise.

But if the unitary theory of literary interpretation is true, and if musical performances are interpretations in the literary sense, the sense in which literary interpretations are "interpretations", then it seems to follow that the plurality theory of musical performance must be false, the unitary theory true; that, in other words, just as there is one, correct interpretation of every literary work (at least as regards meaning), so there is one optimal, perfect, ideal performance of every musical work.

Now there seem to me to be two ways the performance pluralist might resist this implication. The first is to argue that, at least for

---

[6] Ibid.
[7] John Burnet, *Early Greek Philosophy*, 4th edn. (London: Adam and Charles Black, 1952), 142.

literature, meaning interpretation is *not* monistic but pluralistic, and hence has no dire implications for performance pluralism; the second, to argue that even though literary meaning–interpretation implies a monistic view of *it*, it does not imply a monistic view of musical performance, for the obvious reason—obvious at least to many—that performance–interpretation is not meaning–interpretation.

That literary meaning–interpretation is pluralistic is not an uncommon view these days; and, in fact, I exaggerated the intuitive pull of the unitary view of it, in presenting the previous argument. A person might want to argue, after all, that one of the very things that distinguishes literary texts from, for example, philosophical ones, is that, while a philosophical text is assumed to have one and only one correct interpretation, literary texts permit, even invite, a plurality of meaning–interpretations as part of their aesthetic. Joseph Margolis, for one, in a well-known statement of what he calls "Robust Relativism", puts the intuitive pull of interpretative pluralism even more strongly. Beardsley, he avers, "cannot preclude a relativistic conception of [literary] interpretation—which may well be not merely tolerated but *required*".[8] So the argument is that the unitary view of literary interpretation is no threat to the plurality view of musical performance, even though musical performance is interpretation, for the simple reason that the unitary view of literary interpretation is false. As Margolis would put it, literary works of art not only tolerate a plurality of meaning–interpretations, they demand it.

Of course, the dispute between the unitarians and the pluralists as regards the interpretation of meaning in literary works is one of the most complex and protracted in the philosophy of art. And because of the impossibility of resolving it here and now, or in the foreseeable future, I would not want to make the plurality of performance rest on such a resolution. Furthermore, I myself am drawn intuitively towards the unitary view of literary meaning–interpretation, so that if the dispute between literary monists and literary pluralists were resolved in the direction I now favor, my performance pluralism would be defeated.

Fortunately, however, for performance pluralists, such as myself, there is no reason to believe that meaning monism in literary interpretation implies monism in musical performance. And that is because the performance pluralist of my stripe does not believe that absolute music, the performance of which is the point at issue here, has meaning in the

---

[8] Joseph Margolis, "Robust Relativism", repr. in *Philosophy Looks at the Arts*, ed. Joseph Margolis (Philadelphia: Temple University Press, 1987), 397; my italics.

first place. So, if one is strongly drawn, as I am, to meaning monism in literary interpretation, there is absolutely no reason to give up, on that account, performance pluralism, merely because one construes performance as a form of interpretation. For it is clear that since absolute music, on my view, does not posses meaning, what performances of it interpret cannot be meaning, and hence need not be tarred with the brush of the meaning monist in literary interpretation.

What, then, is there left to interpret, in absolute music, it might be objected, if meaning is denied? Well, as I put the case in *Authenticities*, and I will take the liberty of quoting myself, the arranger

starts with a preexistent work, of which a *version* must be contrived; and in order for his or her result to *be* a *version* of the work and not a new work in its own right, it must be, whatever else it is, a possible, a plausible way *that work goes*. Thus the arranger must have an idea of how the work goes in order to make a credible version of it. He or she must, in other words, have an interpretation, be an interpreter. And that gives us just the result we were seeking for performance. Because insofar as a performer is akin to an arranger, he or she too must have an idea of how the work "goes" that is being "arranged." He or she too requires an interpretation, and is an interpreter.[9]

An interpreter of a work of art, then, is someone who explains "how it goes", or "what makes it tick"; and "how it goes", "what makes it tick", may or may *not* include "what it means". In the case of absolute music it does *not* include "what it means". And, as Margolis points out, there is far more to a literary work that an interpreter deals with besides meaning, and that may, quite uncontroversially, bear a plurality of interpretations. As Margolis says of Wordsworth's well-known "Lucy poem", it "does appear to support two different interpretations of the poem's larger meaning or design (that is, roughly the picture of the imaginative world described in the poem, *without different interpretations of the poem's textual meaning*").[10]

Similarly, there is no reason to believe that the "larger design" and functional parts of a work of absolute music cannot support more than one interpretation: more than one story about "what makes it tick". For once meaning is no longer an interpretational issue, the specter of interpretational monism is exorcised. A strong intuition pulls us towards the view that a specific speech act or text can have but *one* meaning, not many, no matter how difficult it may be, perhaps impossible, to ascertain what that meaning is. If it is p, it cannot be not-p as well.

---

[9] Kivy, *Authenticities*, 137–8.   [10] Margolis, "Robust Relativism", 397.

But there is nothing to say that an abstract structure of sound patterns, even the quasi-syntactic ones of Western counterpoint and functional harmony, must have one unitary interpretation of "how things go", "what makes it tick". It may very well be a structure that can be perceived under more than one description; and I see no a priori reason why we must assume that only one of those descriptions is the one and only right one, even if they are incompatible one with another. Jastrow's well-known duck–rabbit is not either a duck or a rabbit—*decide we must.*

And to adduce another example, more to the present purpose, the first movement of Beethoven's String Quartet, op. 132, seems to be in sonata form, but seemingly with *two* recapitulations: what Joseph Kerman calls the "E-minor Recapitulation" and the "A-minor Recapitulation",[11] although he is somewhat skeptical of the former, writing that "To refer to the passage as the 'E-minor Recapitulation' is to stretch terminology hard, for the basic idea of a sonata recapitulation is not only (or even principally) to repeat all the original material, but to repeat or rationalize it all in the tonic key."[12] But if one takes the possibility of an E-minor recapitulation seriously, then here are some possible interpretations. (1) The movement is in sonata form, with an E-minor recapitulation and an A-minor coda. (2) The movement is in sonata form, with an A-minor recapitulation and no coda. (3) The movement is in a non-standard, revolutionary sonata form with two recapitulations. (4) The movement is not in sonata form at all. (5) The movement is in sonata form, but Beethoven, on purpose, left it ambiguous as to whether there are two recapitulations or one, and whether or not there is a coda, and so forth.[13]

Now the point is that it may make as little sense to ask, Which of these is the correct interpretation of this movement? as it does to ask, What is it *really*, a duck or a rabbit? *All* of them are correct interpretations. All of them say "how it goes", "what makes it tick". That of course does not mean that *any* interpretation is a correct one. The movement is not a rondo, or a theme and variations; it is not a double fugue or in minuet and trio form. There is a range of correct interpretations and a slew of incorrect ones. And which of the correct interpretations you choose

---

[11] Joseph Kerman, *The Beethoven Quartets* (New York: Alfred A. Knopf, 1967), 247.
[12] Ibid.
[13] This last is the interpretation of Robin Wallace, in "Background and Expression in the First Movement of Beethoven's Op. 132", *Journal of Musicology*, 7 (1989), 3–20. Wallace also thinks that the movement is ambiguous as to key, which is to say, whether it is in A minor or major.

will, of course, if "you" are the members of a string quartet, inform your performance of the movement in certain respects (although that does not mean there cannot be different good and correct performances even among those who all interpret the movement one way). And it is in this sense that a performance *is* an interpretation.

The urge to insist that one of these five ways of interpreting the first movement of op. 132 and, therefore, one of these five ways of performing it must be the one, the only, the perfect way, stems, at least for many, I think, from the idea that asking whether op. 132 is in this form or that, or the other, is the same kind of question as asking whether some fragment of Heraclitus's *means* this thing, or that, or the other. Many of us feel compelled to say that the text *must* have one and only one of the many meanings attributed to it by different interpretations, but *not* that the first movement of op. 132 *must* either have an E-minor recapitulation and an A-minor coda, *or* an A-minor recapitulation and no coda, and so forth. For once one leaves meaning–interpretation for—What shall I call it?—structure–interpretation, the spell of monism is broken. Why *shouldn't* a structure have more than one interpretation, more than one way it goes?

But—and it is a big *but*—textual meaning–interpretation is not the only source for the performance unitarian. There seems no reason to believe that because performance is *interpretation*, there must be a principle of one work, one performance, because one work, one interpretation. A far more compelling source, however, for the view that there must be only one perfect or ideal performance of a musical work is the stipulation that performance is *intentional*: that, in other words, a performance is always *of* a *work*. A detailed argument to this effect has recently been advanced by Gilead Bar-Elli. In the following sections of my paper I shall concern myself with presenting this argument and responding to it from the side of the performance pluralist.

PERFORMANCE OF ...

Bar-Elli's argument covers a good many points relevant to work and performance; and I cannot go into all of them here. I shall concentrate, naturally, on those I think most central to the question of whether there is one, single, perfect, or, as Bar-Elli prefers to put it, *ideal*, performance of any given work. I shall begin my discussion, *in medias res*, with what I take to be the crucial principles upon which Bar-Elli's position is based.

First of all, of course, there is the motivating principle—the source of Bar-Elli's performance monism—that performances are intentional: that a performance is always a performance *of* a particular work. As Bar-Elli puts it:

According to our assumption, a performance is by its very nature a performance of a specific composition; this is constitutive of its very identity, and is conceived of and evaluated as such. The claim about ideal performance, for which we shall argue below, means that the composition determines its ideal performance uniquely.[14]

Second, Bar-Elli maintains that "A musical composition is constituted by normative properties—properties that determine how it should sound, and which must be realized in performance."[15] Those normative properties he calls "aesthetic-normative" properties, "A-N" properties for short; and they are of two basic kinds: "there are 'absolute' properties, such as the composition's opening with a D-major chord, for instance," and "there are 'gradual' properties: the rate of accelerando, for instance, or the strength of a certain note or entire passage in relation to its surroundings, the balance between different voices and their relative freedom, and so on."[16] It is the latter, Bar-Elli points out, that are crucial to, and controversial for, his claim that for every musical composition there is one and only one ideal performance. The former give no trouble: "for in this instance the 'ideal' is clear—a performance that realizes the composition's ideal properties." But gradual A-N properties are a problem for performance monism: "It is these properties that are usually important for judging a performance, and it is they that fuel our feeling that there is no ideal performance—that there can be different performances, utterly good and correct, of which no one is preferable over the others."[17] (What the problem of gradual A-N properties is for Bar-Elli, we will get to in a moment.)

A third crucial assumption of Bar-Elli's is what he refers to as:

the assumption of coherence, which says that the aesthetic-normative properties of a musical composition are coherent in the sense that they are (objective) properties of the composition itself, and that they do not conflict with one another within a certain composition: if a composition, or a particular part of it, has a certain normative property, it does not have a conflicting one (in the same place).[18]

[14] Bar-Elli, "Ideal Performance", 227.   [15] Ibid. 231.
[16] Ibid. 233.   [17] Ibid.   [18] Ibid. 229.

With these three assumptions in hand, it is time to state, in brief, the position on musical performance that Bar-Elli is defending. It is that "The ideal performance is that one which fulfills correctly all of the composition's A-N properties", and that must include, contrary to what one might think initially the troublesome "gradual" A-N properties as well. If so, and given the "assumption of coherence", then "it follows that it [i.e. the ideal performance] is unique".[19] This startling conclusion—startling at least to common musical sense and the performance pluralist—must now be spelled out.

To begin to understand why Bar-Elli's conclusion would seem the least bit plausible, I will state what I take to be a basic belief, almost universally held, both by musicians and by persons who give any thought to musical performance. It is that there can be two or more—indeed many—performances of a musical work, all of which are correct performances, and each of which is a *different* performance of the same work. Furthermore, some of these performances may be better than others, even if they are all correct, and some of them may be of equal merit. They differ in aesthetically relevant ways; and it is one of the joys of musical listening that there can be these many aesthetically different but equally correct performances of the same work out there to be enjoyed. As I understand Bar-Elli, he flatly rejects this basic belief (or set of beliefs). As he puts it in one place,

if two performances of a composition are to be distinguished as performances of the same composition, then it will be on the basis of at least one A-N property, concerning which at least one performance is incorrect. In other words, if they are different, at least one of them is incorrect in relation to one of the normative properties that constitute the composition.[20]

To understand what this passage means, and what, in my opinion, might be wrong with it, we should begin with the relatively uncontroversial case: what Bar-Elli calls "absolute" A-N properties. These are the properties that we might call, broadly speaking, "the notes": that there is a G-sharp here, that that is an eighth-note, and so forth. They are the properties, as well, that performance pluralists have in mind when they say that two performances can both be entirely correct, yet be different performances of the same work; for what they mean by "entirely correct" is fully realizing in performance the absolute properties. That is why, as Bar-Elli says, "Such absolute properties do not interest us, for in this instance the 'ideal' is clear—a performance that realizes the composition's absolute properties".[21]

It is the gradual A-N properties of a musical composition, then, that are going to be the point at issue between the performance unitarian and the performance pluralist. These are the ones that add the "expression" and the other subtle differences between two "equally correct" performances, as the pluralist would say. But what does Bar-Elli, the performance monist, say? Take, for example, two performances of a piece with a passage marked, in the score, *crescendo*, one of which starts the crescendo at a lower dynamic level than the other, and ends it at a higher, and both of which get all of the absolute A-N properties right. Here is what Bar-Elli says: "if all that this compositional property demands is a crescendo … in a certain passage (without determining the extent), then the two performances are both good and both correct (in this regard)".[22] This sounds okay, uncontroversial, until the additional conclusion is drawn that "it would be wrong to say that the performances differ because of significantly different crescendos, because, as I have already stressed, a performance is a performance *of* a certain composition, and its A-N properties, like its identifying conditions (and its difference from other performances), are derivative of this".[23] In other words, where the common intuition is that what we have here are two *different*, correct performances of the same work, Bar-Elli tells us that we must see them as the *same* performance of the work: that is to say, two tokens of the same correct performance type.

The reason why this must be so, on Bar-Elli's view, is that if the two "different" crescendos are taken to be performances *of* the work in that respect, there must be a feature, the same feature, of the work that they are both performances of, because of the assumption of performance intentionality. So what one thing could two *different* crescendos be performances of? Bar-Elli replies: "if all that this compositional property demands is a crescendo … in a certain passage (without determining the extent), then the two performances are both good and correct (in this regard)"[24]—in other words, they are the *same* performance in this regard, in spite of their acoustic differences. The notion of one ideal performance has been saved, but, of course, at a price. The common way of speaking in the musician's world, which says that there are clearly two aesthetically different, yet correct performances of the same work,

---

[21] Bar-Elli, "Ideal Performance", 233.
[22] Ibid. 235.   [23] Ibid.   [24] Ibid. 233.

has to be given up, which would seem to be a high price to pay. By what appears to be a logical sleight of hand, we are now to call two different crescendos the "same" crescendo, reflecting a single feature of the work. Whether this is the right way to go is a question to which we shall return.

Well perhaps we can "catch" Bar-Elli with a more probing example. At this writing, I am looking over my score of Bach's Sonata for Unaccompanied Violin, BWV 1005, in the *Neue Bach-Ausgabe*, which is generally considered the most authoritative edition to date. The four movements, with repeats, total 626 measures; and there is not a single dynamic marking in the score, not even a *piano* or a *forte*, let alone a crescendo. I cannot imagine any violinist, even an advocate of the so-called historically authentic performance, who would take the complete absence of dynamic markings in the authentic Bach score as a requirement that each movement of the work be played at the same dynamic level throughout. Violinists have, of course, differed widely in their performances of this work as regards handling of dynamics, ranging from the unabashedly Romantic to the austerity of the Baroque performer with a period instrument and bow. And the ordinary, workaday way of describing such performances is that they are all performances *of* the work, differing in various aesthetically significant ways as regards dynamics. How must Bar-Elli describe them?

It would appear, on first reflection, that the way Bar-Elli wants to describe things, none of these performances is a performance of the sonata, in respect of dynamics, since there are no dynamic markings in the score that the dynamics of the performances can be performances of: they are all, in this respect, incorrect.

But wait a bit! There is another string to Bar-Elli's bow. A musician, as is obvious, must, in the Western musical tradition, know how to read a score intelligently. And, Bar-Elli correctly observes, "When we say that one must know how to read a score, we are saying that one must know how to read it in light, *inter alia*, of the conventions (historical, cultural, and individual) according to which it was written".[25] This is precisely right. As I put what I think is the same point, some years ago, " 'the notes' are more than meets the eye. Or, rather, *just* what meets the eye, when it sees within a practice. And without a practice there are no notes at all".[26]

[25] Ibid. 235.
[26] Peter Kivy, "Note-for-Note: Work, Performance and Early Notation", in Kivy, *New Essays on Musical Understanding* (Oxford: Clarendon Press, 2001), 17.

The implication of this line of thought is that if it lies within the practice of Bach's musical notation, if it lies within what Bar-Elli calls its "conventions", that you can, if you want to, or indeed are required to, play crescendos and decrescendos in appropriate places in the Third Sonata for Unaccompanied Violin, then those crescendos, even though not written in the score, are part of the score. As Bar-Elli specifically puts the point, with regard to the "rhythmic variations" the pianist might employ in the performance of (for example) a Chopin mazurka, "such rhythmic variations are in the score no less than the notes themselves, even if they are not represented by a specific symbol. They appear in the score in that it was written according to certain conventions (some subtle and sophisticated, some less) knowledge of which is a condition for correctly reading and understanding the score".[27]

Intentionality of performance is saved, then, for features like a crescendo in a performance or a variation of tempo, even when not notated in the score, by considering them "implicitly" notated in the score, and hence features of the work by virtue of the musical practice, or system of conventions, in which the notation exists. The price, again, is going against what I take to be the common musical intuition that in such cases the performer is adding something of his or her own to the performance, not realizing some odd "property" in the work. Of course, what the performer adds is within a practice, or set of conventions, but that does not make it part of the score or work, without begging the question at issue. The more common way of describing matters is, rather, to say that the manner of performance is within a practice or set of conventions, with no implication that the manner of performance is a work or score property.

We can now see that by a series of steps from the "hard" features that both performance pluralists and performance monists would agree are features of the work, to those "soft" ones that the performance pluralist wants to say are not, the performance monist has attempted to put the pluralist on a kind of slippery slope that can end only in performance monism by way of performance intentionality. For what is *added* by the performer cannot be part of work performance, since there is nothing in the work (or score) that it is a performance of. So we can save what we used to call the performer's "contribution" only by reinterpreting it, in the above manner, as a feature of the work, although the features get more and more peculiar the further down the slope we slide.

---

[27] Bar-Elli, "Ideal Performance", 241.

Must we get on the slippery slope in the first place? Does intentionality, commonsensically construed, really compel us to? To these questions, and some related ones, I intend to devote the remaining sections of this paper.

PERFORMANCE PLANS

Ordinary musical discourse—ordinary discourse, for short—makes a distinction between markings in the score that indicate features of the work and those that indicate how the work might be performed.[28] And I use the phrase "might be performed" to introduce the notion that even where the composer specifically indicates a crescendo, say, or a ritard, it is taken, by many performers, to be not an indefeasible command, like the indication of a sharp or a flat, but a suggestion: part of a tentative performance plan. Whether such a marking is so intended, or is meant to be work-constitutive, cannot be decided, in my view, on the basis of theory, but case by case in practice. Some crescendos, for example, are rightly seen as part of the musical structure; others, though, as defeasible recommendations for performers, not to be taken lightly if they emanate from the composer; not, however, to be taken for stone tablets from Sinai either. And this is not my recommendation as to how performers *should* pursue their art. It is, in my experience, how they *do* pursue it.

The same conclusion applies, *a fortiori*, to unwritten performance possibilities. If the composer's specific performance markings are not to be taken, always, as constitutive of works, but rather as defeasible performance advice, surely the implicit performance "instructions" of a performance practice should have even less of a claim to be an inviolable part of the work.

Furthermore, the notion of a performance practice itself, as Bar-Elli wishes to use it, presents a problem that casts doubt on the use to which he puts it. I can best introduce this problem with an example.

It is generally agreed upon by students of Baroque performance practice that the extensive, ubiquitous presence of vibrato in contemporary

[28] I am assuming here, as ordinary discourse does, but as Nelson Goodman notoriously did not, that dynamic markings, crescendos, tempo indications, and the like, when they are written in words are all part of the score, though not all constitutive of the work. Not all markings on the musical page are, needless to say, part of the score: for example, the name of the publisher, etc. I take it, however, that common sense is adequate to sort these things out, and in no need of philosophy's help.

mainstream performance was unknown in the age of Bach and Handel. It is not that vibrato was not in use at all; but, compared to present-day usage, it was sparing, and by no means the rule rather than the exception.

The so-called historically authentic performer will tell us that since ubiquitous vibrato is not within Baroque performance practice, it should not be employed in the performance of Baroque music today. And Bar-Elli should take the view, if I understand him correctly, that ubiquitous vibrato is not a feature of the musical works of the Baroque, although sparing vibrato *is*, implicitly in the score, by virtue of conventions governing the notation of that historical period.

But suppose I were strongly inclined towards Bar-Elli's musical metaphysics and also a supporter of ubiquitous vibrato in the performance of Baroque music. Could I preserve performance intentionality for ubiquitous vibrato? Indeed I could, by simply expanding the boundaries of what we take to be the "performance practice" in which Baroque music exists to include mainstream performance practice as part of it. And that is not, *prima facie*, a completely unacceptable maneuver, because I could claim that there is an unbroken "laying on of hands" from Baroque performance practice to our own, such that we can think of the whole shebang as one big performance practice, spanning three (or more?) centuries, to include ubiquitous vibrato and all of the other techniques of modern performance practices to the Baroque.

I myself find this a distressingly *ad hoc* policy for defending a metaphysics I don't much sympathize with anyway. It allows one to include almost anything one happens to like in performance as reflecting a feature of the work in Bar-Elli's strict way of construing performance intentionality, just by expanding the boundaries of a performance practice to accommodate the preference in question.

How, then, should a performance of Baroque music with modern vibrato be viewed? Well, I think I know how ordinary discourse represents it. The performance *is* a performance *of* the music without qualification; and that *includes* the vibrato, Baroque performance practice to the contrary notwithstanding. We expect performers to use their artistry in ways that could not have been foreseen or anticipated by composers of generations long past. And when they do, we do not think that they have ceased being performers *of* the work, or have somehow evoked weird "properties" in it.

But that being said, two problems arise for the performance pluralist so described. First, how can performance intentionality be preserved by performance pluralists? And second, what exactly are the properties of a performance properties of, if there is nothing in the score prescribing them? They seem to be dangling in empty metaphysical space. How can they be properties of a performance of a work, in the full intentional sense, without being properties of the work? And so how can they be properties of the work if there is nothing explicitly in the score, or even implicitly in the score's performance practice, sanctioning them?

To answer the first question, we might remind ourselves of Nelson Goodman's notorious claim that a performance with even one misplayed note is not a performance of the work.[29] The outraged reply was that no one construes "performance of" in a way so strict that one wrong note renders an ostensible performance a non-performance. But surely a similar retort can be made to construing the intentionality criterion in the strict way Bar-Elli does. One wants to say, in ordinary discourse, that if a performer plays enough of "the right notes", and the manner of her playing them makes some kind of reasonable stylistic, musical sense of the music she is playing, then it is a performance of the music *sans phrase*, without need of qualification as regards which performance features are, and which are not, explicitly or implicitly sanctioned in the notation. And if the metaphysician should yell and scream that intentionality of performance demands that those features of performance rightly called "performances of" *must* have something in the score, which is to say in the work, answering to them, the performance pluralist's reply will be that *his* concept of performance intentionality makes no such rigorous demand (if "rigorous" is even the right word for it, and not "misplaced rigor"). The performer is quite untroubled in describing a crescendo as a "performance of" the work even though it is the performer's idea, unsanctioned either explicitly or implicitly by the notation or its practice. The metaphysician, he will say, has constructed a philosopher's concept of performance intentionality that does not reflect ordinary discourse, and there is no need for ordinary speakers of the musical language to alter their discourse accordingly. They must be given a reason or reasons for doing so. I will consider what those might be, and whether they are persuasive, in the concluding section of my paper.

But before I get to that, I must face the fact that the performance monist does have some good reason to feel uneasy about the performance pluralist's (to him) loose way of construing performance intentionality. His concern is this. If there are features of performance (musically

[29] See Nelson Goodman, *Languages of Art: An Approach to a Theory of Symbols* (Indianapolis and New York: Bobbs-Merrill, 1968), 186–7.

relevant features, mind!) that have no corresponding features in the score, what relation do these features have to the work? They are not features of the work, it will be insisted, because there is nothing in the score, either explicitly or implicitly, that sanctions them.

This is an understandable worry. My answer is that these features of performance *are* features of the work in the following sense: they are features of the performer's *version of the work*. Now this may have the appearance of a verbal trick, substituting "version" for "performance", while the monist's problem remains. But I think the change is more than merely a verbal one; it is, in my view, genuinely informative. As I argued previously, in *Authenticities*, performances, as artworks, are analogues to the artworks we know as arrangements; and we expect arrangements to have features not possessed by the works they are arrangements of. If they did not, they would not be arrangements of the works, but the unarranged works themselves.

The performance monist may insist that a feature of a version that is not reflected in the score, either explicitly or implicitly, cannot be a feature of the work. The pluralist will reply that it is a feature of a version *of* the work, and that is enough, and there's an end to it. Versions occupy just that metaphysical space, if I may so put it, between work and non-work that is needed to accommodate the ontology of ordinary discourse. And the performance pluralist should resist the pressure by squeaky clean metaphysicians to be pushed to one side or the other. The middle ground exists and should be stubbornly occupied.

This is not to say that there are no ambiguities; that is the human condition here as elsewhere. Is Liszt's piano version of Beethoven's Ninth Symphony a version *of* the work, in a strong sense, or a new work, closely based on it? Is a performance of *Richard III*, in modern dress, with tanks and machine guns, a version of the work, in a strong sense, or a new work based closely on Shakespeare's play? One might be inclined to say that Liszt's version of Beethoven is another work. But I think it would come as a great surprise to working people in the theatre to be told by a fastidious metaphysician that their production of *Richard III* was not a production *of* the Bard's play, even though Shakespeare could not possibly have envisioned such a performance plan.

It is just this metaphysical middle ground that musical performances occupy; and the proper answer to the question of whether their novel features, undreamed of by the composers whose works they are performances of, can be features of the works is "Yes and No". That is all the answer the question deserves, or will get. They are features of versions of works: that is all, and that is enough.

The point of an arrangement is to make a work available to the listener in a certain way. The point of a performance is the same. To make the work available to the listener, it must pass through a human musician, a human consciousness, with tastes, sensibilities, and musical insights that eventuate in a version of the work, if he is a distinguished performer, personally *his*. It is his version of the work, his interpretation of how things go, and includes his contribution as performing artist, a contribution that need not be reflected in the score except in the sense that what the performer presents is a believable interpretation, a believable version of the work, always assuming the possibility that the performer may come up with a manner of performance that, in some aspects at least, was unthought of by the composer. "It's a bad plan that can't be changed."[30]

A THEORY OF EVERYTHING

It would be a mistake to think that my remarks concerning Bar-Elli's attempt to defend the notion of the one and only ideal performance constitute a refutation. I am laboring under no such misapprehension. What, then, is at issue here? I think that the issue is between two very different ways of doing so-called analytic philosophy of art. And I would like to conclude by spelling that out.

You will recall that I began this essay by describing myself as an Aristotelian in my philosophical method. That means, in this case, that I take ordinary discourse as the data which my "theory" of musical performance must fit.

Against this one can place as the contrasting method, theorizing in the grand manner, ordinary discourse be damned, perhaps best exemplified for present purposes by Nelson Goodman's analysis of the relation of performance to score, in which it turns out that a performance with but a single mistake on that account alone cannot be construed a performance of the work. "The practicing musician or composer", Goodman observes, "usually bristles at the idea that a performance with one wrong note is not a performance of the given work at all; and ordinary

---

[30] Publius Syrus, quoted as the epigraph in Kivy, *Authenticities*, p. vi.

usage surely sanctions overlooking a few wrong notes."[31] The question is, for Goodman, "Could we not bring our theoretical vocabulary into better agreement with common practice and common sense by allowing some limited degree of deviation in performances admitted as instances of a work?" His answer is that "this is one of those cases where ordinary usage quickly gets us into trouble", the trouble being that "by a series of one-note errors of omission, addition, and modification, we can go all the way from Beethoven's *Fifth Symphony* to *Three Blind Mice*".[32] And this means, as Goodman concludes: "in view of the transitivity of identity ... all performances whatever are of the same work."[33]

This is not the place to launch into an examination of Goodman's work-performance analysis, ground that has been covered elsewhere by myself and others. The point is that his is a kind of method that favors theoretical elegance over fitting the facts. And, as Aaron Ridley has, I think quite correctly, put it, in terms of what I have been characterizing as the Aristotelian methodology, "The general feeling has been that any theory *this* seriously at odds with intuitions shared by more or less everyone who has ever listened to or played a piece of music must be (and whatever the 'transitivity of identity' might suggest) mistaken."[34]

I think that Bar-Elli must be aware of his own Goodman-like departure from ordinary musical discourse, and the possibility of its being held against his position, for he begins his essay with the frank admission that "Most of us are repelled by the idea of an ideal performance of a piece of music, which seems opposed to reasonable and commonly held positions."[35] And he adds, even more tellingly, "indeed, I too am not sure that this position is mistaken, and my natural tendency, like most of us, I suppose, is to adopt it."[36]

What I take to be something of a defense of theory over practice on Bar-Elli's part comes a bit later on, and I will quote it now. Bar-Elli writes:

the problems discussed here are philosophical and not musical. Obviously one must know something about music to understand the discussion, but the professional musician, as such, has no decisive advantage here. He must avail himself of patience and treat with understanding the *chutzpa* of philosophers for crudely barging into his sphere, for they are not actually invading his territory at all, but rather concerning themselves with their own, with a problem that is fundamentally philosophical.[37]

---

[31] Goodman, *Languages of Art*, 186.   [32] Ibid. 187.   [33] Ibid. 186.

[34] Aaron Ridley, "Against Musical Ontology", *Journal of Philosophy*, 100 (2003), 204.

[35] Bar-Elli, "Ideal Performance", 223.   [36] Ibid. 224.   [37] Ibid. 225.

That philosophical problems are not musical problems, and vice versa, I suppose no one will dispute. But that should not be taken to mean that what musicians say about their own discipline and its activities is somehow irrelevant to philosophers. To invoke *intentionality* in the present context, philosophy *of* music must be philosophy of *music*, philosophy *of* science philosophy of *science*: not music and science as legislated by philosophers, but as they exist, and have existed in practice, in the musical and scientific workshops.

What is the philosophical *chutzpa* of which Bar-Elli speaks, and for which he pleads indulgence? One assumes, given his opening remarks about going against "reasonable and commonly held positions", that it is the Goodmanian *chutzpa* of brushing aside the authority of ordinary discourse in favor of neat and elegant theory. But, then, can we not say to Bar-Elli's analysis, as we said to Goodman's, that, in Aaron Ridley's words previously quoted, "any theory *this* seriously at odds with the intuitions more or less shared by everyone ... must be ... mistaken"? Perhaps we can. That is certainly my inclination, and what I have been suggesting in the preceding discussion. But there is a more charitable response to Bar-Elli's theorizing that, although it does not grant him outright his philosophical *chutzpa*, states our conditions for granting it in the future if those conditions are fulfilled.

Philosophy of art is part of the larger enterprise of philosophy, as philosophy of music is part of the larger enterprise of philosophy of art, philosophy of musical performance part of the larger enterprise of philosophy of music. Now if Bar-Elli had a philosophy of music which implied his philosophy of musical performance, say, then it seems to me, in the interest of theory elegance, I might be inclined to overlook more departures from ordinary discourse than if he had only a philosophy of musical performance alone. Furthermore, if he had a philosophy of art which implied that philosophy of music, then, in the interest of theory elegance, I might be inclined to overlook yet more departures from ordinary discourse than if he had only a philosophy of musical performance and a philosophy of music. And, finally, if he had a broad philosophical viewpoint, a *theory of everything*, if you will, that informed his philosophy of art, his philosophy of music, and his philosophy of musical performance—an impressive accomplishment, needless to say—I would be inclined to be even more cavalier with regard to ordinary discourse in the interests of theoretical beauty and comprehensiveness.

It is given, however, to few philosophers in a century to present us with a compelling philosophy of art, let alone a theory of everything.

And whether Bar-Elli is such a one, only time will tell. If he turns out to be, then perhaps his philosophical *chutzpa* with regard to musical performance will be vindicated. In the meantime, I myself, without even a comprehensive philosophy of music in my tool kit, will go my own plodding, inelegant, Aristotelian way, under-laborer that I am, picking at problems piecemeal, as they come, always with a wary eye over my shoulder at ordinary discourse and what is practiced in the workshop and marketplace, always more than a little suspicious of theorizing in the grand manner.

Thomas Huxley once said that Herbert Spencer's idea of a tragedy was a deduction killed by a fact.[38] My own view with regard to theorizing in the philosophy of art is that a deduction killed by a fact is not so much a tragedy as it is, frequently, rather, justifiable homicide.

[38] Quoted in Herbert Spencer, *Autobiography* (London: Williams & Norgate, 1904), i. 403.

PART IV

INTERPRETATION

9

Another Go at the Meaning of Music: Koopman, Davies, and the Meanings of "Meaning"

> In the beginning was the Word, and the Word was with God, and the Word was God.
>
> John 1 : 1

The *Oxford English Dictionary* gives ten or more meanings for "meaning", depending on how carefully you want to count and how fastidious you are about nuances. Given such a superfluity of meanings, it is hardly surprising that music has "meaning". Indeed, it would be surprising if anything *didn't*. That being the case, it is always with a sigh of resignation that I espy a new book or article intended (or "meant") to prove that, appearances to the contrary notwithstanding, music has you-know-what. And in recent years I have tended to pass over such books and articles in favor of fresher topics. But every once in a while it is a good idea to rethink even a settled opinion, and when a recent article by Constantijn Koopman and Stephen Davies, called "Musical Meaning in a Broader Perspective" crossed my path not too long ago, I decided that perhaps the time had come for me once again to give a little thought to this vexed and perennial question of musical meaning, especially as I was singled out early on in the article of Koopman and Davies as, it seems, their major adversary. As they put it:

One might conclude that, at root, music has no meaning. Peter Kivy argues this way: Because music has no semantic content—despite its quasi-syntactic structure—musical meaning does not exist "as a reality of listening." His conclusion is inescapable only if one restricts the notion of meaning to the linguistic model. Ordinary language allows for a more generous use of "meaning," however. Most people agree that (good) music makes sense and can be said to have meaning.[1]

There is nothing particularly remarkable about the suggestion that meaning can be accorded music if the concept of meaning is construed more generously than I have done. It is a familiar move. What is remarkable to me is how much of what Koopman and Davies say about music I totally endorse. How can I agree with so much of what they say, and yet be taken by them to be in the enemy camp? Are we disputing merely about a *word*? Are we engaged in semantic quibbling?

In fact I think we are, for the most part, disputing about a word. But it is not a "mere" word. It may be, however, that we *are* "quibbling". The thing is that it is an *important* quibble, if I may be allowed the apparent oxymoron. That, in any case, is the theme of my paper.

I

I want to begin with some preliminary remarks on the passage quoted above. It should not be overlooked that there is a rather strong hint of question-begging, and either *vox populi* or the argument from authority (depending upon how you interpret the passage) in the way Koopman and Davies begin their essay. They begin, as I understand them, with the following three claims: (1) Most people agree that good music makes sense. (2) Most people agree that good music can be said to have meaning. (3) There is some connection between most people's claims that music makes sense and their claims that music can be said to have meaning. Either the claim is that most people think they are saying the same thing when they say that music makes sense and that music has meaning, or they think that if music makes sense, then it implies that it has meaning. (I am not sure which.)

Claim (3) is part of the very crux of the matter between Koopman and Davies, and me. So it is best to return to it later on. But claims (1) and (2) require some scrutiny at the outset.

Consider claim (1). On what evidence is it based? It certainly sounds like the kind of claim that would (and should) be made on the basis of empirical research: questionnaires and that sort of thing. But I know of

---

[1] Constantijn Koopman and Stephen Davies, "Musical Meaning in a Broader Perspective", *Journal of Aesthetics and Art Criticism*, 59 (2001), 261.

no such empirical research. And if the claim is based on Koopman's and Davies's own experience, I have to say that my experience is not the same.

First of all, it is essential to determine the range of "most people". I presume that "most people" ranges over the people who listen to classical music of the pure, instrumental kind, because I presume that the issue of musical meaning for all three of us is the meaning of that kind of music. Second of all, it seems obvious that the "most people" who listen to classical music are a varied bunch, ranging from the very naive and unsophisticated to the musically trained and educated. If, of course, the "most" Koopman and Davies are referring to are most musically trained listeners, it may well be, I don't know, that most of *them* claim that music makes sense and can be said to have meaning, but I don't think *that* would carry much, if any, philosophical weight. For these are not folks with "pure intuitions", untainted by theory, and my impression is that what Koopman and Davies are employing here is the familiar appeal to "commonsense beliefs" as something that philosophical theory must respect, and depart from only for good theoretical reasons. In other words, *philosophy* has the burden of proof, not "ordinary intuitions". But if "most people" for Koopman and Davies are people trained in music theory, musicology, and musical speculation in general, then their population is *not* "untainted by philosophy", at least philosophy as broadly conceived. And then their argument becomes a kind of argument from authority cum *vox populi*: "Most informed listeners believe *p*, therefore. ... "

So it looks as if the appeal of Koopman and Davies *is* to "most people" in general—that is, most people who listen to classical music of the instrumental kind, without text, or title, or other literary or pictorial "content". And that being the case, it seems to me that claims (1) and (2) are both false, although I am more certain about the falsity of the former than of the latter. I begin with "making sense", and with an example.

It seems to me that an excellent example of music that I would suspect *doesn't* "make sense" to many musical listeners of the kind under discussion is the atonal serialism of Schoenberg, Berg, and Webern. But my own experience is that *that* is not what people initially say about such music, on first hearing. They usually say such relatively uninteresting things as "How awful", "It's so dissonant and ugly", "Why do people write such stuff?", and so on. In other words, they simply express strong aversion and disapproval.

In understanding what is going on here, it would be useful to introduce at this point the familiar distinction between "first-person" and "third-person" description, which is to say how *I* would describe something about my experience and how someone *else* would. For what I want to claim is that *I* would describe the music as not making sense to the listeners, whereas *they* would describe it as "dissonant", "ugly", "awful", and so forth. A standard third-person response to such first-person exclamations, on the part of someone who appreciates Schoenberg, Berg, and Webern is: "It doesn't make sense to you now, and that is why you find it ugly, awful, dissonant; but after a while it will begin to make sense to you, and then it won't sound that way to you." In the first person, sense does not come first.

When it comes to the second claim, that most people think music can be said to have meaning, it is hard not to agree, on the basis of my own experience, that people often *enunciate* the words "Music has meaning", when asked. But it is *also* my experience that they seldom really *mean* what they enunciate. For when I ask someone *what* he or she thinks a piece of music means, the answer usually is, "Well, it's sad, or happy, or emotional stuff like that." And it is almost always clear from the response that meaning is not what people have in mind in *any* of the standard senses: it is *expressiveness*.

There is no real mystery as to why the untutored music lover usually cashes out music in terms of what philosophers of art have almost universally agreed to call musical *expressiveness*. For the notion of an intimate and special connection supposed to exist between music and the emotions is as widespread among the general musical public as it is the oldest and most persistent claim in the philosophy of music, amounting in many cases to the very basis of musical aesthetics: the *fons et origo* of music's unique power as an art. But if my experience is unbiased, then it gives little if any initial support to the claim that music has meaning, in any of its standard senses. For the pre-systematic "intuition" that is being expressed by most people, my experience suggests to me, is not that music has meaning, although these are the words frequently acquiesced in, but that music is *expressive*, which is quite another thing.

The general conclusion I would like to elicit from these introductory observations is that there is no initial, pre-systematic presumption on that part of the general public that music has "sense" or "meaning". The defender of pure instrumental music as meaningless, and the defender of the view that it has meaning at least in one of the standard senses, start on a level playing field, as far as pre-systematic intuition is concerned: "common sense" favors neither one side nor the other. It is up to the defender of musical meaning to make out his case. So let us now see what Koopman and Davies's case is.

II

Koopman and Davies distinguish in their article two kinds of musical meaning: what they call "formal musical meaning" and what they call "meaning-for-the-subject". Of the latter they say: "Meaning-for-the-subject, as we call it, has to do with the place something takes in the individual's life or consciousness, with the specific way she or he experiences it, and with how this relates to her or his perceptions, feelings, thoughts, and desires."[2] The contrast is, then, between meaning *of* ... , and meaning *to* ... , the meaning of the music and the meaning of the music to this listener or that one (or a specific group of them). Some might be tempted to put it as the difference between "subjective" and "objective" meaning; but I take that to mean no more (or less) than the distinction that Koopman and Davies make.

I myself am not particularly interested in meaning for ... , subjective meaning, and have never denied that music has meaning in the subjective sense. So I will concentrate for the most part on objective meaning, meaning of ... —what Koopman and Davies call "formal meaning"—although I will have a little to say about meaning-for-the-subject at the end.

According to Koopman and Davies, there are two kinds of formal musical meaning, one, which Davies earlier described as "formal significance",[3] the other what Koopman and Davies call "experiential formal meaning".

With regard to formal significance, Koopman and Davies write:

we explain musical works as displaying a kind of internal rationality. Musical works cohere in specific ways that can be explained because, like human action, their progressions are ruled by implications. Explanation here is in terms of coherence. The coherence of the parts of the piece at all levels enables us to explain the function of the various parts in the whole.[4]

---

[2] Koopman and Davies, "Musical Meaning in a Broader Perpective", 268.
[3] Stephen Davies, *Musical Meaning and Expression* (Ithaca, NY: Cornell University Press, 1994), 48.
[4] "Musical Meaning in a Broader Perspective", 263.

With this I think we can all agree. It is the crucial next step, the leap to "meaning", that marks out the first of Koopman and Davies's theses, and enters the realm of the controversial. Here is how that next step goes:

Because we can explain what happens at a given point in the music by reference to what occurs on either side of it, it is not inappropriate to talk of "the meaning" of the music and of its temporal progress. In the context of formal meaning, the question "What is the meaning of event x in piece y?" ... is [typically] a request to elucidate the way event x coheres with the rest of piece y.[5]

We will want to ask ourselves in a moment whether the step from "coherence" to "meaning" is justifiable, and if so, in what way. But before we do that, we had better have the other kind of formal musical meaning before us: the kind Koopman and Davies call "experiential formal meaning".

Understanding the "meaning" of some musical event, in the sense just outlined, is, one might say, a distinctly conscious, intellectual affair. A person who understands the meaning of event x in piece y is conscious of understanding how event x is connected with the events that precede and follow it in piece y, and, presumably, can explain it to someone else: she understands why x coheres with y in a fully self-aware way. This does not seem to be the case with experiential formal meaning. Here it is more an awareness of the music's flow: a sense of the connectedness of musical events, but not accompanied by explicit knowledge of how these events are connected with each other or with the whole of which they are a part.

Here is how Koopman and Davies initially state the contrast between explicit knowledge of musical meaning and the kind called experiential formal meaning:

The fact that we can explain music in terms of reasons provides a sufficient justification for speaking of musical meaning. However, there is a more fundamental sense in which music can be said to have meaning. To understand music as meaningful, it is not necessary that we can explain the progression of the music. Meaning can be understood immediately in the musical encounter, without reasoning at all. ... [W]e experience the musical parts as connected into a dynamic whole. ... One understands a piece's formal musical meaning when one appreciates the internal connectedness of its parts. ... [T]here is formal meaning in response, or *experiential formal meaning*, as we shall call it.[6]

[5] Koopman and Davies, "Musical Meaning in a Broader Perspective", 263–4.
[6] Ibid. 264.

Again, one feels inclined to agree totally with the substance of what Koopman and Davies are saying here. Indeed, it is hard to think of any competent writer on musical aesthetics, from Hanslick, to Gurney, to Zuckerkandl, to Leonard Meyer, to Jerrold Levinson, to myself for that matter, who have not said much the same thing; and Koopman and Davies adduce a number of other examples as well. The question is not whether what they have described *is* something that goes on in the musical experience or whether it as an *important* something. We all agree that it is there and that it is important. The gnawing question for *me* is whether we are justified in calling it "meaning"—the same question that concerns me with regard to the first kind of formal musical meaning that Koopman and Davies discuss. And to that gnawing question I must now turn.

III

Let us look first at the kind of explicit, self-conscious knowledge of "meaning" that is constituted by understanding, and being able to state in what way a musical event coheres with the musical whole in which it functions. Koopman and Davies say, you will recall, that "Because we can explain what happens at a given point in the music by reference to what occurs on either side of it, it is not inappropriate to talk of 'the meaning' of the music and of its temporal progress". And what immediately catches the eye of the skeptic in this initial formulation of their first claim is the extreme caution with which it is framed. It is not *altogether* appropriate or even just *appropriate* to speak of "the meaning" of the music in regard to this kind of understanding. The best Koopman and Davies can say is that "it is not *inappropriate*". To assert the positive by denying the negative is, in English, anyway, the weakest, most tentative, most defeasible way of expressing a proposition.

Why did Koopman and Davies express this proposition with such diffidence, such hesitation? I think I know why. It is because anyone with a "good ear" for "ordinary language" can hear that, in this musical context, questions about meaning do not sound altogether "right": do not sound idiomatic. And one can perceive this clearly by moving on to Koopman and Davies's own way of putting their thesis: to wit, how event x coheres with the events surrounding it in piece y.

As Koopman and Davies put their point, you will recall, " 'What is the meaning of event x in piece y?' ... is [typically] a request to elucidate the way event x coheres with the rest of piece y." Now it may very well be that if someone *were* to ask his theory teacher what the "meaning" of some chord (say) was in a piece, she would understand him to be asking her to explain how it coheres with the rest of the piece. But to my ear, anyway, that sounds like a very odd, unidiomatic, and far from typical way of asking the question. The question is, normally, "What is the *function* of this chord in the piece?", or, "What's this chord *doing* here?", or something of the kind. It is no more idiomatic to ask the meaning of a chord in a musical composition than it is to ask what the meaning of the escapement mechanism is in a clock. One *can* ask the question that way and perhaps be understood. However, it is plainly false to suggest that it is the ordinary way of asking, or even a particularly enlightening way of asking it. I think it is liable to be a misleading way of asking it. And this is why the best we, or Koopman and Davies, can say is that it is not altogether inappropriate: you can, if you want to, ask your question that way; it is not, however, the best way to ask it.

But, you may reply, the analogy of chord function to the functioning parts of a clock may not be the most felicitous one. Koopman and Davies, as a matter of fact, make much of the analogy between the functioning parts of a musical work and human actions. They say, in this regard, that "In terms of the relations among its parts, we can provide reasons why a work develops this rather than that way. Moreover, these reasons have a distinctive character: They are like those with which we explain human actions."[7]

It is certainly true that there are human actions about which it makes perfect sense, sounds altogether appropriate, to ask "What does it mean?" If someone makes a peculiar gesture towards me with his hand, I might well ask, "What do you think that means?" But the problem is that for vast numbers of human actions the appropriate question is not about meaning at all. Just as in the musical case, it is a question, more or less, about function: "What is the purpose of that action?" Or, in other words, "What is she doing?" So invoking human action as the favored analogy to musical events does not, in my view, *ipso facto* bring meaning along with it. And, by the way, where it does, it is just the wrong kind of meaning for Koopman and Davies. For to ask what a particular gesture—say, raising your hand in class—*means*, is to ask the same kind of question that a foreigner might ask if I said, "I have a question". We are right back in the rejected realm of semantic content.

---

[7] Koopman and Davies, "Musical Meaning in a Broader Perspective", 263.

With all of these reservations on the table, we can, I suppose, acquiesce in Koopman and Davies's very weak conclusion that it is at least *not inappropriate* to ask "What does musical event x mean in piece y?", when what one is asking is how x functions or coheres in y, even though there are far more felicitous, *altogether appropriate* ways of asking such questions.

But if asking for the meaning of musical events in pure instrumental music is just marginally appropriate, in Koopman and Davies's words, "not inappropriate", why should one want to describe as *meaning* what can so much more plausibly and idiomatically be described as *function*, or with a host of its other close relatives? I shall tackle that question in the next section of my paper. Before I do that, however, I want to go on to a similar critique of Koopman and Davies's second kind of formal musical meaning: namely, experiential formal meaning.

When a person understands a piece of music in the way of experiential formal meaning, he understands it in the sense of hearing it as "making sense". It progresses in his listening in a way that is coherent (and pleasing?) to him. As Koopman and Davies put it, you will recall, "we experience the musical parts as connected into a dynamic whole". Or, as they describe it in another place: "We take 'experiential formal meaning' to refer to the experiential potential the listener is able to realize when she or he responds to the music with understanding."[8] We "understand" the music—but not as the theoretician or analyst understands it, under concepts and descriptions that he can convey in words. Rather, we "understand" it in the sense of being able to apprehend, follow, and appreciate the musical events we are hearing. When we cannot appreciate it in this way, we may say, to quote a line from an unmemorable movie, "It don't make no more sense to me than Chinese music." It is, in other words, the unconscious understanding, appreciation, that each member of a given musical culture acquires, without being aware of it, as (in much the same way) he acquires his native language.

Now Koopman and Davies quite unapologetically refer, with great frequency, to this kind of understanding as understanding of musical *meaning*. Thus, the reader will recall that they say: "One understands a piece's formal musical meaning when one appreciates the internal connectedness of its parts." And again, in another place: "We take the experience of coherent musical structure as the basis for ascribing

---

[8] Ibid. 264.

meaning to music. ... "[9] All responsible writers on music with whom I am acquainted, agree that such understanding of music exists, as the basis for all musical appreciation; and I certainly acquiesce in that opinion as well (with certain qualifications). But why call it the understanding of *meaning*? There is nothing idiomatic or in any other way compelling in that description. It does not particularly "ring true".

When someone "doesn't get it", listening to a piece of music — for example, a new contemporary work, or music from another culture — she may say, "It doesn't make sense," or "It doesn't hang together," or, indeed, "I don't get it." But it is both unidiomatic and puzzling to say, "I don't understand what it *means*," or "What does it *mean*?" Someone who said *that* would very likely be taken to have mistaken a musical "utterance" for a linguistic one. One *can*, of course, express one's puzzlement, one's lack of musical comprehension that way, and perhaps be understood. What perplexes me is why one would. That the word "meaning" cuts a wide swathe we know. And if one goes far enough away from the central and standard meanings of "meaning", one can probably find one that can be applied to the experience of music we are talking about "not inappropriately". When all else fails, of course, there is always the refuge of metaphor. Metaphorically speaking, the average concertgoer finds the music of Webern "meaningless".

Furthermore, let me add, before closing this section, a word about "making sense". It is a mistake to suggest that because we can say "The music makes (or doesn't make) sense", it follows that we can say that it has (or doesn't have) "meaning". "Making sense" is not coextensive with "having meaning", even in the broad sense of "meaning"; witness the fact that it is perfectly idiomatic to say of a piece of complicated machinery whose workings or purpose one doesn't understand, "It doesn't make sense (to me)," whereas it is not idiomatic to say, "I don't know what it means." In other words, "making sense" is a description made in numerous contexts that have nothing to do with meaning, either in its semantic or non-semantic uses. And the musical context is a case in point: a case where "making sense" is appropriate but "having meaning" (in any of its uses) is not, at least to *my* "ordinary language ear".

The gnawing question for me, I repeat, is why there should be what seems to me to be something amounting to a compulsion, or at least a deep-seated need, to find a way (or ways) to say that music has meaning, while giving wide berth to the generally discredited view that music has

<hr />

[9] Koopman and Davies, "Musical Meaning in a Broader Perspective", 266.

meaning in the form of semantic content. To that gnawing question I now to turn my attention.

IV

Let me begin by acknowledging that in both kinds of formal musical meaning that Koopman and Davies distinguish, it does make sense to ascribe meaning to the musical phenomena in question. The variety of meanings of "meaning" beyond the central, standard ones virtually assures this. And although I find their applications strained, and sometimes departures from ordinary linguistic usage, I can at least acquiesce in the minimal conclusion that these are not totally *inappropriate* applications. But in the face of this barely minimal appropriateness of ascribing "meaning" to musical form and process in the ways that Koopman and Davies advocate, I want to advance some reflections on why they and others feel it so urgent that music be described in these ways and why I think it is a bad idea.

Here is the thrust of Koopman and Davies's article, as I read it: Kivy, and others, are quite right in rejecting the notion that pure instrumental music can "mean", in the semantic sense of the word. (As a matter of fact, Davies himself gives a masterful analysis and refutation of music as a bearer of semantic content in his *Musical Meaning and Expression*.[10]) But—and this, I think, is an unspoken concern lying behind most attempts to rescue *some* kind of meaning for music—it is a very unfortunate conclusion for music that it cannot possess any meaning at all. So if music cannot possess semantic meaning, we had better cast about for another kind that it can possess. After all, doesn't it seem narrow-minded to think semantic meaning the only game in town? It is rather like giving up the pleasures and consolations of a household pet just because you're allergic to cats and dogs. (How about a monkey or a parrot?)

What we first want to know is *why* it is thought to be an unfortunate conclusion that music does not possess meaning. Music, since the end of the eighteenth century, or the beginning of the nineteenth, depending upon whom you read, has been considered a member of the community of "arts and letters". That is a community in which one

[10] Davies, *Musical Meaning and Expression*, ch. 1.

of the busiest and most admired occupations is that of the *interpreter of meaning* (henceforth *interpreter* for short). Literary art works, *belles lettres*, works of the visual arts, works of philosophy and its satellites, are all the subjects of intense interpretational scrutiny by a cadre of academics and independent scholars whose task it is to tell us "what it all means". The arts and letters are supposed to be sources of "humanistic", moral, philosophical, psychological, and other knowledge. The works in which this knowledge is supposed to be conveyed are often obscure to the ordinary reader. The interpreter's job is to aid this reader in understanding these works as well as revealing "new meanings" discovered in them to the intellectual community at large. And the content he or she interprets must needs be *semantic* content—"semantic" at least broadly conceived to include the "implied" messages of literary works as well as the representational content of the visual arts.

It is this interpretational task to which musicologists, music analysts, music theorists, and music critics aspire. It is small consolation to the musically learned that the objects of their love and admiration have been allowed membership in the pantheon of arts and letters only to be denied meaning and, therefore, denied the benefit of the interpretational skills and methods so cherished in the academy and the art world. Musical scholars want to play with the big boys; they want a stake in the philosophy and morality game. In short, they want music to *mean*; and if it can't mean semantically, then they grab for some other way it can mean.

Alas for these musical seekers after meaning, the thing is that finding a kind of meaning other than the semantic for music is *not* like finding another kind of pet if a dog or a cat won't work for you. A monkey or a parrot may give you the pleasures and consolations of a dog or a cat, in the way of a pet, but non-semantic meanings of the kind Koopman and Davies talk about (or any other kinds I am familiar with) will assuredly *not* provide the pleasures and consolations of semantic meaning, which are just the pleasures and consolations that the musical analysts and musicologists are seeking when they seek musical "meaning" in the first place. All they are given is the word. It is about as satisfactory as acquiring a stone and calling it a "pet".[11]

---

[11] Actually, having stones for pets was a craze a few years ago. I don't know what it was all about, but it sounds a lot to me like having meaning for music in a broader perspective.

The reason why I (and others) think that when music is shown to have no semantic meaning, broadly conceived, it has been shown to have no meaning *sans phrase*, is not that we are so myopic or totally obsessed with semantic meaning that we don't know that there are other senses of "meaning", and that some of them may correctly be ascribed to music. Rather, it is that we know the other senses of "meaning" won't do the job. They won't give the musical seekers after meaning what they want: license to talk the talk of the interpreters of the literary and representational arts. They get the word, but nothing more. It is a hollow victory.

It is my belief that nothing Koopman and Davies say about music in their discussion of what they call formal musical meaning, much of which I agree with, requires to be said using the word "meaning" at all. The word is utterly superfluous to the musical phenomena they are describing, and many of the writers whom they quote, and with whose accounts of the musical experience they seem to agree substantially, do not use the word at all. Furthermore, when Koopman and Davies do use the "m" word in *their* descriptions, it always seems to me strained, and at the very outer boundaries of idiomatic English. I have grudgingly acquiesced in the weak conclusion that its use is *not inappropriate*. But that seems just about analogous to damning with faint praise.

Perhaps the friends of musical meaning will reply to my skepticism that there certainly is no harm in describing music as having "meaning" in the senses Koopman and Davies have described. But, in fact, my skepticism extends to even that seemingly uncontentious assertion. There *is* potential for harm, and here is why.

Words have magnetism; they are magical. They wield a peculiar and subtle power over us. And the word "meaning" is one of the most magnetic, magical, and powerful of all. So unless we continually repeat to ourselves the mantra "This is not semantic meaning, this does not license us to talk with the interpreters, this does not bestow philosophical or moral or narrative significance upon absolute music", we are liable to forget how little we gain when we grant "meaning" to music if the meaning is anything but the semantic variety. Thomas Hobbes famously said that "Words are wise men's counters ... but the money of fools. ... "[12] And no word has, in the philosophy of music, been more taken for coin rather than counter than that seductive word "meaning". We would do better to do without it.

---

[12] Thomas Hobbes, *Leviathan*, Part I, ch. iv.

In the conclusion of my paper I shall have some further remarks to make on the reluctance of musical thinkers to give up the "m" word, and the dangers thereof. But before I get to that, I want to make good on a promise I made earlier on to touch at least briefly on what Koopman and Davies call "meaning-for-the-subject" and "meaning-for-us".

V

What Koopman and Davies call "meaning-for-the-subject" is very familiar to us all. "*Meaning-for-the-subject*, as we call it, has to do with the place something takes in the individual's life or consciousness, with the specific way she or he experiences it, and how this relates to her or his perceptions, feelings, thoughts, and desires."[13] In other words, meaning-for-the-subject is what we might describe as the very personal and particular significance this musical composition might have for me, that one for you, because of our different life experiences. "Meaning-for-the-subject is largely subjective," Koopman and Davies say.[14] And, they add, developing this point, "The best example of a dimension of musical meaning that is idiosyncratic concerns the association of music with particular events in a person's life."[15]

Meaning-for-us, like meaning-for-the-subject, is a familiar concept to us all. Just as meaning-for-the-subject is the significance, or importance, of music for some individual, you, me, or whomever, so meaning-for-us is the significance, or importance, of music for some specific group: Americans or Viennese, choral singers or barber shop quartets, teenagers or their middle-aged parents, Quakers or Catholics, or, if you want to really go out on a limb, the whole human race. Koopman and Davies write:

In characterizing the meaning music has for a person, we have stressed its significance for the individual. Now we should ask if musical meaning has a wider scope. As well as meaning-for-the-subject, is there *meaning-for-us*? There is reason to think so. No human society is without music, and there is hardly any individual who would not claim that music plays an important role in her or his life.[16]

What can certainly be acknowledged straightaway about meaning-for-the-subject and meaning-for-us is that the "m" word *is* altogether

---

[13] Koopman and Davies, "Musical Meaning in a Broader Perspective", 268.
[14] Ibid.   [15] Ibid. 269.   [16] Ibid. 270.

appropriate for *both*. For the sense of "meaning" being exploited here is a standard one: "importance" or "significance". To say that music means a lot to me in this sense is to say that it is important to me, a significant part of my life, and, likewise, if I say that it means a lot to the Viennese but not much to rural Americans. I certainly have no problem with that; nor would anyone else that I know of who has denied that absolute music has *meaning*.

But there is a potential problem here, a hidden danger. "Meaning" is just one among a variety of words that describe what Koopman and Davies are referring to when they talk about meaning-for-the-subject and meaning-for-us; and some of the words are better suited, more appropriate for the job, than the "m" word is. Yet *that* is the word they constantly use. The danger to the unwary is that they will be lulled into thinking that something has been accomplished here in the way of redeeming for absolute music that coveted sense of "meaning", the semantic sense, at least broadly conceived, that will allow us to make philosophy and narrative out of music. I do not, for a moment, suggest that Koopman and Davies have deceived *themselves*; they are far too sophisticated for that. But it is easy for others, I fear, to lose sight of the fact that what Koopman and Davies call meaning-for-the-subject and meaning-for-us have absolutely nothing to do with what folks were really looking for and hoping for when they picked up their article to read.

Another way of putting it is this. When I write about what *Billy Budd* means, what moral or broadly philosophical points Melville is making, I am playing the part of interpreter. But when I write about what Beethoven's Fifth Symphony means to me, I am playing the part of autobiographer; when I write about what it means to someone else, I am playing the part of biographer; and when I write about what it meant to the French Romantics, I am playing the part of social and musical historian. There is a world of difference between the first occupation and the other three. And it is the first occupation that many musical scholars, critics, theorists, and analysts desperately long for. Alas, Koopman and Davies can offer them no consolation whatever in that direction.

VI

Koopman and Davies call their article "Musical Meaning in a Broader Perspective." If one were to take "meaning", in the title, to be semantic meaning, broadly conceived to include not only the meanings of sentences in literary works but the implied meanings of literary works; and pictorial meaning, in the sense in which Raphael, for example, was "saying" something about the philosophies of Plato and Aristotle in *The School of Athens*, by having Plato pointing up, Aristotle down—then their article would seem to hold out hope that, viewed in the "broader perspective", meaning in music too would turn out to be semantic meaning, at least broadly conceived. But that would be a false hope, and Koopman and Davies, as one finds out early on, never intended to hold out such hope at all.

Actually, what the title of Koopman and Davies's article really should be, if faithful to its content, is: "The Word 'Meaning', as Applied to Music, in a Broader Perspective". For *that* is what their project really is. What Koopman and Davies have done is shown that numerous aspects of absolute music we have customarily described without using the word "meaning" can be described using that word, if that word is utilized in all of the ways it can be, beyond the semantic way. This is not an unworthy project. But, in the event, one is bound to ask, as I have before, *why* we should describe these aspects of music, which can be described quite adequately without the "m" word, in terms of meaning, particularly as it is frequently strained or even unidiomatic to do so.

Let me make the perhaps outlandish suggestion that the obsession with ascribing meaning to music, after one has come to the awful truth that music cannot possess semantic meaning, even broadly conceived, is something like the compulsion of the person who has trodden the painful path from theism to atheism to still describe *something* as "God". What does it avail the pantheist to call the universe of modern physics God? If he crosses himself, it cannot grant him a good at bat. If he prays to it, it cannot reunite him with his departed loved ones in Paradise. If he does good works, it cannot grant him life everlasting. He may call himself a pantheist instead of an atheist, give Nature a capital "N" and call it God. But with regard to benefits now, or in the hereafter, he is on all fours with the non-believer. What he *does* have is the comfort of a word. And apparently that amounts to something worth having to many people, although I have not found it so.

Likewise, I think that the music lover feels the loss of musical meaning, in the semantic sense, the way the atheist feels the loss of God. And as the atheist, *alias* pantheist, is comforted for his loss, apparently, by calling the universe God, so the music lover who has reached the conclusion that music can have no meaning in the semantic sense, even broadly conceived, finds comfort in his loss in having the "meaning", devoid of substance and nourishment though it may be.

I think it would be the better part to give up the word altogether. Yes, you can view the "m" word, as applied to music, in a broader perspective if you like. But if you view it in a broader perspective, there isn't *anything* that lacks meaning. I don't know what the comfort of that conclusion is.

But no doubt I am shouting into the wind. The Evangelist well knew the power of the Word. And to oppose the power of the word in question, I have a feeling, is a lost cause. So let there be musical meaning, in a broader perspective, for whatever that is worth. I prefer to do without it.

10

Another Go at Musical Profundity: Stephen Davies and the Game of Chess

I

When I decided to conclude my book *Music Alone* with a chapter called "The Profundity of Music", I had no idea that what I said on the subject would raise so many hackles.[1] But I should have known better. For, after all, pure instrumental music, what I called in the book "music alone", is generally agreed upon to be one of the fine arts; and perhaps the highest compliment one can pay to a work of the fine arts, it might be thought, is to call it "profound". So when I cast doubt on whether such music *could* rightly be called "profound", I must have been seen as consigning "absolute music", as it came to be called in the nineteenth century, to a second-class citizenship in the community of arts and letters. A play, a poem, a novel, maybe even a painting, might achieve the highest level, *qua* work of art, the level of profundity. But a work of instrumental music *never*. *Faust*, yes; *Paradise Lost*, yes; the *Eroica*—application denied.

Since I reached this seemingly distressing conclusion, in 1990, numerous replies have been directed at me by the distressed. And in 1997 I tried to answer what I took to be the most philosophically interesting of them. There matters stood, at least as far as I know, until 2002, when the question reemerged again, on the pages of the *British Journal of Aesthetics*, in the form of an article by Stephen Davies called "Profundity in Instrumental Music".[2] Were the article by a "lesser light", I would have been inclined not to read yet another attempt to find a place for absolute music in the Pantheon of the Profound. But when

---

[1] Peter Kivy, *Music Alone: Philosophical Reflections on the Purely Musical Experience* (Ithaca, NY: Cornell University Press, 1990), ch. 10.

[2] Stephen Davies, "Profundity in Instrumental Music", *British Journal of Aesthetics*, 42 (2002).

the attempt is by Davies, one is ill-advised to pass it over without serious consideration. And having read Davies's intriguing arguments, it seemed clear to me that the time had indeed arrived to at least briefly reopen, yet again, the question of musical profundity. Apparently, my "distressing" conclusion continues to distress.

II

It would be well to begin by stating carefully what my distressing conclusion was, and what reasons I had for reaching it. And I want to state it not exactly as I stated it in *Music Alone*, in 1990, but in the way I stated it later on, and now understand it. For although I have not changed my views with regard to the profundity of absolute music, I have become clearer about them over the years, due in large measure to the many critical comments that they attracted.

I begin with the assumptions that, first, we do, from time to time, feel it appropriate to describe certain exemplary works in the canon of Western absolute music as profound, and, second, that we by and large agree upon which works deserve the compliment. The question is why we describe these works as profound, and not others, even though we might well agree that the other works are beautiful or great works of art.

In order to answer this question, I proposed in *Music Alone*, and later in *Philosophies of Arts*, that we first take some clear cases where we can agree what the criteria are for ascribing profundity, and then see if the musical cases fulfill these criteria. My examples were drawn from two obvious sources, philosophy and literature; and since in the case of music we are dealing with one of the fine arts, it was literature that provided my paradigm. With literature in mind, then, this is how I characterized profundity in *Philosophies of Arts*, a characterization that I still think is pretty much on target. I take the liberty of quoting myself:

for a work of art to be profound—and literature is the obvious example here—it must (1) have a profound subject matter and (2) treat this profound subject matter in a way adequate to its profundity—which is to say, (a) say profound things about this subject matter and (b) do it at a very high level of artistic or aesthetic excellence. ... [3]

[3] Peter Kivy, *Philosophies of Arts: An Essay in Differences* (New York: Cambridge University Press, 1979), 145.

But if this is the basic sense of profound, then it is clear why we should be very skeptical of ascribing profundity to any work of absolute music. For it requires that whatever is profound be capable of both reference and sense; and pure instrumental music seems incapable of either.

Against my characterization of profundity in the arts, Davies responds, to start with, that it is, in effect, too exclusionary. But this response is the result, I believe, of a misunderstanding of my position that I would like to clear up before going any further.

Davies writes:

His account of profundity is vulnerable in its insistence on what I will call the "aboutness" criterion. Kivy seems to require for "aboutness" both reference and predication. This makes the expression of profundity essentially propositional, so it is not surprising that instrumental music fails to make the grade. But surely this is too restrictive a standard? (It will exclude, as well as all music and painting, all but the most explicitly didactive literature.) ... There are ways of conveying ideas other than asserting them. These ways might show rather than say how things are.[4]

Now it would, indeed, be an intolerable conclusion, for me, if my account of profundity in literature implied that only "the most explicitly didactive literature" could be profound. If that were really what it implied, I would give up my account altogether. It couldn't possibly be the right account of profundity if it had that implication. But surely it does not.

To begin with, my account implies that most didactic literature is *not* profound—that is to say, not profound *qua* literature, although it might be profound *qua* philosophy, say. Indeed I considered just such a case of works that are philosophically profound, but not profound literature, in *Music Alone*: namely, the dialogues of Bishop Berkeley.[5] They do indeed fulfill criteria (1) and (2a): they are about profound subject matter and say profound things about it. But they do not fulfill criterion (2b): they do not treat their subject matter at a very high degree of artistic or aesthetic excellence. As I remarked in *Music Alone*, "The characters are wooden, and the philosophy sticks out, when the works are read as literature."[6]

Now the problem here seems to me to be this. Davies must, I guess, think that for a work of literature to be, say, philosophically profound,

[4] Davies, "Profundity in Instrumental Music", 344.   [5] Kivy, *Music Alone*, 213.
[6] Ibid.

according to my propositional take on literary profundity, it must contain tons of *sentences* expressing profound philosophical thoughts: which is exactly what didactic literature does (when it is profound). But that, of course, is exactly why "didactic" is a term of abuse when applied to literature. For literature that did contain tons of sentences expressing profound philosophical thoughts would be bad *literature*, although it might, for all of that, be great philosophy.

But the view that for literature to be profound it must express profound *propositions* is not the view that it must express those directly in sentences. On the contrary, that would make it bad, and so not profound, literature. The view that literature can sometimes be profound by expressing profound propositions has always been the view that it expresses these propositions indirectly. It "suggests" or "implies" them in a literary way.

Thus, I thoroughly agree, in spirit, with Davies when he says that "There are ways of conveying thoughts other than asserting them." But what I take that to mean is that there are other ways whereby one can convey thoughts besides directly asserting them in sentences. One can assert them indirectly in the ways literature does. "I don't mean that a novelist's statements about a fictional Mr. N.N. are true claims about a non-existent person, but that such statements *convey* truths about what makes people tick."[7]

I agree, too, in spirit, with Davies when he says that "These ways might show rather than say how things are." But what I take *that* to mean is that we can sometimes express propositions through showing things rather than asserting the propositions directly in sentences. Literature expresses many propositions by showing the ways in which people behave and by various other "showings". I will call this "propositional showing".

Davies, however, is not defending propositional showing in these two remarks I have just quoted. Rather, he is defending the view that I will call "pure showing". For I take him to be saying that there are ways of conveying thoughts that are not propositional at all. And since absolute music, on his view as on mine, if it can express propositions at all, can express only pretty banal ones, propositional showing is out of the question for it as a means of attaining profundity. Pure showing is

---

[7] Susan Haack, "As for the phrase 'studying in a literary spirit' ... ", in *Manifesto of a Passionate Moderate: Unfashionable Essays* (Chicago: University of Chicago Press, 1998), 56; my italics.

the option Davies chooses for it. And he introduces his notion of pure showing with an excellent and intriguing example: the game of chess. To that example, and what follows from it, I now want to turn.

III

I must begin this discussion by making it very clear that I know next to nothing about chess. I know how the pieces move, how they can "take" other pieces, what "check" and "checkmate" are. In other words, I can "follow" a game of chess. But if I were to play a game with Davies, I probably would have to resign after three moves.

To get directly to the point, or, if you will forgive me, cut to the chess, Davies adduces two masterful games of chess which, as he puts it, "illustrate to a jaw-dropping degree the inexhaustible fecundity, flexibility, insight, vitality, subtlety, complexity, and analytical far-reachingness of which the mind is capable".[8] The first game, Fischer versus Byrne, Davies avers, "was a masterpiece of tactical calculation"; the second, Capablanca versus Marshall, "a masterpiece of strategy".[9] I have no reason to doubt Davies's claim that these two games were "masterpieces", or to doubt that if I understood chess more adequately than I do, I would share Davies's thrill in seeing revealed in them the incredible accomplishments "of which the human mind is capable".

But Davies wants, obviously, to go further. These games of chess are not just masterpieces of chess; they are "profound". Thus he writes:

Chess fails Kivy's conditions for profundity. It is not obviously *about* anything and certainly is not about anything that goes to the moral heart of human life. ... In particular, neither Fischer's move nor Capablanca's strategic play could be profound on Kivy's account. Yet I maintain that these abstract, intellectual achievements are profound in their way. And I would say the same of some complex mathematical proofs, for instance.[10]

For Davies, then, there is a kind of profundity, other than propositional profundity, other even than the kind of propositional profundity exhibited by literature, in which the profound thoughts, if there are any, are expressed not for the most part directly, but by what I called propositional showing. It is the profundity of pure showing. In Davies's words, "It is sufficient that profundity is *shown* or *displayed* by

[8] Davies, "Profundity in Instrumental Music", 351.   [9] Ibid. 349 and 350.
[10] Ibid. 350.

an activity or judgement."[11] And the *criterion*, if you will, of purely shown, non-propositional profundity, is that the thing, or activity, or whatever, as Davies so well puts it, "illustrate[s] to a jaw-dropping degree the inexhaustible fecundity, flexibility, insight, vitality, subtlety, complexity, and analytical far-reachingness of which the human mind is capable". When this degree of mental capability is shown or displayed forth by some human accomplishment, it is, by virtue of that, to be called "profound". And pure instrumental music can, surely, qualify as profound, because it can satisfy this criterion: "in creating the very greatest music, composers display to an extraordinary degree many of the general cognitive capacities seen also in outstanding chess; namely, originality, far-sightedness, imagination, fertility, plasticity, refinement, intuitive mastery of complex detail, and so on."[12]

To begin dealing with Davies's concept of non-propositional profundity, of which chess and instrumental music are his principal examples, I want first to point to what I take to be an argument, and a bad one at that, for his position, "suggested", if that is the right word, although not stated outright, in a crucial passage quoted above. Here is what Davies says: "neither Fischer's move nor Capablanca's strategic play could be profound on Kivy's account. Yet I maintain that these abstract, intellectual achievements are profound in their way. And I would say the same of some complex mathematical proofs, for instance."

Now what bothers me here is the adducing of mathematical proofs as examples of non-propositional profundity, and the argument that, it seems to me, lurks therein. For I take it that Davies is trying to convince us of the plausibility of non-propositional profundity by adducing what he takes to be completely non-controversial examples of it: namely, "some complex mathematical proofs". But although complex mathematical proofs are *certainly* non-controversial candidates for profundity, and sometimes anyone would agree, achieve it, they are certainly, when they *do* achieve it, clear examples of *propositional* profundity. Surely they have a subject matter—number, quantity, groups, dimensions, surfaces, and all of the other "things" mathematics is about—although the ontological status of mathematical "objects" is a matter of dispute. Mathematics consists in propositions, even though these propositions are not expressed in ordinary language. And it achieves profundity, one would think, in just the way other human sciences and disciplines do: by dealing with a profound subject matter in a way

[11] Ibid.   [12] Ibid. 351–2.

adequate to its profundity (and, by the way, sometimes exhibiting, as the mathematicians tell us, "elegance" and other "aesthetic" properties). Thus, if Davies is trying to work his passage from mathematical profundity to chess profundity, and thence to musical profundity, I don't think it will work. Indeed, I think a chess enthusiast might have the same problem with chess profundity as I have with musical profundity; we both feel compelled on occasion to call an object of our veneration "profound", and we can't think why. For chess to get us to musical profundity, then, it will have to do it on its own, without the help of mathematics. I don't think it can, and here is why.

The chess games of Fischer and Capablanca that Davies adduces are both, he says, "masterpieces". To a jaw-dropping degree they illustrate the tremendous creative capacity of the human mind. And to the extent that chess games show, not tell about, the great creative capacity of the human mind, they are non-propositionally profound.

Now my problem is that, so far as I can tell, *any* great game of chess, *any* chess masterpiece, by this criterion of profundity, will be profound. There will be no great chess games, no chess "masterpieces" that will *not* be profound games of chess. That is because any truly great game of chess will require the great capacities of the human mind to create, and so any great game of chess will illustrate, display, show forth the unutterable fecundity, and so forth, of the human mind. And so every great game of chess will be non-propositionally profound.

Of course it is absolute music, not chess, that concerns me. It may be my utter ignorance and ineptitude, chess-wise, that makes it seem counterintuitive that if great chess games can be profound, all of them are. But absolute music is my game. And so far as I can tell, the kind of non-propositional profundity that Davies is touting for chess and for absolute music will have the same counterintuitive result for the latter as for the former. On Davies's view, as I see it, all great musical works will be non-propositionally profound musical works. Because all truly great musical works require that awesomeness of mental endowment—"genius" I am not ashamed to call it, in the good old Romantic sense—they will all illustrate, all display forth that awesomeness of mental endowment, that incomprehensible genius that makes jaws drop in stunned wonderment and disbelief. The *Eroica* does it; but so too do Mozart's shimmering wind sextets, with their seemingly endless display of delicate musical beauties in which the individual characters of each of the wind instruments are exploited in a way never equaled, let alone excelled. How can a human mind be capable of creating such a parade of beautiful sounds, in such variety and profusion? These works, no less than the mighty *Eroica*, display forth those mental characteristics of imagination, fertility, plasticity, intuitive mastery of complex detail, and the rest. So it would appear that, on Davies's criterion for musical profundity, Mozart's wind sextets should be counted profound musical works. I take it that they are masterpieces of their genre, but surely not profound. (If you are not familiar with these wonderful compositions, you may work the same argument on Mozart's *Eine kleine Nachtmusik*, or any other work that you may think fits the bill.)

"So what of it?", the convert to Davies's position might respond. "What is wrong with the conclusion that all musical masterpieces are profound? It sounds OK to me." To see what is wrong with it, we will have to get back to basics.

The quest for musical profundity began with the assumption that certain works of absolute music tended to elicit from some the judgment "profound", and that there was agreement, more or less, on the part of people who passed such judgment, on which works deserved it. At least, that is the assumption I began with, and which Davies seems to share.

Given this assumption, my project was to try to pin down just what we might mean to say of an artwork when we call it "profound"; and I took as my model the literary arts, which, I thought, presented uncontroversial and easily made-out criteria for profundity in the fine arts. There is no need to go over that ground in detail again except to point out that what the literary model clearly showed is that we use the term "profound" in such a way as to distinguish between those literary works that are great works of art but not profound, and those that are great works of art and *are* profound. In other words, it turns out that, if literature is taken as our model, according to the way the word "profound" is used, all profound literary works are great literary works, but not all great literary works are profound.

But if we accept that result, if we accept the condition on profundity in the fine arts that not all great works of art are profound works of art, then we must reject Davies's account of musical profundity. He certainly has said something that is important and true: that truly great works of art display forth, illustrate, the awesome fecundity, inventiveness, creativity, and so forth of the human mind when it is functioning at the genius level. Furthermore, I certainly agree with him that it is part of our experience of great works of art to be aware of this, and have written about it elsewhere in my own terms.[13] But it is *not* profundity, even though one can call it that if one wishes, by stipulative definition, or, as R. G. Collingwood would say, as a "courtesy" definition, as when we call the pastry chef's latest creation a "work of art", knowing full well that it isn't.[14] (I have been known to describe the *Eroica* as a "profound human utterance", although I do not think it is either an utterance or profound.)

Suppose, though, someone were to reply in this wise: "Why choose literature as your model? Take, rather, philosophy. With regard to philosophical works, doesn't it seem true that any great work of philosophy is, *ipso facto*, a profound work?"

This may or may not be true of philosophy. But it is manifestly not true of the literary arts; and that is because the literary arts are *arts*. Being arts, they are valued, *qua* art, in ways that philosophy is not valued, *qua* philosophy. Most obviously, they are valued *qua* art, as philosophy is *not* valued, *qua* philosophy, in virtue of their outstanding aesthetic and artistic qualities. That being the case, a literary artwork can achieve greatness without achieving profundity—if it is very high in aesthetic value (say) and without profound subject matter. But it cannot be profound, *qua* art, without being high in aesthetic value, because to be profound, *qua* art, a literary work must be about profound matters, treat them in a way adequate to their profundity, *and* be of very high aesthetic value. That is why we can single out only *some* great literary works as, *qua* literary work, *profound*.

But why choose literature rather than philosophy as the model for musical profundity? The answer is all too obvious. Music, like literature, is a fine art; and, furthermore, we seem to naturally gravitate to the use of "profound" for absolute music that allows us to single out from among the larger class of great musical works those that are *also* profound.

Davies, then, has not, so far as I am concerned, made out a case for absolute music's profundity. He more or less agrees with me that absolute music does not seem able to achieve propositional profundity. And his attempt to make out a case for absolute music's being profound in a non-propositional sense seems to me a failure, because it implies that all great instrumental music is profound music, an implication

[13] See Peter Kivy, *The Possessor and the Possessed: Handel, Mozart, Beethoven, and the Idea of Musical Genius* (New Haven: Yale University Press, 2001).

[14] See R. G. Collingwood, *The Principles of Art* (Oxford: Clarendon Press, 1938), 8–9.

I find highly implausible. (As a matter of fact, Davies's view implies, so far as I can see, that *every* human accomplishment and invention requiring genius or greatness of mind is non-propositionally profound in Davies's sense; and I don't see why one should accept a view that would require the revising of ordinary language to the extent of calling the steam engine, for example, "profound". Yet the steam engine, surely, illustrates, displays forth that very greatness of mind that is displayed forth by both Bobby Fischer's chess game and Beethoven's *Eroica*.)

So where do we go from here? There will be, I am sure, among music lovers of a philosophical bent, further wringing of hands over the "loss" of profundity to absolute music, and further attempts to "restore" it. But what I think would be far more useful than either is resignation and consolation. Absolute music can't be profound. Let's learn to live with that and see it for what it is: not a defect in absolute music but, rather, part of what it *is*, and part of what makes us love it. To that (perhaps impossible) task I would like to devote the final section of this paper.

IV

There was once a kid named Sid whose favorite part of the week was Friday afternoon, after school. It held out the promise of Saturday and Sunday, which were still pristine and unused. Saturday was good: there was still Sunday between Sid and school. But by Saturday morning the glass was *beginning* to be half empty. And although Sunday was OK—no school!—it was, all in all, a rather depressing day. Stores were closed, and Monday was waiting in the wings, like Captain Hook, to cast a pall over Sid's rapidly dissipating freedom. Saturday was good, Sunday OK; but Friday afternoon was the nuts.

While at that stage of his life when Friday afternoon was the favorite part of his week, Sid's favorite color was navy blue. And one day, in a blinding flash of philosophical insight, Sid came to realize that his favorite part of the week could not be his favorite color: Friday afternoons could not be navy blue. Sid's shirt could be navy blue; his pants could be navy blue; even his dirty old pair of socks could be navy blue; but his favorite part of the week could not be his favorite color—could not, indeed, be any color at all.

Sid became profoundly depressed over this; for although Friday afternoons were still his favorites, they did not seem to have quite the charm for him that they once had. Something was missing, or so it seemed.

Sid's parents, realizing they had a problem, a "philosophical" problem, went to the neighborhood philosopher who, providentially, had just read the newly published translation by Miss Anscombe of the *Philosophical Investigations*. (The year of which I write was 1953.) This local guru immediately recalled a passage in the *Investigations* in which the master had tackled the very problem that was poisoning Sid's Friday afternoons. Wittgenstein wrote: "Given the two ideas 'fat' and 'lean', would you rather be inclined to say that Wednesday was fat and Tuesday lean, or the other way round? (I incline to choose the former.)" He added: "Here one might speak of a 'primary' and 'secondary' sense of a word," and provided another example: "If I say 'For me the vowel *e* is yellow' I do not mean: 'yellow' in a metaphorical [but in a secondary] sense,—for I could not express what I want to say in any other way than by means of the idea 'yellow.' "[15]

Sid's parents returned with what they thought would be comforting news for Sid: "Yes, Sid," they said, "Friday afternoons can be navy blue, at least *in a secondary sense*." But Sid was made of sterner stuff; and his distress was by no means palliated by the assurance of the local philosophical practitioner that Friday afternoons could be navy blue, *in a secondary sense*. For the secondary sense gave him nothing that true blue gave him. It was the shadow, not the reality. In the ways that really counted, Friday afternoons remained navy-blueless.

Now Sid, as should be perfectly clear, was involved in a classic case of the category mistake. And I am not for a moment suggesting that it is a category mistake to call a piece of absolute music profound, as it would be to call a Friday afternoon navy blue. Rather, one is inclined to say that profundity is a special case of "aboutness", and, taking Arthur Danto's line on aboutness, say further that it is at least not inappropriate to ask of a given work of absolute music, "Is it profound?", even though (as I believe) the answer will always be "No".[16]

Nevertheless, although Sid was involved in a category mistake in his quest for navy blue Friday afternoons, and the seekers after musical profundity are not, there is something to be learned from the parable

[15] Ludwig Wittgenstein, *Philosophical Investigations*, trans. G. E. M. Anscombe (New York: Macmillan, 1953), 216[e].

[16] See Arthur Danto, *The Transfiguration of the Commonplace: A Philosophy of Art* (Cambridge, Mass.: Harvard University Press, 1981), 82.

of Sid. Sid has let a genuine philosophical discovery, so to speak, cause him to lose his bearings. He has gone from the correct conclusion that Friday afternoons cannot be navy blue to the incorrect conclusion that he has discovered a lack in Friday afternoons: a defect, a gap that must be filled on pain of Friday afternoons losing something of their past luster and delight.

So too with the philosophical discovery—and that is what I think it amounts to—that absolute music can't be profound; or, at least, that there is serious doubt about whether it can be. It seems to make many music lovers of a philosophical bent feel that they have discovered a lack in absolute music that must be filled on pain of absolute music losing something of its past luster and delight. If I had been Sid's parents, though, I would not have gone to the local philosopher in search of ersatz, "secondary sense" ways in which Fridays can be navy blue, to console him for his "loss". Rather, I would have reminded him of what it was he loved about Friday afternoons in the first place, before he discovered that they could not be his favorite color, and that *that* is there still. I would have reminded him, as well, that he never felt any lack in his enjoyment of Friday afternoons *before* he became obsessed with their lack of navy-blueness.

There is an old adage to the effect that you should never tell a child not to stick beans up his nose, the reason obviously being that he may never have had the idea in the first place, but now not only does have the idea but will do it just out of spite. I believe that in chapter 10 of *Music Alone* I committed a similar mistake, and caused grief to a whole lot of philosophically inclined music lovers, who never would have had the idea in the first place that music *could* be profound, until I suggested that it *couldn't* be. Like a huckster creating an artificial "need" for a useless product, I think I somehow poisoned some people's enjoyment of absolute music by making them feel an artificial "lack" in it that not only *isn't* there, but *can't* be there. And if it is not the categorial "can't" of navy blue Fridays, it seems to me to approach it in strength. What absolute music can't be, *it can't be*; and there is something obstinate and deeply irrational about bemoaning and deploring an *almost* metaphysical truth.

Indeed, as I have argued on other occasions, it is part of the wonder of absolute music that it is sound without meaning, *a fortiori*, sound without *profound* meaning, which has the power to move us profoundly, and to engage our intellectual and perceptual faculties in the most arresting and deeply satisfying ways. It is sufficient unto itself.

For profundity we go elsewhere, not because absolute music is not up to the task, but because it was meant for other no less important things.

Let me just add that in rejecting Davies's attempt to rescue profundity for absolute music, I by no means reject his characterization of it as revealing the greatness of the kind of mind that can produce such awe-inspiring creations as the *Eroica* Symphony. I believe I was trying to capture the very same experience as Davies was when I wrote in my book, *The Possessor and the Possessed*: "When we experience great works of art, we find ourselves unable to conceive how (by what means) such works could have been brought into being, and this engenders in us a sense of wonder, a sense of miracle that is a necessary part of our aesthetic experience."[17] We worship the same object. We disagree about the name. But I don't think it is a trivial disagreement. Everything is what it is, and not another thing. And the thing in question is not musical profundity. In my view absolute music, at its greatest, can be profoundly moving and profoundly arresting; but not in spite of lacking profundity; rather, in part, *because of it.*

[17] Kivy, *Possessor and the Possessed*, 249.

11

From Ideology to Music: Leonard Meyer's Theory of Style Change

Leonard Meyer's splendid new book, *Style and Music: Theory, History, and Ideology* provides a rich feast indeed of food for musical thought, and (inevitably) for musical controversy.[1] Theorists will, of course, be drawn to the author's nuts-and-bolts functional analysis of the various musical passages he discusses in making his argument; and music historians, doubtless, will find much to stimulate them, as well as to argue about, in his historical characterization of the Classical and Romantic periods in music, and of their relevant social, political, and philosophical backgrounds. But philosophers of art like myself will surely fasten upon Meyer's bold attempt to connect the purely musical parameters of syntax and structure to the reigning ideologies with which they coexist. Nor, I think, will it be out of place to concentrate on this attempt in the present review essay; for it is the major theme and argument of Meyer's book.

I call the attempt to connect music and ideology a "bold" attempt because, and I think Meyer would agree, this is one of the most difficult and contentious things to make out in the "philosophy of music": in my view, one of the two "master problems" of the discipline, the other, to which it is obviously related, being the problem of making out exactly what the nature is, in the first place, of the aesthetic satisfaction we take in absolute music, given that such music seems, at least on the surface, bereft of semantic or representational content, and yet has come to occupy a place in the pantheon no less prominent than that accorded the semantic and representational arts.

It may sound like a platitude, but the central thesis of Meyer's book, as I see it, is that *musical composition is a process of choice making.*

[1] Leonard Meyer, *Style and Music: Theory, History, and Ideology* (Philadelphia: University of Pennsylvania Press, 1989). Page references to Meyer's book will appear in the text in parentheses.

Such compositional choice making is of (at least) two distinctive kinds: choice among the alternatives that a given style allows, and choices determinative of styles themselves—that is to say, choices that, cumulatively, change a style, as, to take the style change most important to Meyer's book, the compositional choices that eventually traversed the passage from Classic to Romantic.

Composing within a style is a matter of choosing available possibilities, hedged in by a set of constraints that make the given style identifiable as just that style. "The constraints of style are *learned* by composers and performers, critics and listeners." But such *learning* is seldom the result of self-conscious instruction; it "is largely the result of experience in performing and listening rather than of explicit formal instruction in music theory, history, or composition. In other words, knowledge of style is usually 'tacit': that is, a matter of habits properly acquired (internalized) and appropriately brought into play" (p. 10).

Working within a style is, furthermore, a matter of devising what Meyer calls *strategies*. "Strategies are compositional choices made within the possibilities established by the rules of the style. For any specific style there is a finite number of rules, but there is an indefinite number of possible strategies for realizing or instantiating such rules" (p. 20). The spelling out of these strategies, in terms of the possibilities open to the composer, the constraints laid upon him or her by style, and the reasons for consequent compositional choices made, is the goal of music theory and style analysis. Specifically, style analysis asks, "*Why* do the traits described 'go together?' To explain this, it is necessary to relate the strategies employed both to one another and to the rules of the style, including the particular ways in which the several parameters interact." And, "Because such relational sets are understood as being synchronic, style analysis need not consider parameters external to music—ideology, political and social circumstances, and so on" (p. 45). In a word, style analysis is completely self-contained, completely within the purely musical parameters themselves, as, indeed, conventional, "formalistic" wisdom would have it. So far, then, there need be no appeal to anything beyond the "game" of music itself.

But what of style changes themselves, and the compositional choices involved in effectuating them? Here matters are very different. Analysis within a style may be an autonomous discipline. "But the history of style", Meyer writes, "cannot, in my view, be explained without reference to aspects of culture external to music" (p. 45). Why should this be the case?

To answer this question, we must first observe that "the history of style" is, of course, the history of *style change*. For if style did not change, it would not have a history at all. (What would there be for the history to be *about*?) Second, we must ask ourselves why a perfectly obvious, and often cited, "explanation" of style change, which does not require the controversial appeal to extra-musical causes, will not wash. The explanation of which I speak is simply appeal to the desire—the innate desire?—for novelty. And it will not wash, because in explaining *everything*, it in effect explains nothing. Any change, one would think, can be explained as the satisfaction of the desire for novelty. But since there are innumerable ways in which a musical style may change—innumerable directions in which innovation may go—the simple desire for novelty tells us nothing about why a musical style changed *in the particular ways that it did*. Classical style could have evolved in countless ways, and the desire for novelty could "explain" all of them. But the question is, Why did it evolve into the style we call "Romanticism" rather than a hundred other possible styles? This the desire for novelty or innovation cannot explain. And, on Meyer's view, we must reach for factors external to the "game" of the purely musical parameters for such an explanation: in a word, to "ideology".

It is Meyer's working hypothesis that "a musical style changes precisely because some of its constraints *do not reflect* (are not congruent with) some of the dominant parameters of the culture in which it exists" (p. 118). I am going to call this Meyer's *global* hypothesis of style change, and contrast it with two less ambitious hypotheses: the *limited* hypothesis that *some* musical styles have changed precisely because some of their constraints did not reflect (were not congruent with) some of the dominant parameters of the cultures in which they existed; and the *particular* hypothesis that Classical musical style evolved into Romantic style because some of its constraints did not reflect (were not congruent with) some of the dominant parameters of the culture in which it existed. Meyer's major "argument" for the global hypothesis is a detailed attempt to establish the particular hypothesis. My own suspicion—something beyond a gut reaction, but certainly short of a firm belief—is that the global hypothesis is false, the limited hypothesis at least a possibility, and the specific hypothesis quite plausibly defended by Meyer, although there seems to me to be a gap in the argument in some places that needs filling in. My reasons for all of this will emerge as the discussion proceeds.

How does ideology "explain" style change? In general, the explanation goes this way. If ideology and musical style get out of phase—that is to say, if prevailing musical style ceases to "reflect" prevailing cultural ideology—then the prevailing ideology, presumably shared by the composer, will influence him or her to make such compositional choices as counter the prevailing stylistic restraints or tendencies in a way to bring style and ideology back into phase and make the former again "reflect" the latter: thus old style gives way to new, under the pressure of changing ideology.

Of course, it is one thing to enunciate such a hypothesis, quite another to convince anyone of it. For it is just here that the skeptical eyebrow will be raised. How can ideologies, of all things, be "reflected" in musical notes—in the pure parameters of musical structure and syntax? Meyer is well aware of how crucial the question is. As he puts it, "if economic, political or other [external] circumstances are to influence the history of musical style, they must be translated in such a way that they can affect the choices made by composers" (p. 145). So a large portion of his book is devoted to making such "translations," showing how, in musical detail, ideology—for the most part, Romantic ideology—was translated into real, nuts-and-bolts compositional choices.

These nuts-and-bolts "translations" are extensive, and rich in analytic detail. And one cannot possibly give any but the most sketchy idea of Meyer's piling up of detailed examples in the abbreviated format that is all a review allows. I shall have to make do here with just a small sampling.

The overarching ideological principle of the Romantic movement, according to Meyer, is *egalitarianism*. "At its core", he writes, "was an unequivocal and uncompromising repudiation of a social order based on arbitrary, inherited class distinctions. This rejection was not confined to the arts or philosophy; rather it permeated every corner of culture and all levels of society. It was, and is, Romanticism with a capital *R*" (p. 164).

But if, as Meyer believes, "A crucial question for the history of music is how ideological values are transformed into musical constraints and specific compositional choices" (p. 218), then, clearly, the crucial question at hand is how the ideological "repudiation of a social order based on arbitrary, inherited class distinctions" can be "transformed into musical constraints and specific compositional choices". What, in other words, is the real musical payoff, in the coinage of the purely musical parameters, of a basically political ideology?

According to Meyer, as I read him, the link between ideology and the purely musical parameters, in the Romantic era, is *disdain for the established conventions*. In the overarching political and philosophical ideology, it is disdain for the unjust establishment of social classes and conventions, the most obnoxious symbol of which being the inherited nobility. In musical practice this is reflected in the fact, as Meyer puts it, that: "Ideologically, whatever seemed conventional (familiar cadential gestures, commonplace melodic schemata, stock accompaniment figures, and so on) was anathema to Romantic composers" (p. 219).

In *Style and Music* Meyer considers two ways of what he calls "making the claims of [Romantic] ideology compatible with the inescapable conventions of tonal syntax". The first strategy was to use syntactical constraints and conventions, but to "disguise" them. "The second ... involved the use of means less definitely dependent upon constraints and ones less patently conventional" (p. 222). In other words, Romantic composers reflected the ideological rejection of convention in the nineteenth century, not merely by rejecting musical convention in kind but (more cleverly) by using it in camouflage.

The camouflage was of two kinds: what Meyer calls "disguise through emergence" and "disguise through divergence". An example of the former will have to suffice.

The last cadence of Debussy's *Prelude to the Afternoon of a Faun* is "Not surprisingly, the most decisive closure ... " in the piece. "Closure is articulated by an ostensibly normal ii–V^7–I progression that accompanies two coordinate melodic closing gestures" (p. 223). The first cadential gesture is compared to another "instance of such a gesture, from the second movement of Mozart's String Quintet in Eb Major (K. 614) ... ". What distinguishes them is that Debussy's is "disguised" by its organic connection with what goes before, whereas Mozart's is just an out-front conventional tag, tantamount to *finis* at the end of a film. "For Mozart's cadential gesture, unlike Debussy's, does not grow out of earlier events. Indeed, nothing resembling it occurs earlier in the movement; nor does it complete a process begun before. The gesture signifying closure is not essentially part of the intra-opus style of this movement, but rather part of the dialect of Classic music. As such, it is unequivocally and unashamedly conventional." But in Debussy's cadence: "Because the gesture grows out of the melodic, orchestral, and textual process that precedes it, its identity and integrity are masked. And so, as a result, is its conventionality" (p. 224).

Going from the disguise of conventional syntax to its outright rejection, Meyer opines that "The gradual weakening of syntactic relationships, coupled with a correlative turning toward a more natural compositional means, was perhaps the single most important trend in the history of nineteenth-century music" (p. 272). Of this weakening, and even rejection, Meyer has many carefully worked-out examples, each of which not only supports his thesis but invariably casts new light on the music he discusses. Of particular importance in this regard is a whole class of non-syntactic features of music which Meyer calls "secondary parameters". I shall confine my remarks to these.

Of the distinction between primary and secondary parameters, Meyer writes:

The primary parameters of tonal music—melody, harmony, and rhythm—are syntactic. That is, they establish explicit functional relationships. ... Secondary parameters, on the other hand [e.g. "louder/softer, faster/slower, thicker/thinner, higher/lower"], are statistical in the sense that the relationships to which they give rise are typically ones of degree that can be measured or counted. ... [T]he syntax of tonal music, like other kinds of syntax, is rule governed, learned, and conventional. The secondary, stastical parameters, on the other hand, seem able to shape experience with minimal dependence on learned rules and conventions. (p. 209)

Thus, a musical structure based on secondary, rather than primary, parameters would seem to "reflect" more appropriately the Romantic idiology, with its negative attitude towards social stratification and "convention", than would a musical structure based on primary ones. And so it would be altogether expected, on Meyer's view, that, as he maintains, "Complementing the trend toward syntactically weakened harmonic and tonal relationships [in the Romantic era] was an increase in the relative importance of secondary parameters in the shaping of musical process and the articulation of musical form" (p. 303).

At this juncture, with Meyer's general argument well in tow, we can step back and take a critical look at it. I have two major points to make: the first concerning what I have called the *particular* hypothesis, the second concerning what I have called the *limited* and *global* hypotheses.

The particular hypothesis, it will be recalled, is that the parameters characteristic of Romantic musical style can be explained by appeal to the regnant ideology of the times. The "appeal" is by way of the concept of *choice*. The argument is that composers have been influenced by their beliefs in this ideology to choose those musical parameters that "reflect", that are in accord with, the ideology. And because the Classical parameters ceased to be seen by composers as reflecting—as being in accord with—the Romantic ideology, they chose other strategies that were so seen.

Now I said at the outset of this essay that the central thesis of Meyer's book, platitudinous though it may sound, is the thesis: *musical composition is a process of choice making.* We are now about to see how crucial, and how *un*platitudinous this thesis really turns out to be.

I think that if we want to *explain* why someone is behaving, or has behaved, in a certain way by saying that he or she *chose* to do it, we must fulfill certain necessary conditions for such an explanation. First, I shall say that we must be able to "rationally reconstruct" a plausible practical argument leading from thought to choice. So, for example, if I explain why Rudolph is now waddling around on the floor like a duck, going "Quack! Quack!", by saying that he *chose* to do so, and is not (say) under post-hypnotic suggestion, or simply "a nut case", I must make good my claim by reconstructing a rational argument from what Rudolph believes and wants to a "practical" conclusion to the effect that waddling around on the floor and going "Quack! Quack!" is, under the circumstances, the (or a) rational thing for Rudolph to be doing. My explanation is: he wanted to entertain his 5-year-old niece, who was crying; so, since he knew she liked ducks, and had left her rubber ducky at home, he decided on the present (undignified) strategy.

One thing important to notice is that a necessary condition for making the rational reconstruction plausible is that the chooser be just the sort of person for whom the particular reconstruction, whatever it might be, would seem appropriate. Thus if, for example, we knew that Sarah was an extremely selfish person, a rational reconstruction of the deliberations leading to her choice to give a million dollars to charity involving benevolent motives might be rejected in favor of one involving considerations of tax advantage, on the grounds that Sarah is not the sort of person whose deliberations would be likely to involve benevolent motives at all.

Of course, in giving a rational reconstruction of a practical argument leading to choice, we need not necessarily be suggesting that, in the particular instance, the chooser actually went through the steps laid out. Alice *chooses* to run to her right, rather than her left, in order to answer Jim's overhead smash, because she knows that if she does so, she will have a fifty–fifty chance of returning the ball, whereas if she stays in center court, and waits to see whether Jim hits to the right or the left, it will be too late to return the ball at all, no matter which side Jim hits to.

But, clearly, there is no time for Alice to go through this "argument" in the heat of the moment. Rather, as we say, she has "internalized" this strategy, made it "second nature", so that she can act, in the event, instantly, without thinking at all. Nevertheless, *and this is crucial*, if Alice *never* went through the reasoning process, or one like it, that the rational reconstruction lays out, *then* I think we would be loath to call her behavior a matter of *choice*. Presumably, there was a time when Alice was taught to go randomly to her left or her right, and not get caught in center court, because doing that would raise her chances of returning a smash from zero to fifty–fifty. She understood that this was the rational thing to do, and *chose* to internalize that mode of behavior. On the basis of her once having made this conscious choice, we say now that each time she behaves in this way, she *chooses* to do so, for just the reasons cited. However, had she never entertained any practical argument leading to this mode of behavior as its conclusion, had she been born doing this, then, clearly, we would not explain her behavior as the result of choice, but in some other way: "instinct", or whatever.

Forearmed with these commonsensical preliminaries, let us now ask ourselves if Meyer has indeed made it appear plausible to explain the musical parameters of Romanticism as the result of compositional *choice* predicated upon Romantic political and philosophical ideology. I have purposely chosen the examples I have of this compositional choice, not only to illustrate the nuts and bolts of Meyer's argument, but to now suggest that there is a gap in the argument, which one of them exhibits, but the other does not.

Let us take the successful example first. Meyer's explanation, you will recall, for the increasing tendency in the nineteenth century to choose secondary rather than primary parameters as structural features was that they more accurately "reflected" the ideological rejection of conventions and class distinctions, and the endorsement of egalitarianism. For the primary parameters are rule- and convention-based, while the secondary ones "seem able to shape experience with minimal dependence on learned rules and conventions".

Now, if we are to find the choice explanation plausible, I have argued, we must be able to give a rational reconstruction of a practical argument that leads from ideological belief to compositional choice. And we must be able plausibly to imagine the composer as the kind of person who would be likely to have gone through, at one time or another, such a reasoning process. The second condition will become crucially relevant when I come to consider the limited and global hypotheses. But for now

I will put it aside, assuming that it is met in the present instance (which I happen to believe is true), and concentrate on the first. Can we make a rational reconstruction of a practical argument that leads from belief in the Romantic ideology to the compositional choice of secondary over primary parameters? I think the answer is "Yes", and here is how I think it goes, as (I believe) implicitly implied in what Meyer says. Romantic political and philosophical ideology was against class and convention, and basically egalitarian. The Romantic composers shared this ideology, wished to write music that "reflected" their ideological convictions, and tried to do so. So they chose, among other things, to reject the primary, rule- and convention-governed parameters, in favor of the secondary ones. But what made this a *rational* choice, given their ideological commitment?

Well, to put it bluntly, if you are ideologically an egalitarian, then it is reasonable to assume that you endorse music for the "masses", not music for the elite. But the "masses" will not have the musical education and experience of the elite, so, if the music you write is to be accessible to them (more exactly, in Meyer's terminology, the audience of "elite egalitarians"), it must be music that can be enjoyed without any considerable learning or experience. The favoring of secondary over primary parameters now follows as a natural egalitarian strategy. For, as Meyer points out, the primary parameters, being syntactical, which is to say convention- and rule-governed, must be learned, and can only be appreciated by an elite, musically sophisticated audience, whereas the secondary parameters, being more "natural", do not depend for their appreciation upon learned rules and conventions. Thus, given their egalitarian sentiments, the choice of secondary over primary parameters on the part of Romantic composers seems an entirely rational one.

But can the same be said for the choice of "convention disguised"? Here I have problems.

Can we derive from Meyer's text a rational reconstruction of a practical argument that goes from Romantic ideology to the use of such disguised conventions as are illustrated by the close of Debussy's *Prelude to the Afternoon of a Faun*? If we cannot, then with regard to these numerous, and important, parameters of Romantic musical style, of which the example from Debussy is of course but one representative instance, the explanation Meyer gives us, of the change from Classical to Romantic style, is incomplete, and in need of fleshing out. I do not say, I hasten to add, that such a fleshing out is impossible. I certainly have no argument to that effect. All I am going to suggest is that with regard to the Romantic compositional strategy of disguised conventions, as Meyer describes it, there is a crucial missing step in the practical argument from ideology to compositional choice, which it may or may not be possible to provide, and without which the rational reconstruction necessary for a plausible choice-based explanation is impossible.

The problem is this. I see no rational connection between embracing Romantic ideology—in particular, the rejection of social rules and conventions—and choosing, as a compositional strategy, to use and to disguise rule- and convention-driven musical parameters. Indeed, if one pursues the line of argument just outlined to explain the choice of secondary over primary parameters, the choice of disguised primary parameters seems positively to contradict Romantic ideology. For if the secondary parameters are "egalitarian", *disguised* primary parameters are even more elitist than undisguised ones, since, one would think, they require even more musical sophistication to appreciate. Whatever musical learning and experience an undisguised musical convention may require for its perception, a masked one cannot require less; and, common sense suggests, it must require something more, for the result of camouflage is, obviously, to make things more, rather than less, difficult to make out. It would be rational for an adherent of Romantic egalitarianism to choose as few conventional formulae as possible. But to disguise the ones chosen would not soften the blow—it would, on the contrary, rub salt in the wound.

What has gone wrong here? The culprits seem to be such vague ways of expressing the relationship between musical parameters and ideologies as "reflect" and "compatible" and the like. *Why* should it be a rational strategy for a composer to choose parameters that "reflect" or are "compatible" with his or her political and philosophical ideology? Well, that all depends upon what the cash value of "reflect" or "compatible" is. For under some interpretations of these terms, it would not be a rational, which is to say plausible, understandable strategy at all, and hence the rational reconstruction of a practical argument from ideology to compositional choice could not go through, leaving a gap in the explanation. To illustrate what I am getting at, let me suggest two possible interpretations of "reflect" that do make for rational strategies, although, in the event, neither seems an acceptable one for disguised conventions.

We might say that the musical parameters reflect an ideology just when there is a "practical" connection between the parameters and the ideology: when the ideology implies some musical strategy for effectuating an end that the ideology endorses or recommends. The choice of secondary over primary parameters, because it makes music more accessible to the masses, is just such an example of practical "reflection" as, in a later day, and reflecting a similar ideology, was Hanns Eisler's "proletarian" musical style. But, as we have seen, that particular mode of reflection will not work for the strategy of disguised conventions. Indeed, from the point of view of accessibility considerations, it would seem that the strategy of disguising conventions reflects, on the contrary, the opposite, elitist ideology, and indeed reflects it even more strongly than the Classical employment of conventions "out front".

There is, however, another, obvious way of construing "reflection", staring us in the face, that might indeed provide a very plausible "practical" connection between Romantic ideology and the disguising of conventions. Why do we not say that the disguised conventions present us with aesthetic "symbols" or "representations" of the ideological rejection of class distinctions, and the ideological endorsement of natural Man? What better way, after all, of symbolizing these things in music than by weaving a musical fabric that, although held together by convention-driven parameters, gives the *appearance* of being purely natural and conventionless, because those parameters have been artfully hidden. And to undertake the aesthetic symbolization or representation of the ideology, since it can be seen, at least if certain other conditions obtain, as a rational strategy aimed at promulgating what is symbolized or represented, the reconstruction of a practical argument from ideology to compositional choice is accomplished, and the explanation complete.

But alas, the step to symbolization or representation, where pure instrumental music is concerned, is a dangerous one that no music theorist of Meyer's sophistication is likely to take very cheerfully. Indeed, I would venture to guess that one of Meyer's reasons for choosing such vague and noncommittal words as "reflect" and "conform" is just to avoid making a commitment to anything so dangerous and problematic as either symbolization or representation, where "pure" instrumental music is concerned. For the problems of making such claims stick are legion. At the very least, one must prove that the composers *intended* to symbolize or represent, even if they did not succeed, to make the practical argument from ideology to compositional choice complete. And, so far as I can see, Meyer provides no such proof. So we are again at a loss for a rational connection between espousing the Romantic ideology and making use, in musical composition, of disguised conventions.

Without such a connection, the explanation of how these parameters became prevalent, based on ideology and choice, remains importantly incomplete, although, as I have said before, perhaps not necessarily so.

At this point, I imagine, the lure of the "unconscious" will strongly beckon. One will be tempted to claim that, although there seems to be no plausible reason why an adherent to the Romantic ideology should *consciously choose* disguised conventions as a compositional strategy, there is an unconscious desire, or compulsion perhaps, impelling one to use them, driven by some unconscious set of "reasons" and "motives" that connect the two. Might the disguising of the musical conventions be the expression of guilt feelings due to a mistaken (and unconscious) belief that to use musical conventions is to betray the ideological directive against social conventions? We could then liken Debussy's disguising of the conventional close in *Prelude to the Afternoon of a Faun* to the compulsive washing of hands thirty times a day by a gentleman who unconsciously believes that he is responsible for the death of his mother in childbirth and is driven to this useless, even damaging behavior by the again unconscious and mistaken belief that the washing of hands is the cleansing of sin. (You don't have to take my example seriously to get my point.)

But such a path, the path of the unconscious, is not open to Meyer. For it is the very heart and soul of his book, as I understand it, to divert us from such causal explanations, based on the paradigms of natural science, to explanation based on the assumption, which I share, that "human behavior is the result of intelligent and purposeful—though not necessarily deliberate, fully-informed, or even judicious—choice" (p. 76). An individual choice may indeed not be "deliberate", and in that perfectly innocent and non-technical sense be "unconscious", as is Alice's choice of instantly running to the right rather than the left, to maximize her chance of returning Jim's smash. But that is not "unconscious causation" in the Freudian, or any other psychologically deterministic, sense. And in order for Alice's response to be correctly described as "choice", there must have been some point in her past, as we have seen, before such responses were internalized, at which Alice's choice was "deliberate".

Nor, I should point out as a caveat, can one translate this unconscious practical argument into a conscious one, to evade the vagaries of the unconscious and solve the present problem, because it will not, if a consciously entertained train of thought, pass muster as a "rational" one, for the crucial premise that explains the *disguising* of the conventions cannot be thought plausibly to be held consciously, which is to say reflectively, by a rational, indeed a sane, person. Who could rationally, consciously, reflectively believe that guilt felt over breaking a rule can be expiated by hiding the breach from prying eyes (in this case, ears)? As Meyer points out, the composer's choice need not be either "fully-informed, or even judicious" for his argument to go through. But it must be at least within the bounds of what we can plausibly believe a rational and sane human being might hold in the relevant time and place; and to believe consciously what I have just laid out as a set of unconscious beliefs is not within those bounds.

The perception that there is some kind of "rightness of fit", some kind, therefore, of rational connection between believing in the Romantic rejection of social conventions and choosing the compositional strategy of convention disguised, remains, I admit, a beguiling one. But we should not be beguiled too soon. We are owed here, as in any other explanation of human behavior in terms of choice, the spelling out of a plausible, rational scenario that makes it plain to us why a person who believes p should be expected to choose q. I do not think that, either explicitly or implicitly, Meyer has given us such a scenario to connect belief in the Romantic ideology with the compositional choice of disguised conventions. To that extent, his explanation of how Romantic ideology might "explain" Romantic compositional practice is incomplete, though not, perhaps, fatally flawed, if completion is possible.

This brings me to my second problematic. How successful has Meyer been in establishing either the *particular*, the *limited*, or the *global* hypothesis?

The particular hypothesis, that Romantic ideology can, through the concept of rational choice, explain the evolution from Classical to Romantic musical style, fails to be supported whenever there is a gap in the rational reconstruction of a practical argument from belief in ideology to choice of musical strategy, as there is, so I have argued, in the case of convention disguised. But, contrariwise, whenever that reconstruction is complete, as it appears to be in the argument from ideology to choice of secondary parameters over primary ones, the particular hypothesis is confirmed. In this particular regard, do Meyer's successes outweigh the failures? My own estimate is that more, rather than less, of the time, some kind of plausible reconstruction can be made. So this part of Meyer's argument in support of the particular hypothesis appears to me to merit a cautiously favorable judgment.

But the rational reconstruction is not, it will be recalled, the only necessary condition for a successful explanation connecting ideology to musical parameters by way of choice. Another is that the choosers be the kinds of people whom we can reasonably assume would go through the kinds of deliberation from ideology to musical choice that Meyer describes. How does the explanation fare against that requirement?

Very well, one would think, given how articulate, and how prone to aesthetic theorizing on the grand scale, the Romantic composers were. As Meyer quite rightly observes, "artists as well as aestheticians believed in and fostered the ideology of Romanticism" (p. 180). And composers were not laggards in this regard, not by any means mere followers, but in the forefront of Romantic philosophizing, at the cutting edge. Berlioz, Schumann, and Wagner, to name merely the most prominent of the musical "thinkers", were not content to receive the Romantic ideology as a gift from the philosophers, but helped in its forging, through their considerable theoretical writings and musical criticism. Thus the Romantic composer represents just that type of artist–thinker whom one can well imagine going through the kind of cerebration from ideology to compositional choice that Meyer's account seems to require. Here, without a doubt, Meyer holds a winning hand.

But there's the rub. For just that very special character of the Romantic composer, and his penchant for theorizing and speculation that make him so plausible a subject for Meyer's account of the relation of ideology to compositional choice in the nineteenth century, make one skeptical of finding his like in all musico-historical periods, or perhaps even in any except the one in which the prototype flourished. Given what we know about society, musical culture, and the intellectual climate in the late seventeenth and early eighteenth centuries, for instance, or in the fifteenth, can we plausibly picture to ourselves a J. S. Bach or a Johannes Ockeghem making rational compositional choices regarding the pure musical parameters, based on serious consideration of philosophical, political, or other such overarching ideologies? Indeed, in the case of Ockeghem, or any other composer who did not work in a period in which pure instrumental forms were an important compositional option, it seems problematic whether Meyer's explanation of style change can be applied at all, since, as Meyer himself points out, in explaining why, for the most part, he concentrates on instrumental music in his discussion of the nineteenth century, "the connection between compositional restraints and ideological ones can be more easily traced when it is not complicated by the further, not necessarily congruent, constraints of text setting and theatrical performance" (p. 219). Furthermore—and perhaps this is just another way, really, of making the same point—no one thinks it difficult to show how a composer of any period responds in musical parameters to the meaning of a text that he or she is setting. And no one thinks it difficult to show how the meaning of a text "reflects" the regnant ideology of its time, since it has the cognitive resources to fully express such an ideology. So that where a text intervenes between an ideology and the purely musical parameters, we are not accomplishing the really hard and controversial trick of showing how the purely musical parameters respond *directly* to ideological considerations, being, as they are, bereft of representational or semantic possibilities.

But putting this added complication of text intervention aside, can we plausibly picture composers other than those of the Romantic era, who lived, after all, in an intellectual climate of just the right kind to nourish and nurture the "speculative" artist, going through the ideological deliberation necessary to make Meyer's account really work? This is not, I hasten to add, merely an idle, groundless question, aimed at raising a little skeptical dust. For there is at least some historical evidence to support the notion that before the late eighteenth century, just the time when Meyer begins in earnest to apply his explanation of style change through ideology and choice, the intellectual climate would not have been such as either to produce or to encourage the necessary speculative composers, whereas the late eighteenth century is just when one would expect such composers to appear. I do not say the evidence is conclusive; but it is highly suggestive.

What I have in mind here is the seminal two-part article by Paul O. Kristeller in which he argued convincingly that what he called "The Modern System of the Arts" was a product of Enlightenment thought.[2] The cash value, of Kristeller's discovery, for present purposes, is that before the eighteenth century music was not considered a "fine art" at all, and composers, in consequence, were not considered, *and did not consider themselves* "artists". Of course this does not imply that, before the eighteenth century, music was not an art or composers not artists. But it does imply, I want to urge, that because composers were considered artists neither by others nor by themselves, they would not have had the training or the inclination, the encouragement or the precedent, to

---

[2] See Paul O. Kristeller, "The Modern System of the Arts (I)", *Journal of the History of Ideas*, 12 (1951); *idem*, "The Modern System of the Arts (II)", *Journal of the History of Ideas*, 13 (1952).

make them think about ideological questions at all, let alone think them relevant to their compositional choices of the purely musical parameters. If you think of yourself as in the social and intellectual class of jewelers and furniture-makers—which is to say, craftsmen—rather than in that of poets, you are hardly the sort of person likely to speculate in the grand manner, like a Berlioz or a Wagner, or even in the clumsy, somewhat illiterate, but nonetheless serious and sincere, manner of a Beethoven. Indeed, you are not likely to "speculate" at all. Plumbers think about pipes, not principles.

Thus, it was a profound social and intellectual change, during the eighteenth century, that made the "speculative" composer possible. That, I argue, is why it seems unlikely that a composer living before this revolution took place, would have the kind of relation to ideology necessary for Meyer's account to go through (allowing always, of course, for exceptions and historical anomalies). And that is why, in consequence, it also seems unlikely to me that the global hypothesis could be true, or the limited hypothesis be anything but *very limited.*

However, and this brings me to my conclusion, I do not think that the argument I have advanced above is in any way conclusive, but merely suggestive. What we must do, if we are to verify or refute either the global or the limited hypothesis, is to dig into the historical and musical materials, the way Meyer has done so splendidly for the Romantics, and see what we come up with. Indeed, it is one of the many virtues of Meyer's challenging book, and one of its most valuable accomplishments, that it leaves musicologists and analysts with a research program to pursue for many years to come. And I cannot express this aspect of Meyer's study more cogently or incitefully than Meyer has himself. Of his conclusions, Meyer writes:

They are hypotheses. Some may be downright wrong, others will require refinement. All need to be tested through applications to genres and repertoires not considered here. It is a program of work to be done, of ideas and hypotheses to be evaluated and perhaps rejected, explored and perhaps extended. (p. 352)

Say "Amen" to that.

12

Sibley's Last Paper

The same dream came to me sometimes in one form, and sometimes in another, but always saying the same or almost the same words: "Cultivate and make music," said the dream.

Socrates (according to Plato (according to Jowett))

It is no exaggeration to assert that Frank Sibley's celebrated paper of 1959, "Aesthetic Concepts," defined my early work in the philosophy of art between 1966, the year I received my doctorate, and 1973, the year I published my first book, *Speaking of Art*, which was an extended critique of Sibley's position. After my Sibley years, my interests turned to what I thought was a neglected topic in the philosophy of art: namely, musical aesthetics.

Unfortunately, it was not until 1989 that I finally met the man whose work had inspired my first project in analytic philosophy. The occasion was an invitation, while on sabbatical leave in the United Kingdom, to give a talk at Lancaster University. And although what almost immediately became a fast friendship, was cut short by Frank's tragic death, it is a friendship I will always treasure.

On my first visit to Frank's home, I discovered, both in conversation and from the array of recordings that lined his walls, that Frank shared my love of music. So it came as no surprise to me that, on my last visit to Lancaster, he gave me a reprint of a paper of his called "Making Music Our Own", which had just appeared in a volume of philosophical essays on music edited by Michael Krausz. It is this essay, Sibley's last published work, that I want to talk about today.

I have chosen to discuss Frank Sibley's last paper for two reasons, not unrelated. Naturally, when one thinks of Frank, one thinks of "Aesthetic Concepts", the work of his that most profoundly affected the practice of philosophy. But being immersed myself, now, in very different projects, the task of thinking myself back into a problem that I had not thought about for twenty years, seemed to me impossible. And as I can anticipate that there will be many hands here to do this work, I thought it appropriate to turn mine to something else.

That that something else should be *music* is, of course, altogether appropriate. For it was Sibley's last project, and one of the projects that now occupies *me*. Of course, the central concern at this commemorative meeting is likely to be (and rightly so) "Aesthetic Concepts", although I hope Frank's important contribution to the philosophy of perception will not be overlooked even if our topic is, as it should be, aesthetics. But my task here, given what Frank's last paper concerned, and what has been my central concern for many years, seems absolutely predestined to be a discussion of Frank Sibley's last thoughts on music, which, as it has unfortunately turned out, were the last thoughts he made public.

My talk will quite naturally fall into two parts. In the first I will present Frank's position, as I construe it, in his last paper, "Making Music Our Own". In the second part I will offer some critical comments on what I take to be three of his main conclusions. That I make *critical* comments hardly requires excuse. The last thing Frank would have wanted would have been that in a meeting like this one his work should be piously commemorated and then let alone. Like all of us here, he wanted to contribute to the ongoing debate that is philosophy; and it is in light of that, the sincerest and best compliment any of us can pay Frank Sibley, his life, his work, to vigorously engage him in that debate, even though to our great misfortune, he cannot be here to gently but firmly correct our mistakes.

I

Sibley's last paper begins, very much like his first. In "Making Music Our Own" a distinction is drawn between two different kinds of terms or descriptions that we might employ to characterize works of art. In "Aesthetic Concepts", as all of you know, that distinction is between what Sibley called "aesthetic" and "non-aesthetic" terms or expressions, the former requiring for their correct employment "the exercise of taste, perceptiveness, or sensitivity, of aesthetic discrimination or appreciation …", the latter not.[1] In "Making Music Our Own", Sibley first tells

---

[1] Frank Sibley, "Aesthetic Concepts", *Philosophical Review*, 67 (1959); repr. in George Dickie, Richard Sclafani, and Ronald Roblin (eds.), *Aesthetics: A Critical Anthology*, 2nd edn. (New York: St Martin's Press, 1989), 356.

us something very important: what kinds of terms he is *not* going to talk about. He intends to "ignore the much discussed descriptions that employ the language of feelings and emotions ... ", as well as " 'aesthetic' terms like *beautiful* and *graceful*, [and] the technical vocabulary of music ... ".[2] The significance of this will be important to return to later on, but need now only be duly noted.

The distinction that I mentioned just now in Sibley's last paper, which suggests the distinction in "Aesthetic Concepts", between "aesthetic" and "non-aesthetic" terms, cannot be neatly stated. Sometimes Sibley expresses it as between extra-musical and musical terms, sometimes as between figurative and literal terms, and sometimes technical musical terms seem to stand in for literal or musical terms, suggesting that he thought they were the only purely musical, or literal, terms of musical description. Again, the significance of this blurriness in Sibley's distinction will be returned to later on. But for now I will give it as Frank first states it, which is to say, as between the musical and the extra-musical. And it is well to point out that Frank does not make the distinction by giving examples of musical and then extra-musical terms. Rather, he assumes we know what the former are, and gives us a long list of the latter, extra-musical terms. Here is his list, and I quote:

extracted from typical descriptions, to exhibit their variety: from light—*sparkling, shimmering, bright, luminous, glowing*; from weight—*light, ponderous*; from movement—*sinuous, abrupt, soaring, turbulent, placid*; from sound and speech—*thundering, murmuring, sobbing, conversing, arguing*; from smell and taste—*bitter, sour, sweet*; from atmosphere—*sinister, threatening, spooky*; from feel, touch, and texture—*soft, supple, gritty, thick, melting, liquid, brittle, sinewy, icy, silky*; from physiognomy—*smiling, laughing*; from gait—*ambling, strutting, striding, plodding*; from character—*gentle, bombastic, aggressive, plaintive, tender, wistful, bold, good-humoured, solemn, animated*.[3]

Now I said earlier that Sibley sometimes calls these terms extramusical, and sometimes figurative. Each appellation has its problems. I will return to them later.

The next step in Frank's argument is a sustained answer to those who would claim, for one reason or another, that music is inherently indescribable. I will skip the details of this, because Sibley's answer is right on the mark, and I can't think of any philosopher who needs

[2] Frank Sibley, "Making Music Our Own", in Michael Krausz (ed.), *The Interpretation of Music: Philosophical Essays* (Oxford: Clarendon Press, 1995), 165.
[3] Ibid. 165–6.

convincing. But there are plenty of other folks who theorize about music who could read this part of Sibley's paper with profit.

To pick up the argument from here, Frank is at pains to make out that what he calls figurative or extra-musical descriptions of music are indispensable for both our characterization and our appreciation of it. As he puts the point: "Either much that matters to us in music is genuinely indescribable, or we must, without qualms, employ the extra-musical language that comes so naturally, recognizing that to eschew it would be as much a self-inflicted impoverishment as denying ourselves figurative language elsewhere, both within and outside the arts."[4] Sibley opts for the second term of the disjunction, as do I.

Frank, however, goes far further than I would, in underscoring the importance of figurative and extra-musical descriptions. Indeed, he goes so far as to actually deny to literal descriptions, and these, remember, include or comprise technical descriptions—that is to say, the music-theoretic ones—any role in music *appreciation*. He writes:

> But now it must be asked what these literal descriptions can achieve. ... [T]hey fail to articulate what, following others, I have been calling the 'character' and 'qualities' of music, and do little to explain why music may engage us as appreciative listeners—which is why non-musicians and musicians alike employ figurative characterizations.[5]

Sibley supports this claim against the importance for musical appreciation of technical musical language with an argument very reminiscent of those deployed in "Aesthetic Concepts" to contrast aesthetic with non-aesthetic terms. He says, after quoting a typical passage of musictheoretic analysis, "It seems possible that, suitably trained, someone who had never appreciated music could give a purely musico-auditory description of a performed piece. ... " But, he continues, "By contrast, listeners incapable of technical description who felt impelled to describe music in the figurative ways illustrated might convince us of their genuine grasp and appreciation".[6] Again, here is a point to which I will return in my succeeding critique.

We come, now, to Frank's main thesis. It is essentially, that somehow or other, understanding and appreciating music consist in, or are deeply involved with, or are evidenced by, the listener's ability to describe it. As Frank puts his thesis:

---

4 Sibley, "Making Music Our Own", 168.   5 Ibid.   6 Ibid.

Could there be reason to think that, even when we listen wordlessly (and non-pictorially), when no one offers or seeks descriptions, we nevertheless make sense of music by, without realizing it, bringing it under verbalizable concepts, and without thinking of the words that might verbalize them? Equally failing to understand it and misunderstanding it would be either failing to bring it under such concepts or bringing it under inappropriate ones.[7]

With this thesis I cannot but heartily concur; for I espoused a similar thesis myself and spelled it out at some length in 1990, in my book *Music Alone*.[8] Here is how I put it, at least in one of my formulations:

> To understand music, then, seems in significant part to be able to describe it. And so we accept as evidence for an affirmative answer to the question, Do you understand music? correct and convincing descriptions of it.[9]

Perhaps this is the *Zeitgeist* at work. Be that as it may, Frank's position and mine are crucially different in one very important respect, as will become apparent in my critical remarks to come. But before that I must complete my exposition of Frank's argument.

Both Sibley and I realized that the thesis we were proposing has two very obvious problems. One is that many people we would want to say appreciate music, particularly among the laity, cannot describe it—music, after all, is notoriously difficult to describe. Furthermore, it seems as if we may be committed to the absurd position that people who appreciate music must, perforce, have descriptions of it running through their heads when they listen to it.

We each dealt with these two problems in rather different ways. And as this is not to be one of the main points of my talk, I will give Sibley's way of doing the business, with very little comment of my own.

With regard to the first problem, that many true lovers of music cannot describe the music they listen to, Sibley replies:

> Certainly, unless we are critics we rarely attempt to articulate in words the qualities we hear in a piece. The more common case is where someone else gives a description and we feel that it is exactly right, or hits off the music rather well,

---

[7] Ibid. 169.

[8] Peter Kivy, *Music Alone: Philosophical Reflections on the Purely Musical Experience* (Ithaca, NY: Cornell University Press, 1990). That the publication of my book predates the publication of Sibley's essay by about five years should in no way be taken to suggest that Sibley's essay was at all influenced by my book. To think that someone of Frank Sibley's philosophical talent needed a suggestion from me to stimulate his creative juices is ludicrous; and, in any case, I have good reason to doubt that Frank ever read my book.

[9] Ibid. 97.

or must be rejected as unsuitable. When this happens, it is, I suggest, a criterion of our having previously heard it in such and such a way that we sincerely assent to the proffered description.[10]

I think that perhaps Frank underestimates the frequency with which music lovers who are not musically trained attempt to and succeed in describing their musical experiences. Such people do, after all, talk about the music they have heard, after a concert, just as they talk about movies they have seen. But that aside, what Sibley gives as an answer to the problem of music lovers who do not or cannot describe the music they enjoy is perfectly consistent with what I had to say in *Music Alone*. So I gladly acquiesce in it.

As for the second problem, that he might be committed to the "absurd" view that people must have the words of musical descriptions running through their heads when they listen to music, Frank, unsurprisingly, takes a distinctly Rylean line—unsurprisingly, of course, because, as we all know, Ryle was Frank's teacher; and when one has a teacher of *that* stature, one never quite gets free of the influence. Thus, Frank argues that "to think, and equally to realize, understand, or hear that something is ϕ, and to experience, see, or hear it as ϕ, need not involve the saying or thinking of any words."[11] Nor does he leave us to speculate about Ryle's influence here. What I have just quoted has a footnote attached, referring us to Ryle's posthumously collected essays *On Thinking*.[12] And what I am about to quote, which goes even further in a Rylean direction, has the same Rylean source. Sibley writes: "I suggest that just as we do not think in anything, we do not experience or listen in anything, either words, pictures, music, or musical terms".[13]

Frank, I think, was still haunted by the ghost in the machine. Contemporary philosophers of mind (and I am thinking here of Searle in particular, but many others as well) have naturalized the ghost. And although our fear of flying has, quite understandably, increased in recent years, our fear of consciousness has been in steep decline. So my own picture of what goes on "in the head" when we listen to music is far more luxurious than Frank's. But that topic must be left for another occasion. It suffices for present purposes to state that, like Frank, I have an answer to the charge that the view we share implies

---

[10] Sibley, "Making Music Our Own", 171.   [11] Ibid.

[12] Gilbert Ryle, *On Thinking*, ed. Konstantin Kolenda (Totowa, NJ: Rowan & Littlefield, 1979).

[13] Sibley, "Making Music Our Own", 172.

the absurdity of thinking that people must always have descriptions of music self-consciously running through their heads as they listen to it. So I want to press on, now, to the two further points that Sibley makes, which will complete my account of his argument.

Besides giving at least a sketch of what musical appreciation consists in, Frank saw himself as doing two other, closely related, things: confuting what he called the musical "purist", and answering the question as to what human beings find so appealing in "absolute music", which is to say, music without title, text, or program. I conclude my account of Frank's position by stating briefly what he has to say on these two issues.

I gather that Frank takes the musical purist to be someone who believes something like "that genuine descriptions [of music] should be literal, in 'purely musical', not borrowed terms".[14] What, then, is the answer to the purist?

Essentially, Sibley's answer to what *he* takes to be the musical purist (and more of that anon) is everything we have talked about up till now. The answer to the musical purist is that we need what Sibley calls figurative or extra-musical terms to describe music, and the ability to describe it in such terms constitutes exactly what musical appreciation is, or at least signals its presence. Furthermore, in a sense, this is *also* the answer to the question of absolute music's human appeal. It is just because music possesses these extra-musical characteristics that it is not remote from human beings, as it would be, Sibley apparently thought, if the purest were right, and music describable only in purely musical, literal, or technical terms, completely remote from human life and experience.

Here is how Frank put it (and I will quote at some length to get the full flavor of his thought):

The view, that grasping the character of a piece involves hearing it in such a way that some possible extra-musical description(s) would be appropriate to our experience would stand sharply opposed to the belief that extra-musical description is always improper. Much that is appealing about music would be, paradoxically, essentially extra-musical.

... But were it true, anyone obviously devoted to music who refuses, unlike many musicians, to countenance extra-musical descriptions must presumably be subject to some purist dogma. The supposition I am considering, however, if defensible, would lessen the 'mystery' of musical understanding by questioning the supposed 'isolation' or 'purity' of music and the 'discontinuity' between it and the rest of experience.[15]

[14] Ibid. 167.   [15] Ibid. 169.

Briefly put, then, Sibley's answer to the musical purist is that extra-musical descriptions of absolute music are both appropriate and indispensable. And his answer to the problem of musical appreciation and understanding, where absolute music is concerned, is that if the problem arises from what he calls "the alleged hermetic and isolated nature of [absolute] music",[16] then it dissolves into a pseudo-problem, since the appropriateness of extra-musical description refutes the notion of absolute music as "hermetic" or "isolated".

This, then, completes my account of Sibley's position in his last published paper, "Making Music Our Own". As anyone who has read the paper will know, I have scarcely done justice in this bare outline to the richness and complexity of Frank's thoughts. For it was characteristic of his style to pack a dense philosophical substance into a very small package. "Aesthetic Concepts" is one instance of that, and "Making Music Our Own" is another. But, as I have not the time to make my account more thorough, I will press on now to a critical discussion of three of Frank's major points. First and foremost, I want to discuss the claim that the technical, literal descriptions of absolute music, employed by musicologists and music theorists, are irrelevant to musical appreciation; that, as Frank put it, "Figurative criticism is alive, where, appreciatively, literal comment is inert."[17] For this conclusion seems to me both paradoxical and dangerously false. Second, I want to discuss the claim that the appropriateness of extra-musical descriptions is an answer to musical purism, along with, third, the claim that it helps us explain the appreciation and love of absolute music. For although I am, in general, sympathetic with both, I think some comments and caveats are in order.

II

1. In my book *Music Alone* I presented, as I have already said, a view of musical understanding and appreciation not unlike Frank's. But whereas Frank took technical description of music to be, as he put it, appreciatively inert, I took it to constitute an example of perhaps the highest form of musical appreciation and understanding. And the reason I find Frank's conclusion not only false but paradoxical is that I think that not only the musically trained would agree with me, but the musical *laity* as well.

---

[16] Sibley, "Making Music Our Own", 176.   [17] Ibid. 169.

My own problem, as I then saw it, was to make certain that I avoided the equally paradoxical position of denying musical appreciation and understanding to those *without* technical training in music; and I did so by pointing out that we *all* have an adequate vocabulary for describing many of the same musical events the music-theoretic vocabulary describes, even though there are, without a doubt, many events that *only* that vocabulary describes, and, to be sure, some that only the lay vocabulary can.

I cannot, here, give a full account of my own view, any more than I could of Sibley's. But perhaps the following will suffice. I argued in *Music Alone* that we enjoy, appreciate, and understand absolute music in a process of perceiving musical events under whatever descriptions we as listeners have at our command. Some of us have more, and some less. Music is an intentional object of musical perception, and the broader and more detailed the descriptions under which we perceive the intentional object, the more elaborate and more interesting and more rewarding that intentional object will be. Thus, on my view, far from being "inert", from the appreciative point of view, as Sibley believes, music-theoretic descriptions are an extremely powerful means of expanding and deepening musical enjoyment. And that, I think, is *understating* the case. My own initiation into music theory was nothing short of a revelation, and my appreciation of music, as a result, increased exponentially.

Why, then, should Frank have thought false what seems to me so obviously true: that music-theoretic descriptions, far from being appreciatively inert, are, quite to the contrary, appreciatively explosive? And how can I support my own view against his? To answer these questions, we must, I think, go back to the very beginning: back, that is, to "Aesthetic Concepts".

You will recall that "Making Music Our Own" begins, much in the same manner as "Aesthetic Concepts", with a distinction between two very different kinds of terms. In the latter, it is the distinction between aesthetic and non-aesthetic terms, in the former that between literal or technical and figurative or extra-musical terms. And to the reader of "Aesthetic Concepts", the distinction in "Making Music Our Own" looks to be, indeed, just a special case of the distinction in "Aesthetic Concepts": a distinction, that is to say, between *musical* aesthetic terms and *musical* non-aesthetic terms.

But this distinction is—or at least seems to be—thwarted at the very outset by Sibley's disavowal, in the very first paragraph of "Making

Music Our Own", that he is talking about " 'aesthetic' terms like *beautiful* and *graceful* … ".[18] *Aesthetic* he puts in inverted commas, seeming to suggest that he is using the word in the way he introduced in his first paper.

Why does Frank, then, seem to be saying that he is not talking about aesthetic terms, as defined in "Aesthetic Concepts", when it seems so apparent that, in "Making Music Our Own", he *is* doing just that? Let me suggest that when he puts *aesthetic* in inverted commas, in the previously quoted disavowal, he is *not* signaling, as he may seem to be to readers of his first paper, the Sibleyan concept formulated there, but rather, signaling the very opposite: the pre-theoretic use of ordinary people for whom the word connotes such typically evaluative aesthetic terms as his two stated examples: *beautiful* and *graceful*. His disavowal, then, is not meant to suggest that the aesthetic terms of "Aesthetic Concepts" are not those being discussed in "Making Music Our Own"; rather, that he will not be discussing such more or less evaluative terms as "beautiful", "graceful", and the like, which, indeed, he does not do. That, in any case, is the most plausible explanation I can come up with for what otherwise seems a puzzling inconsistency between Frank's first paper and his last.

With this offputting denial now, I hope, out of the way, we can find two pretty convincing reasons for believing that the distinction Frank is making at the outset of "Making Music Our Own", between literal musical terms and figurative or extra-musical ones, is a special case of the distinction in "Aesthetic Concepts" between non-aesthetic and aesthetic terms. First, many of the figurative or extra-musical terms that Frank contrasts with literal musical terms are just the kinds of terms as were described in "Aesthetic Concepts" as *aesthetic terms*. But second, and more important, as we have seen when Frank comes to explain why literal and technical descriptions of music are appreciatively inert, he uses the same argument as he used in "Aesthetic Concepts" to make the contrast between non-aesthetic terms and aesthetic terms coextensive with the distinction between terms the correct application of which do not require taste, or aesthetic sensitivity, and those whose correct application does require that special "aesthetic" or "appreciative" faculty.

Non-aesthetic terms and literal musical terms, so this argument goes, can be correctly applied by rules (presumably), without any true artistic appreciation or taste being present or employed. As the view is stated in "Aesthetic Concepts", "Such [non-aesthetic] remarks may be made by,

---

[18] See Sibley, "Making Music Our Own".

and such [non-aesthetic] features pointed out to, anyone with normal eyes, ears, and intelligence."[19] And what I claim is a special case, in music, of this general view, finds expression, in "Making Music Our Own", in the following way: "It seems possible that, suitably trained, someone who had never appreciated music could give a purely musico-auditory description of a performed piece, and even someone deaf from birth who had seen music only in score might learn, however profitlessly, to give such descriptions ... ", which is to say, technical descriptions of music.[20]

But now, I think, we are in a position to understand just why Frank came to what I take to be the paradoxical and counter intuitive conclusion that music-theoretic description is appreciatively inert. He was driven to it, I would suggest, by the doctrine of "Aesthetic Concepts", that, in spirit, if not in letter, informs "Making Music Our Own". For if, as I have supposed, the distinction between literal descriptions of music (including technical descriptions) and figurative or extra-musical descriptions is more or less a special case of the non-aesthetic/aesthetic distinction, then the conclusion is forced upon Sibley that music-theoretic descriptions must be inert as regards appreciation. For, being non-aesthetic, they can be applied without taste or aesthetic sensitivity, without, that is to say, the *appreciative faculty*. Indeed, even deaf people—people without the ability to become aware of any sound at all, let alone musical sound—can, on Sibley's view, learn to apply music-theoretic terms.

Now this conclusion seems to me to represent a serious misunderstanding of music-theoretic language. Such language is always learned in conjunction with musical hearing. The first course in basic musical grammer is called, in most conservatories and music departments, "ear-training and harmony", or something like that. One does not just learn on paper what a minor third is, one learns what it sounds like. One does not just learn on paper what a modulation to the dominant is, one learns to hear it. One does not just learn on paper what a plagal cadence is, one learns it by ear. I do not know what a deaf person would be learning in a theory class. But it would not be theory in the same sense in which a person with the auditory faculty in tact learns it; and he would not "know" what the hearing person "knows".

Really, though, the thought experiment of a deaf person learning music theory is a bit of a red herring. Who knows *what* he or she would

[19] Sibley, "Aesthetic Concepts", 356.
[20] See Sibley, "Making Music Our Own", 168.

make of music theory? The essential question is what a person would
make of music theory who could hear, but not hear *music*; someone
who had no *appreciation* of it; in other words, what is sometimes called
a *tone-deaf* person. My own view is that such a person, a person capable
of hearing sounds, but not capable of hearing music, not capable of
appreciating it, could no more hear minor thirds, modulations to the
dominant, plagal cadences, than a deaf person. He or she could hear the
sounds (of course), but not the intentional objects these descriptions
have reference to. That being the case, *pace* Sibley, whatever he or she
might learn in a theory class, it would not be music theory; he or she
would not "know" music theory. As Kendall Walton aptly puts the
point I am making, in an essay in the same volume as Frank's, "Analysis
is continuous with appreciation, and explaining or understanding how
it is that one hears a piece is not to be separated from the experience of
hearing it."[21]

Furthermore, the last tribunal, in a music-theoretic dispute, is the *ear*.
When two theorists disagree, they do not just "talk" their arguments;
they "play" them. They go to the keyboard. "Don't you hear it as
such-and-such a chord in this key rather than such-and-such a chord in
that one? Don't you hear this as the real recapitulation rather than as a
long coda?" And so on. That is what music theorists do and say. Sibley
describes technical descriptions as "dry".[22] But they are only dry when
seen, and not heard—which is to say, when not musically understood.
To *hear* music under a music-theoretic description is no less to have
a living, breathing musical experience as to hear it under a figurative,
extra-musical one; and it is music *appreciation* in the full-blooded and
highest sense of the word.

And that brings us to another, related and important, point. Many
of the terms Sibley describes as figurative *and* extra-musical may be
extra-musical, but are decidedly *not* figurative. In Sibley's collection,
there seem to be four different kinds of extra-musical terms: those that
are clearly figurative, like "murmuring" or "sobbing"; those that are
dead metaphors, like, perhaps, "light" or "ponderous"; those that are
literal, but derivative from a sense modality other than hearing, like
"bright" or "sour" or "sharp"; and those that are just plainly literal, *sans
phrase*, like "turbulent" or "tranquil".

---

[21] Kendall Walton, "Understanding Humour and Understanding Music", in Krausz
(ed.), *Interpretation of Music*, 269.
[22] Sibley, "Making Music Our Own", 168.

Of metaphors, alive or dead, I will not speak, except to point out that many would count dead metaphors—for example, table leg—as literal. But it is important to point out that the transference of predicates from one sense modality to another is a well-studied phenomenon of linguistics, and does not constitute a figurative use of language. "Bright" is literally true of the sound of the trumpet in its clarino register, as it is of sunlight, even though the predicate migrated from sight to sound.[23] And as for words like "tranquil" or "turbulent", I do not see that they are any more literal when applied to water or air than when applied to sound or the emotional lives of human beings.

Now these may seem like verbal quibbles, but that is by no means the case. For they show that what is important about Sibley's distinction between theoretical terms and the others is *not* that the former are literal, the latter figurative, but that the latter are *extra-musical*, the former applicable solely to music. And that *some* of the latter are also *figurative* turns out to be of little importance. What *is* important is that *all* of these terms, the literal, the music-theoretic (a subclass of the literal), the extra-musical that are literal, and the extra-musical that are figurative, have one thing in common: *they describe musical events*; and in so doing, they perform the same function of making plainer to us, or, another way of putting it, helping to constitute for us, the intentional object of musical appreciation. There is no discontinuity of purpose between them. They *all* motivate musical appreciation.

This brings us, then, to the second and third of Frank's points that I want to discuss: his answer to the musical purist and his attempt to explain the appeal of absolute music. With these points I can be briefer. I will deal with them together.

2. If Frank is correct, and I am certain he is, that extra-musical descriptions are both appropriate and indispensable for our characterizations, understanding and appreciation of absolute music, then he is certainly correct in thinking that this constitutes a conclusive answer to one version of musical "purism". But I think it must be pointed out that it is a particularly *austere* version of purism thus refuted, a version that I doubt anyone today would subscribe to. Or, to be more exact, there are two versions, one more austere than the other. In one version, musical purism is the view that music can be appropriately described only in literal, never in figurative, terms. In the other, it is the view that

[23] See Peter Kivy, *Sound and Semblance: Reflections on Musical Representation*, 2nd edn. (Ithaca, NY: Cornell University Press, 1991), 61–71.

music can be described only in musical, never in extra-musical, terms. Clearly, the latter is the leanest of the two, since it would leave only music-theoretic terms for musical description, whereas in the former version we could use terms that also have application outside music, just so long as they are literal, not figurative, when applied to music.

I myself would certainly be described, and have been, as a musical *purist* by most philosophers, musicologists, and music theorists who are familiar with my work. Yet I have always insisted that extra-musical terms, figurative terms, and even the notorious expressive terms can and must be used in our descriptions of music, if we are to be faithful to the full musical experience. But if *I* am a musical purist, what *is* musical purism? And what is its opposite?

Musical purism I take to be the view that absolute music is a sound structure and surface that has no semantic or representational or narrative *content*. Thus, when I describe music in extra-musical terms, I take myself not to be ascribing content to it (in any of the above senses), but to be merely making use of every resource of language to describe the musical structure and surface adequately. As musical purism is currently construed, then, at least in my crowd, Frank Sibley *was* a musical purist.

But if the debate, as currently carried on, between musical purists and their opponents, is not one between those who do not and those who do countenance descriptions of absolute music in figurative or extra-musical terms, what exactly is at stake? Clearly, it is whether absolute music is absolute: whether it has representational, narrative, or propositional content of any kind, or whether it is pure musical structure—whatever that will ultimately turn out to mean—with no semantic or representational component at all.

In contrast to musical purism, as today understood, are a growing number of strategies for extracting narrative, ideological, and representational content from the absolute music canon. And at least one perceived goal that motivates these strategies, I believe, is the notion, which I share, that the appeal of absolute music to human beings is a phenomenon desperately in need of philosophical analysis. And this, of course, brings us to the last of Frank's points that I want to comment on.

3. What is it that human beings so deeply appreciate and value in something that at least *appears* to be pure musical structure? What is it that they so deeply appreciate and value in something that we *call* "fine art", but yet seems to be so different from those other things—novels,

plays, poems, representational paintings, and statues—that we call by the same name, and have done since the eighteenth century?

The non-purists, following Schopenhauer, have taken the line, as I see it, that since the other arts are appreciated and valued in a process deeply involved with the representational or narrative or semantic content of those works, the same must be the case for music. And their project then becomes that of putting interpretations on this apparently contentless musical structure that can reveal a content capable of explaining our deep appreciation and intense enjoyment of this structure. In so doing, they face the formidable task of producing interpretations that reveal a content interesting and elaborate enough to really explain our enjoyment of absolute music without, on the other hand, producing interpretations that stretch credulity to the breaking point: that suggest invention rather than interpretation.

On the other side, the purist faces the formidable task of providing a believable explanation of how our enjoyment and appreciation of pure musical surface and structure can reach an intensity and depth that impels us to place Bach and Beethoven at the same level of veneration in the pantheon of the arts as Homer and Shakespeare, while at the same time doing without the resources of content available to the other arts.

Frank Sibley thought that recognizing the appropriateness and indispensability of extra-musical descriptions could, if not provide an explanation for our enjoyment of absolute music, at least prepare the ground for one. This, I take it, is the cash value of the concluding sentences of "Making Music Our Own":

But we do, after all, characterize natural and extra-musical sounds in similar ways [to music], as mournful, sighing, chattering, cheerful, murmuring, harsh, sweet, and so on. This at least suggests some continuity between music and other sounds, and so questions the alleged hermetic and isolated nature of music. [24]

I believe Frank is right that musical surface and structure possess "human" and "natural" qualities, and that this does indeed add an attraction in music for us beyond what a surface and structure without them might have. Elsewhere, I have called attention, in this regard, particularly to the humanizing effect of music's expressive qualities. [25] But surely it cannot be the whole answer—only part of a very much larger one—as Frank clearly recognized.

[24] See n. 16 above.
[25] See Peter Kivy, "The Fine Art of Repetition", in *The Fine Art of Repetition: Essays in the Philosophy of Music* (Cambridge: Cambridge University Press, 1993).

I am convinced, and have repeated it over and again, that the problem of absolute music is one of the deepest, most difficult, and most neglected problems that face contemporary philosophy of art. That Frank should have turned his hand to this problem in his last paper, and been tragically prevented from contributing further to the project, is a calamity for us all. We will, of course, have to soldier on without his help and counsel. But we will always hold before us the ideal of philosophical perfection and integrity that Frank set for himself, and that we must, following him, set for *ourselves*. That he set this example for us we should always preserve in memory, and for it always be grateful.

13

In Defense of Musical Representation: Music, Representation, and the Hybrid Arts

I

The importance of Marx Wartofsky's contribution to our understanding of visual representation hardly needs advertisement, being well known to all his admirers. It is in the spirit of that work, although not, obviously, as a direct contribution to it, that I offer some brief remarks on the problem of musical representation.

It seems to me apparent enough, and hardly controversial, that Beethoven musically represented the risen Christ, in the *Et resurrexit* of the *Missa Solemnis*, with rapidly ascending scale passages. And it also seems to me apparent enough that the rapidly ascending passage, a so-called *coup d'archet*, with which Mozart opens his Symphony no. 31 in D (K. 297), the Paris Symphony, does not represent anything at all.

Mozart's Paris Symphony is a work of what the nineteenth century came to call "absolute music", and what I sometimes like to call "music alone", which is to say, music without text, program, programmatic title, or any other such extra-musical paraphernalia.[1] It is my view that absolute music, music alone, has no representational or semantic content whatever. Many historical figures, and some contemporary ones, disagree. I have defended my own view of music alone, which might be described as "enhanced formalism",[2] elsewhere, and will not undertake

---

[1] Mozart's Symphony no. 31 is called the "Paris" Symphony because it was written to be performed in Paris, not, as in the case of Mendelssohn's "Scotch" Symphony, because it was meant to evoke any geographic location.

[2] Philip Alperson so describes it because, unlike traditional formalism, it countenances expressive properties as part of the musical fabric. I gladly adopt Alperson's nomenclature.

to rehearse that defense here.[3] For present purposes, I simply assume that my view of absolute music, enhanced formalism, is true.

It is also my view that music with text or program or programmatic title sometimes contains musical passages palpably "representational", in more or less the same sense of that word in which we would want to say that a certain painting by Van Gogh represents sunflowers or one by Botticelli a woman standing in a seashell. The rising scale passages in the *Et resurrexit* of Beethoven's *Missa Solemnis* are such passages. Their number is legion.

But just as there are many, both past and present, who demur from the view that absolute music is absolutely non-representational, there are those, both past and present, who, appearances to the contrary notwithstanding, demur from the view that some passages of music—those occurring in compositions with text, program, or programmatic title are truly representational in the full-blooded sense of the word. Again, I have defended the possibility—indeed, the actuality—of musical representation elsewhere, both against the old as well as the new arguments to the contrary.[4] But musical representation is apparently in need of eternal vigilance. For new enemies, with fresh arguments, are ever on the march. And one such reinforcement to the anti-representationalist camp, with a new and intriguing argument, is the subject of the present paper.

My good friend Stephen Davies has recently come forth with an array of new arguments against the notion that passages such as the one from Beethoven cited at the beginning of my paper are truly representational.[5] I have dealt with all but one of them on another occasion.[6] But the one I have not yet dealt with has given me pause. In brief, and without any adornments, it is that if music cannot be representational without a text, program, or programmatic title, as, indeed, I claim, then it cannot become representational merely by the addition of one of them.

[3] On this, see Peter Kivy, *Music Alone: Philosophical Reflections on the Purely Musical Experience* (Ithaca, NY: Cornell University Press, 1990). See also Peter Kivy, "The Fine Art of Repetition", "A New Music Criticism?", and "Is Music an Art?", in *idem, The Fine Art of Repetition: Essays in the Philosophy of Music* (Cambridge: Cambridge University Press, 1993).

[4] On this, see Peter Kivy, *Sound and Semblance: Reflections on Musical Representation*, 2nd edn. (Ithaca, NY: Cornell University Press, 1991).

[5] Stephen Davies, "Representation in Music", *Journal of Aesthetic Education*, 27 (1993), 16–22.

[6] Peter Kivy, "Listening: Responses to Alperson, Howard and Davies", *Journal of Aesthetic Education*, 26 (1992).

Even unadorned, the argument has a certain intuitive appeal, although, clearly, it is not the case that in general, something lacking a property in one set of circumstances cannot gain the property in another set, without there being any change in *it*. I may not be rich in New York, but may be in Outer Mongolia. A mere change in venue here does the trick (assuming that what is to become my "wealth" is portable).

What drives Davies's argument, then, is not merely the general principle, which appears to be false, that something lacking a property in one context cannot gain it merely by a change of that context. Rather, it is his conception of what kind of an artwork a musical work is when it possesses text, program, or programmatic title, or, in the case of opera, a *mise-en-scène* as well. Such works are what Davies calls, following Jerrold Levinson, "hybrid art forms". And to appreciate Davies's argument fully, we must first, therefore, turn to Levinson's account of just what a hybrid art form is.

II

According to Levinson:

An art form is a hybrid one in virtue of its development and origin, in virtue of its emergence out of a field of previously existing artistic activities and concerns, two or more of which it in some sense combines. ... The components of a putative hybrid must be locatable somewhere in the preceding culture and must be plausibly seen as having come together in the result. In short, hybrid art forms are art forms arising from the *actual* combination or interpenetration of earlier art forms. Art forms that have *not* so arisen, though they may be intellectually analyzable into various possible or actual structural or mediumistic components, are not hybrids in the primary sense.[7]

Among such artistic hybrids, Levinson wants to distinguish three different kinds, "which can be labeled *juxtaposition* (or addition), *synthesis* (or fusion), and *transformation* (or alteration)".[8]

Juxtapositional hybrids, on Levinson's view, are art forms in which "the objects or products of two (or more) arts are simply joined together and presented as one larger, more complex unit".[9] In such an amalgam,

---

[7] Jerrold Levinson, "Hybrid Art Forms", repr. in *idem, Music, Art and Metaphysics: Essays in Philosophical Aesthetics* (Ithaca, NY: Cornell University Press, 1990), 27–8.

[8] Ibid. 30.   [9] Ibid.

each element maintains its individual character, as, for example, in song accompanied by an instrument or instruments; and thus the "elements [are] imaginable in isolation from the others to which they are joined and which, so isolated, would count as bona fide (if peculiar) instances of the arts entering into the hybrid".[10]

In synthetic hybrids, on the other hand, "two (or more) arts are brought together in such a way that the individual components to some extent lose their original identities and are present in the hybrid in a form significantly different from that assumed in the pure state."[11] An example of such a synthetic hybrid—a very controversial example, one might add—is, Levinson suggests, Wagnerian music drama.

Finally, Levinson describes the transformational hybrid as "closer to the synthetic model than to the juxtapositional one, but which differs from the former in that the arts combined do not contribute to the result in roughly the same degree".[12] An example of a transformational hybrid might be, Levinson suggests, kinetic sculpture, which he sees as "sculpture modified in the direction of dance. It is not an equal fusion of the two, but rather an incorporation of some of the special or distinctive *characteristics* of dance into what remains recognizably *sculpture*, though in an extended sense".[13]

As I said, Davies bases his denial of the possibility of representational music on Levinson's account of hybrid art forms. It would be well, therefore, to suggest at least parenthetically, that as a foundation, Levinson's account is seriously flawed in one rather crucial respect. For, if Levinson's historical criterion for hybrid art forms is adopted, it then turns out that all forms of vocal music with text, which is to say, all music sung to words, with the exception of opera and music drama (and, of course, "melodrama", which is not sung), will turn out, on Levinson's view, *not* to be hybrid art forms in any of its three variations. But as vocal music with a text is usually thought of, and is so thought of by Levinson, as a paradigmatic example of the hybrid, such a conclusion is highly unpalatable, to say the least, and, many would say, a *reductio* of Levinson's historical criterion, although not necessarily of the threefold hybrid concept itself.

The criterion, it will be recalled, for being a hybrid art form, is not merely that two or more art forms be recognizable in the compound, but that they get there in a certain way: "The components of a putative

---

[10] Levinson, "Hybrid Art Forms", 31.   [11] Ibid.   [12] Ibid. 32.
[13] Ibid. 33.

hybrid must be locatable somewhere in the preceding culture and must be plausibly seen as having come together in the result." But such is *not* the case with instrumentally accompanied song, in the Western musical tradition, or of unaccompanied vocal music. It is certainly not the case that, historically, accompanied song is the putting together of a previously existing vocal music with a previously existing, independent instrumental idiom. On the contrary, it is quite the other way around. Instrumental music, in the West, as an autonomous musical art form, is a late development, and comes out of vocal music; in the Renaissance, this is apparent in the fact that a good deal of what instrumentalists played was arrangements of vocal music for instruments.

Furthermore, neither polyphonic a capella vocal music nor unaccompanied monodic song can be thought of as historically being put together out of one art form, music, and another art form, "literature" or "words". For there *never* was a time, in the memory or recorded history of Western civilization, when music was not sung music with a text, with or without musical accompaniment. Of course, opera and music drama, which certainly are on everyone's list of hybrid art forms, do qualify on Levinson's historical criterion. For they are, historically, the self-conscious result of just the kind of putting together that Levinson has in mind. But they are not the threefold putting together of the "pure" art forms of text, music, and dramatic representation, but, rather, the putting together of vocal music and *mise-en-scène*. Yet, even though opera and music drama do survive as hybrid arts on Levinson's historical criterion, texted vocal music of other kinds does not. And this latter result seems too high a price to pay.

Of course, Levinson's general classification of hybrid art forms, and the concept of the hybrid art form itself, need not fall with the historical criterion. But the criterion itself is in need of either repair or replacement, if we are to fully understand just what an artistic hybrid really is. And to that extent Davies's attack on representational music has been launched with one seriously defective weapon. Nevertheless, it may well have merits of its own. And with that in mind, and Levinson's notion of hybrid art forms in hand, I turn now to Davies's critique.

III

It is Davies's thesis that "an illustrative title or an accompanying text could not make a musical work representational if it could not be representational without them."[14] And he asks: "Why, then, does the debate about musical representation concentrate on program music?"[15] His answer and his argument, based on Levinson's analysis of artistic hybrids, are as follows.

Most people, Davies points out, would take opera, for example, to be representational. But opera, he avers, is, to use Levinson's terminology, a "synthetic hybrid". And, he continues:

In a synthetic hybrid the combination of constituents results in a new entity, rather than merely a mixture. It would involve a fallacy of decomposition to argue from the representational character of opera to the representational character of its constituents. It does not follow from the cake's being sweet that the salt which goes into it is sweet.[16]

Thus, even though opera is representational, it is not a *bona fide* example of *musical* representation, because it is *emergent* from its parts, and if one of its parts, *music*, cannot be representational on its own, it certainly would be fallacious to infer that it is representational in the emergent art form which *is* representational: namely, the synthetic art form of opera. Opera, not music, is the representational art here. That is how I understand Davies's argument. I will return to it in a moment.

But what of program music? Davies characterizes it as a transformational hybrid in which "music plays the dominant role". And, he continues:

Titles and accompanying texts may possess a narrative function, but I take it that they are not representational (as paintings are). If program music were to be representational, the representational component would have to be supplied by the music. If "pure" music is not representational, then program music could not be representational, given that program music is not a synthetic hybrid.[17]

So program music, as I understand the argument, because it lacks any representational component whatever, and is not a synthetic hybrid with emergent representational features, fails to be representational at all. Furthermore, the musical part of program music, not being representational in its pure form, and not even being, in program music, part of a representational art form, doesn't even have the consolation of being "representational" falsely so-called as the non-conclusion of a fallacious decomposition argument from whole to part. Nor can it gain representationality from the text, because the text is not

---

[14] Davies, "Representation in Music", 21.   [15] Ibid.
[16] Ibid.   [17] Ibid. 22.

representational. And how, good Simmias, can the non-representational gain representation from that which is not representation itself? Nay, good sir, it flees from its opposite.

So, to sum up Davies's argument, as I understand it: With regard to what might be called, stretching the point a bit, the musical arts of "dramatic representation", in which I include not only opera and music drama but cantata, oratorio, and most "art song", music in those art forms cannot be representational, even though the art forms themselves are. For, first, it does not follow from the whole of a synthetic hybrid being representational that any of its parts is; and second, if music cannot be representational in its pure, absolute form, then it cannot be made so by the addition of text, *mise-en scène*, or anything else. Further, with regard to program music, in which I would also include tone poem and simply titled music like "Scotch" Symphony or "Pastoral" Sonata, here even the work as a whole is not properly speaking representational, although it may be narrative. For the text is not representational, properly so-called, nor is music, in its pure, absolute form. Nor can putting them together in program music make a synthetic hybrid, so there can be no emergent representation in the case. Program music is not representational, nor is either of its parts; and because it is not representational, it can present no temptation to commit the decompositional fallacy on music's behalf. Such, as I understand it, is Davies's whole argument against the possibility of representational music in its texted forms.

IV

I believe that Davies is mistaken across the board. That is to say, I believe that both opera and program music present instances of representational music properly so-called, and that Levinson's account of hybrid art forms provides no reason to think otherwise. Let me turn to opera and opera-like art forms first.

Now, as a matter of fact, Classical and Romantic opera present few real cases of musical representation. (Not surprisingly, Baroque opera is a richer source.) So in my previous work on the subject, *Sound and Semblance*, I adduced my examples mostly from Baroque cantata and oratorio. But since Davies has used opera as his paradigm of the synthetic hybrid, and has based his argument in this regard on it, I see no reason not to follow suit in my reply. So let me begin by adducing an example from the standard operatic repertory of what I take to be a *bona fide* musical representation. On it I shall base my subsequent argument.

In the second act, second scene, of Beethoven's *Fidelio*, Leonore and Rocco, after a bit of huffing and puffing, succeed in moving a heavy boulder (*einer grössen Stein*) from one place to another, for reasons it is not necessary here to relate. The task is accomplished, to be precise, in the Andante con moto section of no. 12: *Melodram und Duett*. The opera *Fidelio* represents, in the place just stipulated, two people rolling a heavy boulder. But, of course, this representation is made up of diverse representational elements. The act of rolling the boulder is represented by two singers pretending to push and shove what appears to be a heavy object. This large object, the boulder itself, is represented by a lump of painted papier-mâché. And, *pace* Davies, the *sound* of the boulder is *represented* by a "grumbling" figure in the celli, double basses, and contrabassoon, over which figure in the score is the stage direction: "*Hier lassen sie den Stein über die Trümmer rollen.*"

Now I would like to call attention to two compelling reasons why I think it makes perfect sense—is indeed correct—to describe the grumbling figure as musically representing the sound of the boulder being moved in the "world" of *Fidelio*. First of all, this is the way I think listeners experience the figure, once they notice it. Of course, it is a very small detail in a very big artwork. And I doubt not that it passes unnoticed among most listeners until some pedant like me points it out. But once it is pointed out, it is then experienced as a representation of the sound the boulder must make in the fictional world of *Fidelio*. To appropriate a concept from Richard Wollheim's account of visual representation, the listener "hears in" the grumbling figure the sound of the rolling stone.[18]

Second, ever since such phenomena as the grumbling figure in *Fidelio* have been discussed, which, in my reading, anyway, goes back to the sixteenth century, "representation" words are the ones that critics, composers, and listeners have consistently used to describe them. "Picture", "tone painting", "imitation" (in the Platonic and Aristotelian sense of "mimesis") are, prior to the twentieth century, the more common words in use, "representation" being, I think, the word of choice in more contemporary "logical" and "analytical" circles. In *Sound and Semblance*

---

[18] On "hearing in", see Kivy, "Afterword: Pictures, Representations and Hearing-in", in *Sound and Semblance*, 2nd edn., 217–26. For Wollheim's account of "seeing-in", See Richard Wollheim, *Painting as an Art* (Princeton: Princeton University Press, 1987), 46–75.

I made a distinction between what I called there musical "pictures" and musical "representations"; and I am certainly not denying that the words "picture", "tone painting", "imitation", and "representation" all possess individual nuances and connotations. Be that as it may, for the purposes of the present discussion I think we may say that the word "representation", in a broad enough sense to take in the historical periods in which "picture", "tone painting", "imitation", and the like, were current, captures the core concept that all of those words implied, the concept that the current argument is about. So "representation" (in this broad sense) is what, I am arguing, people seem to think they experience in cases like the grumbling figure in *Fidelio*, and "representation" is how they refer to it; furthermore, the experience and description have been more or less in place since at least the late Renaissance.

Now it is perfectly possible that people have been both mistaken about what they are experiencing, and logically inaccurate in their referring to things like the grumbling figure as "representations", "tone paintings", "pictures", and the like. So let us now see if Davies provides us with any conclusive argument to think so.

It seems to me that we are offered two basic reasons for rejecting the common notion that things like the grumbling figure in *Fidelio* are *bona fide* representations. First, the notion is reached by the fallacy of "decomposition", and second, it is just evidently the case that, as Davies puts it, "an illustrative title or an accompanying text could not make a musical work representational if it could not be representational without them".

Let us take the fallacy of decomposition first. Here's how Davies illustrates it. "It does not follow from the cake's being sweet that the salt which goes into it is sweet." But nor does it follow from the cake's being sweet that the sugar which goes into it is sweet. And, of course, the sugar *is* sweet. Which just goes to show, as everyone knows, that an invalid argument can have a true conclusion.

But in any case, we do not reach the conclusion that the grumbling figure in *Fidelio* is representational by decomposition, any more than we reach the conclusion that the sugar in the cake is sweetening that way. We conclude that the cake is being sweetened by the sugar and not the salt from what we know of cakes and sugar and salt. And we know that the grumbling figure in *Fidelio* is representational by what we know of such musical figures and what we know of just how this one functions in its place. So we can dismiss the fallacy of decomposition out of hand. It may be a snare for the feet of others, but not for ours.

If anything is going to dislodge me, then, from my belief that the grumbling figure is representational, properly so-called, and that that is the way I experience it, it is going to have to be the contradictory belief that, to refine Davies's axiom a bit, an illustrative title or text cannot make a melody token of a given melody type representational if other melody tokens of the same melody type can not be representational without them. But is this axiom true?

I am calling it an "axiom" because, so far as I can see, no argument is offered for it. But as an axiom, I must confess that it does not tug at my heartstrings. It is far from self-evident to me. Indeed, it is far *more* evident to me that the grumbling figure in *Fidelio* has become representational by the addition of text, where it would not have been otherwise, merely as a figure in a symphony or sonata, than it is evident to me that the axiom which denies this possibility is true. As far as I am concerned, I have just refuted the axiom.

But why should it be even initially plausible to think it impossible that a scrap of music not representational in a piece of absolute music can *become* representational with the addition of text or title? I can think right now of only two possibilities: the first trivial, the second at least of some interest, although, in the event, unconvincing.

Suppose a real nitpicker should argue as follows. Closely considered, and precisely put, the grumbling figure did not become representational when it was not before; it is, indeed, no more representational in the second act of *Fidelio* than it would have been in a sonata or a symphony. What *is* representational is the whole—that is, the whole segment of time—of which it is a part: the segment that includes the scene, the action on stage, etc.

Well this way of "closely" and "precisely" putting the case just seems to me to be wrong: unfaithful to our experience. What is doing the work of representing the sound of the rolling boulder just *is* the grumbling figure in the bass instruments, and there's an end on't. The text and *mise-en-scène* (perhaps) are *necessary conditions* for the representationality of the grumbling figure. *It* wouldn't be representational without *them*; but *it* is what is representational of the sound, not *they*. However, the above way of putting the matter does, I think, point up a more plausible, although in the event inconclusive, reason for thinking the passage of music from pure to representational impossible. That reason requires some consideration.

It may be thought that there is some alchemical sleight of hand going on here. How, it might be queried, can some "object", without there being any change in *it*, be non-representational in one place and representational in another? It sounds like black magic. (Or quantum mechanics.) Of course, many "Cambridge changes" may occur. But certainly the change from non-representation to representation cannot merely be that. So it looks as if we are being asked to accept mysteries. Only someone prepared to believe the doctrine of the real presence, it might be argued, could believe that the *same* musical figure is non-representational in one place, representational in another, while, like the wafer and the wine, keeping the selfsame perceptual qualities in both.

Well there is a kernel of truth in this objection, and it is, simply, that we still have an imperfect understanding of artistic representation *tout court*. Certainly I do not pretend to have presented a full account of the musical kind, here or elsewhere. But that being readily granted, it must nevertheless be insisted that there is no divine mystery in the passage of an "object", musical or otherwise, from non-representational to representational. It is just too common a phenomenon, and too commonly thus described, not merely as regards music, but in the most ordinary circumstances, to be thought arcane or occult. It just happens.

A thumbtack lies on the general's desk and is just a thumbtack. He puts it on his map, and it represents the Third Army. A squiggle is just a squiggle; but in a diagram it represents a coil, on a road sign a dangerous curve. An ordinary chair becomes the throne of a king in an informal run-through of *Lear*. A broom is a horse when it is between the legs of a child, a rapidly ascending scale passage a *coup d'archet* in Mozart's Paris Symphony, but the risen Christ in the *Missa Solemnis*. These are all too common, too ordinary for black magic, and too deep, no doubt, for facile explanations. But if they are not *all* "representation", properly so-called, then I don't know what they might be.

I find no plausibility whatever, then, in the "axiom", as I have called it, that a melodic token of a given type cannot be made representational by the addition of a text or a title. It seems to me to happen all the time. And unless the "axiom" can be shown to follow from some higher principle that I do accept, I am inclined simply to dismiss it as patently false, because in conflict with some of the most familiar and obvious experiences of my musical life, and of musical life in the Western classical tradition at least as far back as the sixteenth century. That said, I think I can now make quicker work of the question of whether program music is properly representational, and press on to my conclusion.

V

The *Harvard Dictionary of Music* (1st edn.) defines "program music" as "Music inspired by, and suggestive of a program, i.e., an extramusical idea indicated in the title of the piece and sometimes substantiated in explanatory remarks or in a preface".[19] And the first two musical compositions that are adduced as examples are, not surprisingly, Beethoven's Pastoral Symphony and Berlioz's *Symphonie fantastique*, which, I would think, are the first examples that would occur to anyone having even a passing acquaintance with the standard concert repertory.

But these are examples, it is worth noting, of two *different* kinds of composition, both of which fit the broad definition quoted. For Berlioz's "program" is a narrative, while Beethoven's is merely a series of titles that set pictorial scenes. But in *both* cases, I would insist, the music generally performs the same function: to "represent" or "illustrate". As I have argued elsewhere,[20] it is not in the power of music to tell stories. What it can do is illustrate scenes from stories, much in the way that pictures do in those deluxe, illustrated versions of novels which used to be popular, and of which Rockwell Kent's beautifully illustrated *Moby Dick* is a notable example.[21] And it can do it, to some extent anyway, "temporally", which "still" pictures cannot but which motion pictures can, silent film with titles thus providing another visual analogue to narrative program music.

But in any case, the "problem" of representation in program music, even in its narrative form, is no different from and no more troublesome than the same "problem" in opera, opera-like vocal music, or any other texted musical form.

Davies, it will be recalled, makes the following claims with regard to program music. First, programs and titles and texts, although they may be narrative, are not representational. Second, therefore, if program music were representational, the representationality would have

[19] Willi Apel, *Harvard Dictionary of Music*, 1st edn. (Cambridge, Mass.: Harvard University Press, 1951), 604.

[20] See Kivy, *Sound and Semblance*, ch. 9.

[21] Herman Melville, *Moby Dick* (Garden City, NY: Garden City Publishing Co., 1930). Many of Rockwell Kent's illustrations are, actually, more decorative than directly relevant to the narrative. Better examples—better not from the aesthetic but from the "logical" point of view—are the illustrated versions of the "classics", *The Three Musketeers, Treasure Island*, etc. that were issued for children in my boyhood.

to come from the music. But third, since pure, absolute music is not representational, program music cannot be either, because program music is not a synthetic hybrid, and thus cannot "emerge" as representational from non-representational parts, the underlying assumption of course being here, as elsewhere, that the mere addition of text cannot make the music representational, where it was not before.

With the first and second claims I have no quarrel at all. They are both, on my view, correct. From the third, however, I demur, as the argument that has gone before should have made readily apparent.

Since, as the previous argument makes clear, I have no trouble with the notion that the addition of a text, whether narrative, descriptive, or otherwise, can make a melodic token of a given type representational, where another token of the type, without the text, was not, and, thus, since I thoroughly reject the "axiom" to the contrary, there is little need for me to say much more in defense of the view that program music, in both its narrative and non-narrative varieties, can, at times, in places be representational. It is so where the text makes apparent *what* the music is representing, and the music makes it apparent *that* the music is representing this by facilitating our experience of hearing the object of representation in the musical fabric. More examples of this would be otiose, as would further argument. What was said of the grumbling figure in *Fidelio* in the previous section applies, *pari passu*, to unnumbered examples in the program music repertory. And the nuts and bolts of how music facilitates our hearing representations "in" it I have treated in detail in *Sound and Semblance*, as regards both the representation of sounds and the representation of other phenomena.[22] For music is by no means limited to the representation of sounds, as my very first example, Beethoven's representation of the risen Christ in the *Missa Solemnis* makes clear. For other such examples I can only refer the reader to my previous work on musical representation and to his or her own musical experience.

VI

To conclude, let me point out and comment briefly on what I take to be a puzzling resurgence in recent years of very old suspicions regarding the genuine possibility of representation in music. Three times in the past

---

[22] Kivy, *Sound and Semblance*, ch. 3.

fifteen years, philosophers in the modern analytic tradition have found logical or metaphysical reasons for affirming that so-called musical representation is not a *bona fide* instance of the phenomenon. In 1976 Roger Scruton argued that musical "representation" was defective because it did not maintain a viable distinction between subject and medium of representation, and because, on his view, any piece of so-called representational music can be fully understood without our being aware of the supposed representationality at all.[23] In 1987 Jenefer Robinson argued that musical "representation" was defective because it did not facilitate "hearing in", the musical version of Richard Wollheim's "seeing in" in visual representation, which Robinson took to be a necessary condition for genuine representationality.[24] And now Stephen Davies (1992) has argued that musical "representation" is defective because, essentially, it is said to exist (for the most part) only with the help of a text, and the mere addition of a text cannot make absolute music, which, by hypothesis, is not representational, into a representational thing.

I have tried, I hope with some success, to answer the arguments of Scruton and Robinson elsewhere,[25] and the argument of Davies here. And although it would be disingenuous of me not to express satisfaction with my responses, I still find myself puzzled by this recent resurgence of doubt, by philosophers of deep insight, about the real possibility of musical representation. The old, historical debate was very much a normative one, in the heat of battle, over whether representation in music was a desirable aesthetic goal. Furthermore, within that debate it is sometimes very difficult to know whether what is being claimed is that composers ought not to pursue musical representation because it is impossible, or that it *is* possible, but not worth pursuing. But in any case, it is clear that the debate was driven by a fierce disagreement over what the "music of the future" should be.

I take it that no contemporary philosopher would be prone to confuse the normative with the "possibility" question, or to be driven by the former to take a stand, one way or the other, on the latter. What, then, drives the debate today?

I can only conjecture that the exponential increase in, and understanding of, representation in the visual arts, of which Marx Wartofsky's work

[23] Roger Scruton, "Representation in Music", *Philosophy*, 51 (1976).

[24] Jenefer Robinson, "Music as a Representational Art," in Philip Alperson (ed.), *What is Music?: An Introduction to the Philosophy of Music* (New York: Haven Publications, 1987).

[25] See Kivy, *Sound and Semblance*, 146–59, and 217–26.

is a prime example, has made it increasingly clear what representation in its most paradigmatic form *is*, and at the same time made it increasingly clear that the musical cases are *peripheral* ones. A hard-headed sense of parsimony will do the rest. It is very tempting, I suppose, to want to get rid of the peripheral cases by drumming them out of the corps altogether.

But I feel obliged to play the role of gadfly in the present debate, and press upon those of a parsimonious bent in representational matters that peripheral cases are *cases* nonetheless. A philosopher of the distant past said, "What is is." A philosopher of the more recent past said (with almost equal pith), "Everything is what it is." I fondly hope, and seriously doubt, that if the skeptic contemplates these two excellent sayings while listening intently to a cantata by Bach, it will settle for him or her forever in the affirmative the question of whether music *truly* "represents".

14

Music, Language, and Cognition: Which Doesn't Belong?

INTRODUCTION

When the topic of "Music, Language, and Cognition" was first proposed to me by the organizers of this Colloquium, I was at once reminded of the game in which a child is shown, for example, pictures of an apple, a banana, and a trumpet and asked "Which one doesn't belong?" I assume you all know the answer.

But which doesn't belong in the triad of music, language, and cognition? If you answer that they *all* belong, as some people might, then you are in disagreement with me. For my answer is: *language* doesn't belong. Music is, indeed, language-like in certain respects. Nevertheless, it is not language; it is not a language or part of a language. And thinking it is any one of these things has caused a good deal of confusion.

Certainly, though, music and *cognition* belong together. For, on my view anyway, the enjoyment and appreciation of music are deeply involved with the cognitive processes. As I put the point some years ago, "music is not a stimulus ...: it is an object of perception and cognition, which understanding opens up for ... appreciation."[1]

My talk today will be solely concerned with absolute music—that is to say, pure instrumental music without text, title, or program—and it will naturally fall into two parts. In the first I want to explore the music–language analogy, emphasizing the while that it *is* an *analogy*: that music is not language, not *a* language, not part of a language. In the second part I want to outline *some* of what I mean when I say that the enjoyment and appreciation of music are concept-laden activities: *cognitive* activities, if you will. Whether such cognitive activities are

---

[1] Peter Kivy, *Music Alone: Philosophical Reflections on the Purely Musical Experience* (Ithaca, NY: Cornell University Press, 1990), 41.

what cognitive science is all about, I do not know. But I dare say this is the place to find out. First, then, to the music–language connection.

MUSIC AND LANGUAGE

When Franz Joseph Haydn, "papa" Haydn to his friends, decided, in 1790, at the advanced age of 58, to make an extended trip to England, Mozart is supposed to have exclaimed: "Oh, Papa, you have had no education for the wide world, and you speak so few languages." Haydn's legendary reply was: "But my language is understood all over the world."[2]

What is it about this famous statement that sounds so true? And what is it that is so palpably false?

In answering these questions, there are three aspects to Haydn's claim that we should look at: what he would have meant by his music, which is, of course what he is talking about, constituting his language; closely related to that, what he would have meant by someone's understanding it; and finally, why he would have felt so confident that his music was understood by listeners "all over the world", "the wide world", as Mozart called it—a fairly audacious claim, one feels compelled to say.

Well, to start with the last aspect of Haydn's remark, his reference to the whole world, it becomes far less grandiose when one considers what the "world" of Haydn and Mozart was. It consisted, after all, of Austria, Germany, Bohemia, France, Italy, and England—certainly not much more than that: that was it. And it does not seem unreasonable to think that *that* "world" could "understand" Haydn's music (although we do not yet quite know what "understand" might mean in this context). In other words, an Englishman who understood no German could still "understand" the *musical* "language" that Haydn "spoke". It was, in other words, an "international language"—the true *lingua franca*.

Of course *we* all know perfectly well that, had Haydn taken his music to Japan, or China, or India, he would have found in those places no understanding of his musical "language"; nor would *he*, genius though he was, have understood the musical "languages" of Japan, China, or India. And in that respect, then, music is language-like. For just as someone brought up in a French-speaking country understands French but not German, so someone brought up in China understands Chinese music but not the music of Haydn and Mozart.

[2] Karl Geiringer, *Haydn: A Creative Life in Music* (London: George Allen & Unwin, 1947), 89.

Someone might object here that the language analogy in this respect is not a very good one, since the French understand French but not German, the Germans understand German but not French, and so on, whereas *all* Europeans understand Haydn, which is to say, Viennese classical music. Well, I am not sure just how important this difference is, or what the reasons for it are. One reason, obviously, for the broader understanding of European music, as opposed to European languages, must be that natural languages have a semantics as well as a grammar. You have to know what French words mean to understand French. But you don't have to know what the themes (or whatever analogue to words you choose) of a classical symphony mean to understand *it*. They don't *mean* anything. One way of putting this is to say that, unlike natural languages, music of the kind Haydn wrote has a "syntax" without a semantics.

Since you are not reading this lecture, you cannot see that in referring to the "syntax" of music, I have put "syntax" in quotation marks—scare-quotes as they are sometimes called. I do this to alert the unwary to the fact that, at least so I believe, musical "syntax" may not be syntax in the literal sense, but syntax-like, as music is language-like, but not language.

It looks, then, as if music may have been understood in the whole of Haydn's world, while German and English were not, because to understand Haydn's music, you needed to know only a syntax, whereas to understand German or English or French you needed to know a semantic as well, and a different one for each language. Furthermore, the grammars of these natural languages differ, even though there are aspects they have in common, so that if you understand French grammar, say, you will also understand at least some of the principles of English and German grammar as well. (I am leaving out here the whole issue of Chomskian deep structure, and its supposed analogue in tonal music, as laid out by Lerdahl and Jackendoff.[3])

In any case, we can reach the reasonable conclusion, to return to Haydn's response to Mozart, with which we began these reflections, that Haydn was right in claiming that his music was understood all over the world, but only because the world to which he referred was *his* world, a very restricted, homogeneous world, which shared his musical culture.

[3] F. Lerdahl and R. Jackendoff, *A Generative Theory of Tonal Music* (Cambridge, Mass.: MIT Press, Bradford Books, 1983).

(Multiculturalism was not something that Haydn and his century had to worry about.) And in that, unlike French, or German, or English, Haydn's music *was* understood throughout his world, and still is, it is very *un*-language-like. On the other hand, in that it was not understood in China, Japan, or India, where very different musics flourished, it *is* very language-like. For it is of the nature of natural languages to be understood only by those who, one way or another, have learned them. And the common way to learn a natural language is to be born into it and be immersed in it throughout one's life. It is the same, needless to say, with music, whether it be Chinese music, Japanese music, Indian music, or the music of the West. You aren't likely to be aware that you are learning it. You just *are*.

But what, after all, does it really mean to say that all the world, Haydn's world, *understood* Haydn's music? What does understanding such music amount to? If I am right—and I am not alone in thinking this—that music has no vocabulary, has no semantic content, then we clearly cannot mean that music is understood in the way French or German or English is. Understanding the meanings of words is, after all, a substantial part of linguistic competence. You have to have a vocabulary. But there are no words in music: there is no vocabulary. So what could we plausibly construe Haydn as saying when he averred that the whole world *understood* his language, which is to say, his *music*?

In the second part of this lecture, when I come to talk about music and cognition, I will go into this matter a little more deeply. But for now it will suffice to say that what it means to understand music is to enjoy and to appreciate it for the right, relevant reasons: that is to say, to enjoy and appreciate in it those aspects of it that the composer intended you to enjoy and appreciate, and to enjoy and appreciate them in the way or ways intended. Thus, for example, if I enjoy and appreciate the way Bach combines the two themes together in a fugue, after developing each of them separately, or the way Beethoven brings in the horn, "in the wrong place", just before the recapitulation in the first movement of the *Eroica*, I am displaying enjoyment and appreciation of the music; and that is what I mean by understanding it. But if I am completely unacquainted with the music of southern India, and am enjoying the exotic jangle of the instruments while eating a curry in an Indian restaurant, I am neither enjoying nor appreciating that music. And that amounts to saying that I am not understanding it. I am certainly enjoying and appreciating *something*; but not *it*.

So far, then, in our exploring of the music–language analogy, we have reached the following conclusions. Music is language-like in that it is *not*, as Haydn is sometimes quoted as having said, an international language. The music of India, like the language of Germany, is not generally understood beyond national boundaries. The understanding of Indian music, like the understanding of the German language, is learned, not innate: learned, to be sure, naturally and effortlessly, within a culture, at least to a certain degree of minimal competence; but hardly cross-culturally understood, the way pictorial representations apparently are. Of course, a German can learn to understand Indian music, as an Indian can learn the German language. And that too marks music out as language-like.

Furthermore, music is language-like in having something *like* a syntax. On the other hand, it is surely far from language-like in its total lack of a semantic component. And that lack alone is sufficient for concluding that music is not language, *a* language, part of a language, or however you want to put it.

Nevertheless, there is *another* aspect of Western music, possessed by it since the beginning of the seventeenth century, that has been adduced so frequently as evidence of its linguistic credentials that no discussion of the music–language analogy would be complete without considering it. The two most frequent characterizations of music as language are that music is an "international language" and that music is "the language of the emotions". We have looked at the former claim already, and I turn now to the latter one. They are not, it turns out, unrelated, as we shall see.

The notion that music is an emotional (as opposed to a conceptual) *language* became so widespread by the end of the eighteenth century that it amounted to more or less a philosophical consensus. Kant, to adduce a prominent example, simply took it for granted. Music, he asserted without any argument at all, is a speech or language of the emotions: *Sprache der Affekte.*[4] Where did this view originate, and what, if any, plausibility attaches to it?

To answer the former question, I must mention two momentous events in music history that transpired in the second half of the sixteenth century. The first, an event not merely of musical significance but of world significance as well, was the so-called Counter-Reformation, the second the invention of the musical art form we know as opera.

---

[4] Immanuel Kant, *Kritik der Urteilskraft* (Hamburg: Felix Meiner Verlag, 1959), 186 (§ 53).

The Counter-Reformation was the attempt on the part of the Roman Catholic Church to, in effect, clean house, in response to the criticism of the Protestant Reformers. What this had to do with music was that the music of the liturgy, by the beginning of the sixteenth century, the heyday of Flemish polyphony, had become so elaborate and complicated that the text was all but unintelligible. And it was the *text*, the Church Fathers reminded the composers, that was the whole point of the exercise.

The villain was the polyphony itself: the combining of five or more long, sinuous melodies in such a way as to prolong a sentence or phrase of text beyond the point where a listener could tell what words were being sung. And if you couldn't understand the words, obviously the religious sentiments they expressed would be lost to you as well, and the very purpose of your presence at worship was defeated.

The fate of Catholic liturgical music, along with the many other issues of the Counter-Reformation, were debated at the Council of Trent, which sat from 1545 to 1563. Here, in part, is the admonition that was directed by the Council to the composers: "The whole plan of singing in musical modes should be constructed not to give empty pleasure to the ear, but in such a way that the words may be clearly understood by all, and thus the hearts of the listeners be drawn to the desire of heavenly harmonies, and the contemplation of the joys of the blessed."[5]

How was this admonition to be executed in practice? Well, if the best way of making words intelligible to a listener is to speak them, then the best way of making them intelligible to a listener, when they are sung, is, one might well suppose, to *represent* the speaking voice in music. What the Council of Trent accomplished, perhaps unwittingly, was to make of vocal music a representational art. I cannot prove that this is what the so-called post-Tridentine composers of Catholic liturgical music had on their minds. But when I listen to their works, especially those of Palestrina, that is what the music sounds like to me: the representation in music of human speech.

In any case, if the representation of the human speaking voice was implicit in the practice of composers of liturgical music in Italy after the Council of Trent, it quickly came to be *explicit*, with a vengeance, in the writings of the so-called Camerata in Florence at the close of the sixteenth century: the group of poets, theoreticians, composers, and noblemen who were in the process of inventing musical theater: *dramma*

---

[5] Quoted in Gustave Reese, *Music in the Renaissance* (New York: Norton, 1954), 449.

per musica, as it was originally called, opera, as we call it now. Their idea was that the only way you could emotionally move the listener—and the moving of the emotions was the most important aim of music, so they thought—was to represent in your music the declamation of a speaker whose utterances are being made under the influence of some powerful emotion. As Giulio Caccini, one of the earliest composers of opera, described his practice: "for, unless the words were understood, they could not move the understanding, I have endeavored in those[,] my late compositions to bring in a kind of music by which men might, as it were, talk in harmony ...".[6]

The basic idea behind the musical representation of impassioned speech in early opera was that the listener would empathize with the character thus expressing herself, and thereby experience the very emotion being expressed. I doubt that the empathy theory is in very good repute these days, and for our purposes it is irrelevant. What is important to observe is that in lockstep with the establishment in Western music of the major–minor tonal system, in the seventeenth century there evolved a whole arsenal of musical themes and harmonic techniques whose emotive character became instantly recognizable to the competent listener. Furthermore, this fundamental recognizability endures to this day. As long as the composer remains within the major–minor tonal system, he or she can still rely on the competent listener to recognize when the music is sad, when joyful, when ominous, and so on. These emotive building blocks are stock-in-trade of the film composer, the composer of popular songs, and are part and parcel of the whole classical music repertoire from the beginning of the seventeenth century to the breakdown of tonality in the twentieth.

I have avoided doing so on purpose, but it is almost impossible to refrain from calling these emotive building blocks I have been alluding to an emotive "vocabulary", making up an emotive musical "language". And as a *façon de parler* it is perfectly harmless. Music is certainly language-like in having these universally recognizable emotive qualities. Where we get into trouble is taking the language analogy too seriously—which is to say, too literally. It is one thing to say that this passage of music is sad, that one triumphant. It is a different thing, and a profound mistake, to say that the one passage *means* "sad", the other

---

[6] Oliver Strunk (ed.), *Source Readings in Music History: From Antiquity through the Romantic Era* (New York: Norton, 1950), 378.

"triumph", and that the music is *saying* something about sadness and triumph. *That* is not a part of what music does.

There has been lively debate among philosophers over the last fifty or so years about what exactly we mean when we describe music in emotive terms. But a general consensus has emerged from this debate that we are *not* ascribing to the music dispositions to arouse emotions in us but, rather, are ascribing phenomenal, heard properties *to* the music. As the American philosopher O. K. Bouwsma once wittily put it, "the sadness is to the music rather like the redness to the apple, than it is like the burp to the cider".[7]

This being said, we might now look, finally, at the relation I suggested there might be between the notion that music is an international language and the notion that it is a language of the emotions. Might not the latter feed the former? For if emotions are universal to the species, in expression and experience, common to all cultures, then if music *were* a language of the emotions, it would, it might be argued, be a cross-cultural—which is to say, an international—language.

There was a time when this argument would have been rejected on the grounds that emotions and their expression are *not* universal to the species, but culturally conditioned: culture-specific. However, there is mounting empirical evidence that at least the basic emotions and their expression are not matters of culture and conditioning; rather, biological endowments.

What *is* wrong with the argument is its reliance on the false assumption that the emotions *in the music* are universally recognized across cultural boundaries. They are not, because they are aesthetic qualities of the music. Being so, they can be perceived only by musically competent listeners, and musical competence, as we have already seen, is not species-universal, but culture-bound. An Indian, unacquainted with Western musical culture and idioms, cannot tell us that a passage in one of Haydn's symphonies is sad rather than happy, not because she experiences sadness and happiness differently from the way we do, or expresses them differently. She cannot perceive that the music is sad or happy because she cannot yet perceive *the music*, of which the sadness or happiness are aesthetic components. It is Western *musical* sadness and happiness, not Western sadness and happiness that are opaque to her.

---

[7] O. K. Bouwsma, "The Expression Theory of Art", in Max Black (ed.), *Philosophical Analysis* (Ithaca, NY: Cornell University Press, 1950), 100.

The notion that music is a language of the emotions, then, like the notion that music is an international language, has a kernel of truth in it: it reveals to us one of the ways in which music is language-like. It *is* language-like in that the competent listener to Western music—and I make no claims in this regard about any other music—can recognize the emotive qualities of the music in a consistent manner. And in this regard it is language-like too, in that the ability to "read" the musical emotions, like the ability to read French or German, is not innate or cross-cultural. Just as you must learn to read French or German, so you must learn to "read" the emotions in Western music. Music is not a language or the language of the emotions. But its emotive character makes it language-like in that respect.

I conclude this section of my talk, then, with the general observation that music is *not* a language but is *language-like* in the ways I have just enumerated. In the triad music, language, and cognition, language is the one that doesn't belong. But music and cognition, on the other hand, are an inseparable pair. And I go on, now, in the second section, to make some observations about their cordial relations.

MUSIC AND COGNITION

There has been prominent in our thinking about music, absolute music, since the eighteenth century, what appears to me to be a false dichotomy between the view that music is content-less, and therefore concept-less, and the view that music must be concept-laden and therefore content-laden. Concept-less or content-laden have been the two alternatives on offer.

For contemporary philosophers the *locus classicus* of the content-less, therefore concept-less, alternative is Kant's definition of music as "the art of the beautiful play of sensations".[8] And perhaps the same role is played by Schopenhauer for the content–concept view in his claim that music is an image or likeness of the will: *Abbild des Willens*.[9]

In the contemporary world, the ascribing of content to absolute music has, after long eclipse in the shadow of formalism, become a flourishing business. To give you an idea of what kind of thing I am referring to, I quote from a well-known practitioner.

---

[8] Kant, *Kritik der Urteilskraft*, 180 (§ 51).
[9] Artur Schopenhauer, *Die Welt als Wille und Vorstellung*, in *Sämtliche Werke*, i (Stuttgart: Suhrkamp, 1986), 359 (Book III, § 52).

By following the events of the first movement carefully, the listener becomes engaged in a process yielding a truth at the end. The forces used here are genuinely dramatic ones. In strictly musical terms, the opposition can be reduced to a conflict between stability and instability, a process not unlike that of any significant dramatic work. But instead of using characters or ideas or beliefs, the symphonist embodies his conflict in musical gestures which, in an archetypal way, parallel human conflicts. In the conclusion of the first movement of [Symphony] No. 83, Haydn can be seen to be demonstrating a very fundamental but difficult truth: opposition is inevitable, and the highest form of unity is not the one which eliminates conflict. On the contrary, it is one in which opposing forces can co-exist. The best minds of Haydn's age aspired to tolerance, not dogmatism. It is precisely this message that can be heard in Haydn's late symphonies.[10]

Now if music possessed this kind of semantic or representational content, there would be at least one obvious sense in which the enjoyment and appreciation of music would be a cognitive process. For I think all will agree that the perceiving of semantic or representational content in a work of art is a cognitive process if ever there was one. And if it is true, as the author just quoted suggests, that "messages" and philosophical theses can be heard in symphonies, and other such forms of music, then clearly we are obliged to acknowledge that the appreciation of such music is a palpably cognitive affair.

Speaking for myself, and for at least a substantial number of others, such semantic and representational interpretations will not withstand critical scrutiny. But I have neither the time nor the inclination right now to present arguments for my skepticism, although I have presented them in other places. Rather, what I want to do in the time remaining to me is to confront the disjunction, no content, therefore no cognition, *or* cognition, therefore content. It is a false disjunction. There *is* a third thing. There *is* cognition without content.

There are, as I see it, *at least* three kinds of cognitive processes going on when someone like me, who perceives no semantic or representational content in music, enjoys and appreciates it. I shall call them, not very surprisingly, conscious cognition, self-conscious cognition, and non-conscious cognition. It is the first two that I want to talk about here; but I mention the third because I do not want to be taken as denying that there may well be processing going on, when we listen to and enjoy

[10] David P. Schroeder, *Haydn and the Enlightenment: The Late Symphonies and their Audience* (Oxford: Clarendon Press, 1990), 88.

music, that we are not aware of, but that can fairly be described as cognitive.

Indeed, the idea that there is non-conscious cognition taking place in the enjoyment and appreciation of music is not a new idea at all, but a very old one. For if I read him aright, it was what Leibniz was saying, when famously he wrote of music, "even the pleasures of sense are reducible to intellectual pleasures known confusedly. Music charms us, although its beauty consists only in the agreement of numbers, and in the counting, which we do not perceive but which the soul nevertheless continues to carry out, of the beats or vibrations of sounding bodies which coincide at certain intervals".[11]

As I say, it is not non-conscious cognition, however, that I want to talk about. And that may come as a disappointment to many here. But, quite frankly, I do not know *how* to talk about non-conscious musical cognition—non-conscious computation, as Leibniz apparently saw it. So I had much better stick to what I think I do know how to talk about: namely, conscious and self-conscious cognition.

I think I mean something pretty obvious by the distinction between conscious and self-conscious cognition. When I see a cat, I take it that I am in the conscious state of seeing the cat. But I also take it that I am not necessarily conscious *that* I am seeing the cat.

However, I may also become aware of my seeing the cat. In other words, my conscious state may have as its intentional object the cat, or it may have as its intentional object my conscious state of seeing the cat. Assuming, as I do, an epistemic view of perception, I call my perceiving of the cat conscious cognition and my awareness of perceiving the cat, with my perceiving of the cat as the intentional object, self-conscious cognition. Both kinds of cognition are at work in enjoying and appreciating music. Here is how I see them operating.

I begin with the commonsensical notion that the performance of a musical work—that is to say, the "sounding" of a musical work—is a series of "sound events". What the events are, and how many there are, is indeterminate, depending as it does upon what descriptions they are perceived or understood under and how one individuates the sounding, event-wise. So to ask how many events a work-sounding is composed of

[11] Gottfried Wilhelm Leibniz, "Principles of Nature and Grace", in *idem, Philosophical Papers and Letters*, trans. and ed. Leroy E. Loemker (Chicago: University of Chicago Press, 1956), ii. 1042.

is very much like asking how many "things" there are in a room. It all depends on how you carve it up.

But the basic point is this. Serious enjoyment and appreciation of classical music is an activity of perceiving, sometimes consciously, sometimes self-consciously, musical events under musical descriptions. Classical music is not, and is not meant to be, merely a pleasing stimulation of the auditory faculty. Furthermore, classical music, when correctly listened to, does not gain its effect solely by non-conscious processing, as Leibniz seems to have believed, although such non-conscious cognition no doubt occurs, and is vital to the experience. The enjoyment and appreciation of classical music is concept-laden *and* content-less, then, in that the entertaining of concepts, both consciously and self-consciously, on the part of the qualified, attentive listener, is essential to its full enjoyment and appreciation, but the concepts entertained are purely musical concepts, even though they may be described in ordinary, non-musical language. In other words, the concepts are not expressive of semantic or representational content. The enjoyment and appreciation of classical music, then, is both a conscious and a self-conscious cognitive process without being one in which the cognition is of either semantic or representational properties.

Now the problem that many people, particularly the musically untrained, have with this position, so stated, is that they believe it over-intellectualizes the musical experience. Yes, it may be granted, the musically learned—musicians, music theorists, musicologists—listen with a whole array of music-theoretic concepts and terminology at the ready. No doubt they very consciously and self-consciously apply these concepts to music as they listen to it. But, so the argument goes on, the untrained classical music lover *just listens*. How can she listen cognitively, either consciously or self-consciously? She doesn't have the concepts that such cognition requires. Only the "expert" does.

There are two points that should be addressed here. The first is the claim that only the expert's listening is cognitive, concept-laden listening, because only the expert has the concepts. The second is the distinction between conscious and self-conscious listening and how I think it gets played out in musical listening, both that of the experts and that of the laity.

I think the best way to address both points is by way of a musical example.

W. A. Mozart, String Quartet in A, K. 464.

Now there are many notable events taking place in this short but musically dense composition (which some of you may be familiar with). And the first thing to say about it is that one has not heard this composition unless one has consciously heard at least some major portion of these events as the events they are. Someone, for example, who has just been vaguely aware of the music, as background to something else he is doing, or as part of the ubiquitous musical "white noise" that pervades airports and bus and railroad stations these days, to relax the nail-biting traveler, on the assumption that classical music is boring, and therefore anxiety-reducing, has not "heard" *the music* in a perfectly well-understood use of perception words. For I am using "hear" in "hear the music" in a sense that I referred to a while back as the "epistemic" sense. In that sense, when one hears something, one hears it *as* something; one takes it to be something. In other words, one hears *it* under some description. It is the intentional object of one's conscious state.

Now what *does* one hear in this miniature compositional *tour de force?* Well, let me just say what *some* of the things are that *I* heard in the first few measures. I heard the opening theme as two separate four-measure phrases, the second kind "answering" the first. In measures 9–12 I heard a variation of the theme's first phrase. But I also heard that the second phrase of the theme was being used to accompany the first phrase. In other words, the main theme is so constructed that the first phrase and the second phrase can be played together, in counterpoint. In measures 13–16 I heard the first four notes of the theme in stretto. That is to say, one instrument begins the theme, and before it has finished playing it, another instrument begins to play it: violin 1, then viola, then violin 2, then cello. At measure 17 things get even more complicated. Now the second part of the theme occurs in a stretto, but violins 1 and 2 begin the theme together, in octaves, and after a measure, before they are finished with it, the viola and cello enter together, the viola playing the second phrase of the theme while the cello plays the second phrase of the theme in inversion: that is, where the original theme ascends, it descends, and vice versa. So whereas the first phrase of the theme can be played with the second phrase as its accompaniment, we now discover that the second phrase of the theme can be combined, in stretto, simultaneously, with itself and its inversion.

These are some of the events I heard in the first twenty measures of the movement. There are many more events of this kind in the rest of it. But it would be pointless to go on enumerating them. I am sure you have gotten the general idea. But I do want to mention one further thing that I heard before I go on. So far, I have been talking about what might be called the "internal" happenings in Mozart's minuet. However, the piece also follows a well-known plan or pattern, if you will. It is constructed of two sections. The first section modulates to the dominant key of E. The second section, twice as long as the first, eventually modulates back to the tonic key of A. Each section is repeated. That is the general, very familiar plan or pattern working itself out as I listened, the while, to the internal events, some of which I have just described. And of course, hearing that plan or pattern helped me to orient myself to the internal events I was hearing within it. I had the map.

Now when I say that I enjoy and appreciate this minuet of Mozart's, I mean, in part, that I enjoy perceiving these musical events playing out the general plan of the work. I enjoyed discovering them in my first hearings of it, and I enjoy rehearing and rediscovering them now, as well as, of course, sometimes discovering new events that I had not heard before. So what I mean by the enjoyment and appreciation of music of this kind being conscious cognitive processes is, in part, illustrated by the way I listen to and enjoy the Mozart minuet. For, I take it, it is obviously a conscious cognitive activity to hear that the theme of the minuet is in two phrases, that the first phrase is treated in stretto, beginning at measure 13, that the second phrase is combined with its inversion at measure 18, and so on. And to hear that these things are happening in the way I described, I must of course possess the concepts of theme, phrase, stretto, inversion, counterpoint, and so forth. So that is what I mean when I say that listening to music is concept-laden: that, further-more, enjoying and appreciating music are concept-laden, but the music content-less. For the concepts that I deploy in enjoying and appreciating music are not its content: are not concepts that the music expresses. The music is not saying "stretto", "inversion", and so on.

But it is just here that the charge of *over-intellectualizing* the musical experience is liable to be made. For, so the argument goes, lots of people, genuine, serious music lovers all, enjoy and appreciate this minuet without possessing any of the concepts I have mentioned. They don't know what a stretto or an inversion is. They don't have any musical training. So how can they have any musical concepts at all to apply to the music? The expert's or trained amateur's listenings to music may be concept-laden, but the average music lover's are concept-*less*. Does that make the average music lover completely inconsequential from the aesthetician's point of view? That would be a hard saying indeed.

There is an element of truth in the charge. It is quite correct to say that the average, untrained music lover does not possess the music-theoretic concepts of the expert or trained amateur. Where it goes wrong is in suggesting that *therefore* the average, untrained music lover does not possess any musical concepts at all, and, as a consequence, is a completely "mindless" listener. Musical events need not be described in music-theoretic terms or be understood only under music-theoretic concepts. For many purposes ordinary language and non-technical concepts can suffice for rich enjoyment and appreciation.

So what does the serious but untrained music lover hear in Mozart's minuet? In the non-epistemic sense she hears, of course, the same musical events that the trained listener hears. But in the epistemic sense she hears some of these events under different descriptions from those of the expert, perhaps less satisfactory descriptions, and misses hearing some of them altogether.

Thus, for example, where I hear a stretto, the untrained listener will not hear what is going on under that description but may very well hear that *something* unusual is going on which she may want to describe as "crowding" or "clumping" or something like that. But she may well miss the inversion of the theme altogether, under any description, because I think it is hard to hear the inversion of a melody as a version of that melody at all unless the technique is pointed out and conceptualized. Anyway, the general idea is that music is describable in terms other than those of a music-theoretic kind, and can be heard under concepts other than those of a music-theoretic kind; and that, it appears to me, is sufficient to answer the charge of over-intellectualizing the musical listening experience, if it is a charge motivated by my use in my original description of that experience of music-theoretic terms and concepts.

But suppose the skeptic continues to press his claim, albeit in a somewhat scaled-down version. He will say something like this. Granted there are *both* trained *and* lay listeners who enjoy and appreciate music in the cerebral, concept-laden, cognitive way you have described, nevertheless there *also* are large numbers of listeners who enjoy and appreciate music in a purely "mindless" way—at least, mindless in the sense that they are not consciously or self-consciously perceiving musical events: rather, they are simply pleased by the sounds, bathing, so to speak, in their fragrance, without a thought in the world *about* the music, although, of course, their minds (or brains) are very busy in cognitive and conceptual processes, *à la* Leibniz, of which these "mindless" listeners are completely unaware.

Now with this skeptical response to my views I have no quarrel at all. Doubtless it is true that there *are* mindless listeners, so described by the skeptic. Nor am I here to read them a sermon on how they ought to change their mindless ways and listen to music the way I and my friends do. There is, indeed, music designed for mindless listening, and it pervades our aural space. The music of which I speak, however—the music of Bach and Haydn and Mozart, of Beethoven and Mendelssohn and Brahms, of Mahler and Schoenberg and Stravinsky—was not meant to be mindlessly enjoyed and appreciated, but enjoyed and appreciated in something like the cognitive, concept-laden way I have been describing. Of course, it can also have a payoff for mindless listening. That is beside the point, which is that when it is listened to as intended, it has a different payoff, and one that has been found rich and rewarding by three centuries of listeners, both trained and untrained in its mysteries. That is the kind of music, and the kind of enjoyment and appreciation, I am trying to understand. That there is other music, other kinds of enjoyment and appreciation, I am not here to deny, although if Clive Bell is to be credited, those so-called mindless listeners of which I have been speaking—at least some of them, anyway—may very well at least be aware that they are missing something important. As Bell put it, "About music most people are as willing to be humble as I am. If they cannot grasp form and win from it a pure aesthetic emotion, they confess that they understand music imperfectly or not at all."[12]

This brings us to the second point I said it was necessary to address: the distinction I have been assuming all along between conscious listening and self-conscious listening. I turn to that now, briefly, in conclusion.

It seems to me to make perfect sense to say that someone is aware of something in his visual or aural field, but is not aware of his being aware. In the musical case, to return to my previous example, I may be perceiving that the second phrase of the theme is now accompanying the first phrase without being consciously aware that I am so perceiving. However, it sometimes happens in my own listening, and I am sure in other people's, that I start thinking about what I am perceiving as I am perceiving it; in this case I start thinking about the fact that the second phrase is now accompanying the first, and perhaps marvel over the skill and workmanship displayed. This is what I call self-conscious cognitive enjoyment and appreciation.

I believe that this kind of self-conscious, cognitive activity is very common among serious, sophisticated listeners. And I think it is common not merely among musically trained listeners, because I take it that a musical listener can be sophisticated to a high degree *without* being musically trained.

Now it may be—it very probably is—the case that technical musical training increases the tendency to listen to music self-consciously: to think about what one is hearing while one is hearing it. I know it increased that tendency in me. Is that a good result? Is it better to hear music self-consciously as well as consciously? I think it has been in my experience. Certainly it seems to add a layer of pleasurable experience to the enterprise.

---

[12] Clive Bell, *Art* (New York: Capricorn Books, 1958), 31.

It may be objected to what I am suggesting, however, that thinking about what one is hearing while in the process of listening to the music, even though it does occur, is not only not essential to the musical experience but downright destructive of it. If you think too much about what you are hearing, it will, so the objection goes, distract you from the hearing itself.

My own view is that you can't think too much about what you are listening to when listening to music. What I do think is that thinking too much is frequently confused with thinking about the wrong things. A composer may become so intrigued with a musical event she is perceiving that she will start thinking about how to use it in her own work. An oboist or violinist may become so intrigued with the techniques of players he is listening to that he starts thinking about his own playing technique. These are not cases of thinking too much about the music, but of ceasing to think about the music altogether. It is, I suppose, thinking too much. What it is not is thinking too much about *the music*. Even though they are musical thoughts, they are as irrelevant to and distracting from musical listening as letting oneself think about the poetic or philosophical ideas that the music might suggest. Again in Clive Bell's words, "Tired or perplexed, I let slip my sense of form ... and I begin weaving into the harmonies, that I cannot grasp, the ideas of life".[13]

I have been arguing, then, that there are two kinds of conscious cognitive activity going on in serious, concentrated listening to classical music. There is the conscious hearing of musical events, hearing *that* certain musical things are going on. And there is what I have been calling self-conscious hearing: hearing *that* certain musical things are going on, and, the while, thinking about these goings on and about your hearing them. These together seem to me to play a very large role in serious music listening. This is not to deny that undoubtedly there is also cognitive processing going on of which I am completely unaware while I am listening to music. I have said nothing of substance about such non-conscious cognition because, as I said before, quite frankly, I don't know how to do that. I have simply spoken about that of which I *can* speak. What I can't speak of, I can't speak of; and that's that. But there probably *are* folks at this congress who *do* know about what I have been calling non-conscious musical cognition. And from them I am anxious to learn what I can.

13 Ibid. 30.

CONCLUSION

Let me press on now to my brief and overdue conclusion. The topic proposed to me, and to Laird Addis, was Music, Language, and Cognition. I have argued that these are strange bedfellows, in that language should not be in the same bed. The enjoyment and appreciation of music is thoroughly imbued with conscious and self-conscious cognitive processes, and, no doubt, non-conscious processes as well. But the connection between music and language is purely analogical. Music is language-like in being culturally conditioned and being vaguely, but not literally, describable as a "language of the emotions". That, so far as I can see, is where the connection ends. And a tenuous connection it is.

I have not really said here anything beyond what I have talked about and written about on various other occasions. But I am not apologetic for that. I am reminded of Groucho Marx's remark that there is no such thing as a new joke: a new joke is just an old joke someone hasn't heard yet. I told you all an old joke. My hope is that you haven't heard it yet, and can give me some new responses. Anyway, I presume that whenever one tries to reexpress his views, as I have done for this occasion, the views change, if ever so slightly, in the reexpressing. For, as Heraclitus said, you can't step in the same joke twice.

Bibliography

ADDISON, JOSEPH, *The Spectator*, ed. A. Chalmers, 6 vols. (New York: D. Appleton, 1879).

ADORNO, THEODORE, and EISLER, HANNS, *Composing for the Films* (London: Dennis Dobson, 1947).

ALPERSON, PHILIP (ed.), *What is Music?: An Introduction to the Philosophy of Music* (New York: Haven Publications, 1987).

ANON, Review of Mainwaring's *Memoirs of the Life of the Late George Frederic Handel*, Critical Review, 9 (1760).

APEL, WILLI (ed.), *The Harvard Dictionary of Music* (Cambridge, Mass.: Harvard University Press, 1951).

AVISON, CHARLES, *Essay on Musical Expression*, 3rd edn. (London, 1775).

BACON, FRANCIS, *Essays, Advancement of Learning, New Atlantis, and Other Pieces*, ed. R. F. Jones (New York: Odyssey Press, 1937)

BAR-ELLI, GILEAD, "Ideal Performance", *British Journal of Aesthetics*, 42 (2002).

BAZELON, IRWIN, *Knowing the Score: Notes on Film Music* (New York, Cincinnati, Toronto, London, and Melbourne: Van Nostrand and Reinhard, 1975).

BEARDSLEY, MONROE C., *The Possibility of Criticism* (Detroit: Wayne State University Press, 1970).

BELL, CLIVE, *Art* (New York: Capricorn Books, 1958).

BLACK, MAX (ed.), *Philosophical Analysis* (Ithaca, NY: Cornell University Press, 1950).

BÜCHER, KARL, *Arbeit und Rhythmus*, 4th edn. (Leipzig and Berlin, 1909).

BURNET, JOHN, *Early Greek Philosophy*, 4th edn. (London: Adam and Charles Black, 1952).

BURNEY, CHARLES, *A General History of Music*, ed. Frank Mercer, 2 vols. (New York: Dover, 1957)

CARROLL, NOEL, *Mystifying Movies: Fads and Fallacies in Contemporary Film Theory* (New York: Columbia University Press, 1988).

CATTELL, JAMES MCKEEN, "On the Origin of Music", *Mind*, 16 (1891).

COLLINGWOOD, R. G., *The Principles of Art* (Oxford: Clarendon Press, 1938; repr. 1955).

COMBARIEU, JULES, *Music: Its Laws and Evolution* (London, 1910).

CONE, EDWARD T., *Music: A View from Delft: Selected Essays*, ed. Robert P. Morgan (Chicago: University of Chicago Press, 1989)

DANTO, ARTHUR C., "The Artworld", *Journal of Philosophy*, 61 (1964).

_____ *The Transfiguration of the Commonplace: A Philosophy of Art* (Cambridge, Mass.: Harvard University Press, 1981).

DARWIN, CHARLES, *The Descent of Man*, 2nd edn. (New York, 1897).

—— *The Expression of the Emotions in Man and Animals* (London: John Murray, 1872).

DAVIES, STEPHEN, *Musical Meaning and Expression* (Ithaca, NY: Cornell University Press, 1994).

—— "Profundity in Instrumental Music", *British Journal of Aesthetics*, 42 (2002).

—— "Representation in Music", *Journal of Aesthetic Education*, 27 (1993).

DESCARTES, RENÉ, *The Passions of the Soul*, trans. Lowell Bair (New York: Bantam Matrix Books, 1966)

DEUTSCH, O. E., *Handel: A Documentary Biography* (New York: Norton, 1954).

DICKIE, GEORGE, SCLAFANI, RICHARD, and ROBLIN, ROBIN (eds.), *Aesthetics: A Critical Anthology*, 2nd edn. (New York: St Martin's Press, 1989).

GEIRINGER, KARL, *Haydn: A Creative Life in Music* (London: George Allen & Unwin, 1947).

GOODMAN, NELSON, *Languages of Art: An Approach to a Theory of Symbols* (Indianapolis and New York: Bobbs-Merrill, 1968).

GURNEY, EDMUND, "On Some Disputed Points in Music", *Fortnightly Review*, new series, 20 (1876).

HAACK, SUSAN, *Manifesto of a Passionate Moderate: Unfashionable Essays* (Chicago: University of Chicago Press, 1998).

HAMPSHIRE, STUART, *Two Theories of Morality* (Oxford: Oxford University Press, 1977).

HOBBES, THOMAS, *Leviathan*, ed. Herbert W. Schneider (Indianapolis: Bobbs-Merrill, Library of Liberal Arts, 1977).

HUME, DAVID, *Essays, Moral, Political and Literary* (Oxford: Oxford University Press, 1963).

—— *The Philosophical Works of David Hume* (Boston and Edinburgh: Little, Brown, 1854).

KANT, IMMANUEL, *Critique of Aesthetic Judgement*, trans. James Creed Meredith (Oxford: Clarendon Press, 1911)

—— *Kritik der Urteilskraft* (Hamburg: Felix Meiner Verlag, 1959).

KERMAN, JOSEPH, *The Beethoven Quartets* (New York: Alfred A. Knopf, 1967).

KIVY, PETER, *Authenticities: Philosophical Reflections on Musical Performance* (Ithaca, NY: Cornell University Press, 1995).

—— "Charles Darwin on Music", *Journal of the American Musicological Society*, 12 (1959).

—— *The Corded Shell: Reflections on Musical Expression* (Princeton: Princeton University Press, 1980).

—— *The Fine Art of Repetition: Essays in the Philosophy of Music* (Cambridge: Cambridge University Press, 1993).

KIVY, PETER, "Listening: Responses to Alperson, Howard and Davies", *Journal of Aesthetic Education*, 26 (1992).

—— *Music Alone: Philosophical Reflections on the Purely Musical Experience* (Ithaca, NY: Cornell University Press, 1990).

—— *New Essays on Musical Understanding* (Oxford: Clarendon Press, 2001).

—— "Opera Talk: A Philosophical 'phantasie' ", *Cambridge Opera Journal*, 3 (1991).

—— *Osmin's Rage: Philosophical Reflections on Opera, Drama and Text* (Princeton: Princeton University Press, 1988).

—— *Philosophies of Arts: An Essay in Differences* (New York: Cambridge University Press, 1979).

—— *The Possessor and the Possessed: Handel, Mozart, Beethoven, and the Idea of Musical Genius* (New Haven: Yale University Press, 2001).

—— *Sound and Semblance: Reflections on Musical Representation*, 2nd edn. (Ithaca, NY: Cornell University Press, 1991).

—— *Speaking of Art* (The Hague: Martinus Nijhoff, 1973).

KOOPMAN, CONSTANTIJN, and DAVIES, STEPHEN, "Musical Meaning in a Broader Perspective", *Journal of Aesthetics and Art Criticism*, 59 (2001).

KRAUSZ, MICHAEL (ed.), *The Interpretation of Music: Philosophical Essays* (Oxford: Clarendon Press, 1995).

KRISTELLER, PAUL OSKAR, "The Modern System of the Arts (I)", *Journal of the History of Ideas*, 12 (1951).

—— "The Modern System of the Arts (II)", *Journal of the History of Ideas*, 13 (1952).

LEIBNIZ, GOTTFRIED WILHELM, *Philosophical Papers and Letters*, trans. and ed. Leroy E. Loemker, 2 vols. (Chicago: University of Chicago Press, 1956).

LERDAHL, F., and JACKENDOFF R., *A Generative Theory of Tonal Music* (Cambridge, Mass.: MIT Press, Bradford Books, 1983).

LEVINSON, JERROLD, *Music, Art and Metaphysics: Essays in Philosophical Aesthetics* (Ithaca, NY: Cornell University Press, 1990).

LEWIS, C. S., *A Preface to Paradise Lost* (New York: Oxford University Press, Galaxy Books, 1961).

LONGINUS, DIONYSIUS, *Dionysius Longinus on the Sublime*, trans. William Smith, 2nd edn. (London, 1743).

[MAINWARING, JOHN], *Memoirs of the Life of the Late George Frederic Handel. To which is added a Catalogue of his Works and Observations upon them* (London, 1760).

MALCOLM, ALEXANDER, *A Treatise of Musick* (Edinburgh, 1721).

MARGOLIS, JOSEPH (ed.), *Philosophy Looks at the Arts*, 3rd edn. (Philadelphia: Temple University Press, 1987).

MATTHESON, JOHANN, *Der vollkommene Capellmeister*, trans. Ernest C. Harriss (Ann Arbor: UMI Research Press, 1981)

MELVILLE, HERMAN, *Moby Dick* (Garden City, NY: Garden City Publishing Co., 1930).

MILLINGTON, BARRY, "Nuremberg Trial: Is there Anti-Semitism in *Die Meistersinger?*", *Cambridge Opera Journal*, 3 (1991).

MONK, SAMUEL H., *The Sublime* (Ann Arbor: University of Michigan Press, 1960).

MOZART, W. A., *Letters of Mozart and His Family*, trans. Emily Anderson, 3 vols. (New York: Macmillan, 1938).

MUELLER VON ASOW, HEDWIG and E. H. (eds.) *The Collected Correspondence and Papers of Christoph Willibald Gluck*, trans. Stewart Thomson (New York: St Martin's Press, 1962).

NEWMAN, ERNEST, *The Life of Richard Wagner*, 4 vols. (London, 1933–47).

—— *Musical Studies* (London and New York, 1905).

—— "A Note on Herbert Spencer", *Weekly Critical Review*, 2 (1904).

—— *A Study of Wagner* (London, 1899).

NORTH, FRANCIS, *A Philosophical Essay of Musick* (London, 1677).

NORTH, ROGER, *Memoirs of Music*, ed. E. F. Rimbault (London, 1846).

—— *Roger North on Music*, ed. John Wilson (London: Novello, 1959).

REESE, GUSTAVE, *Music in the Middle Ages* (New York: Norton, 1940).

—— *Music in the Renaissance* (New York: Norton, 1954).

RIDLEY, AARON, "Against Musical Ontology", *Journal of Philosophy*, 100 (2003).

RORTY, AMÉLIE OKSENBERG (ed.), *Explaining Emotions* (Berkeley, Los Angeles, and London: University of California Press, 1980).

ROUSSEAU, JEAN JACQUES, *Œuvres Complètes* (Paris, 1788–93).

RUSSELL, BERTRAND, *Mysticism and Logic, and Other Essays* (London: George Allen & Unwin, 1951).

RYLE, GILBERT, *On Thinking*, ed. Konstantin Kolenda (Totowa, NJ: Rowan & Littlefield, 1979).

SACHS, CURT, *The Rise of Music in the Ancient World* (New York: Norton, 1943).

SANTAYANA, GEORGE, *Three Philosophical Poets* (Garden City, NY: Doubleday Anchor Books, 1953).

SCHOPENHAUER, ARTUR, *Die Welt als Wille und Vorstellung*, in *Sämtliche Werke*, i (Stuttgart: Suhrkamp, 1986).

SCHROEDER, DAVID P., *Haydn and the Enlightenment: The Late Symphonies and their Audience* (Oxford: Clarendon Press, 1990).

SCHUELLER, HERBERT M., "Immanuel Kant and the Aesthetics of Music", *Journal of Aesthetics and Art Criticism*, 14 (1955).

SCRUTON, ROGER, "Representation in Music", *Philosophy*, 51 (1976).

SIBLEY, FRANK, "Aesthetic Concepts", *Philosophical Review*, 67 (1959).

SPENCER, HERBERT, *Autobiography*, 2 vols. (London: Williams & Norgate, 1904).

SPENCER, HERBERT, *Facts and Comments* (New York: D. Appleton, 1902).

⸺ *First Principles*, 6th edn. (London: Williams & Norgate, 1904).

⸺ "On the Origin of Music", *Mind*, 16 (1891).

⸺ "The Origin and Function of Music", *Fraser's Magazine*, 56 (1857).

⸺ "The Origin of Music", *Mind*, 15 (1890).

SPINGARN, J. E. (ed.) *Critical Essays of the Seventeenth Century*, 3 vols. (Bloomington, Ind.: Indiana University Press, 1957).

STEVENSON, CHARLES L., *Ethics and Language* (New Haven: Yale University Press, 1941).

STRICKER, SALOMON, *Du Language et de la musique* (Paris, 1885).

STRUNK, OLIVER (ed.), *Source Readings in Music History: From Antiquity through the Romantic Era* (New York: Norton, 1950).

TARUSKIN, RICHARD, *et al.*, "The Limits of Authenticity: A Discussion", *Early Music*, 12 (1984).

THAYER, ALEXANDER WHEELOCK, *The Life of Ludwig van Beethoven*, 2 vols. (Carbondale, Ill.: Southern Illinois University Press, 1960).

TOLSTOY, LEO, *What Is Art?*, trans. Aylmer Maude (Oxford: Oxford University Press, 1959).

WALLACE, ROBIN, "Background and Expression in the First Movement of Beethoven's Op. 132", *Journal of Musicology*, 7 (1989).

WALLASCHEK, RICHARD, "On the Origin of Music", *Mind*, 16 (1891).

WITTGENSTEIN, LUDWIG, *Philosophical Investigations*, trans. G. E. M. Anscombe (New York: Macmillan and Oxford: Blackwell, 1953).

WOLLHEIM, RICHARD, *Painting as an Art* (Princeton: Princeton University Press, 1987).

WOODWORTH, R. S., and SCHLOSSBERG S., *Experimental Psychology* (New York: Holt, 1954).

Index to *Music, Language and Cognition*

Note: Footnote numbers in brackets are used to indicate the whereabouts on the page of authors who are quoted, but not named, in the text.